Management Consultancy and Banking
in an Era of Globalization

Management Consultancy and Banking in an Era of Globalization

Andrew Jones
Lecturer in Human Geography, Birkbeck College, London

First published 2003 by
PALGRAVE MACMILLAN
Houndmills, Basingstoke, Hampshire RG21 6XS and
175 Fifth Avenue, New York, N. Y. 10010
Companies and representatives throughout the world

PALGRAVE MACMILLAN is the global academic imprint of the Palgrave Macmillan division of St. Martin's Press, LLC and of Palgrave Macmillan Ltd. Macmillan® is a registered trademark in the United States, United Kingdom and other countries. Palgrave is a registered trademark in the European Union and other countries.

ISBN 0–333–98201–0 hardback

This book is printed on paper suitable for recycling and made from fully managed and sustained forest sources.

A catalogue record for this book is available from the British Library.

Library of Congress Cataloging in Publication Data
Jones, Andrew, 1973–
   Management consultancy and banking in an era of globalization / Andrew Jones.
     p. cm.
   Includes bibliographical references and index.
   ISBN 0–333–98201–0
   1. International business enterprises. 2. Globalization. 3. Business consultants. 4. Investment banking. I. Title.

   HD2755.5.J662 2003
   001—dc21

2002192951

10 9 8 7 6 5 4 3 2 1
12 11 10 09 08 07 06 05 04 03

Printed and bound in Great Britain by
Antony Rowe Ltd, Chippenham and Eastbourne

To Linda and my parents, for getting me through the realities of transatlantic research

Contents

List of Tables and Figures

Tables

Figures

Preface and Acknowledgements

This book is an attempt to take a different approach to theorizing transnational corporations and their activities in the global economy – different because I try to break the conventional and accepted mould used by most academic writers working in this area within management and business schools. In that sense, in some ways it represents a rejection (either explicitly or implicitly) of many of the methodological and conceptual norms used in the academic disciplines that have dominated theories of global corporations. Such a stance didn't 'come from nowhere' but is based both on my experience of the research process itself and in the strong dissatisfaction I found amongst the business managers I talked to through the project. These people often felt that a lot academic theory has little or no use or relevance to them as they go about running the world's largest companies. This book is thus intended as a challenge to the way academics (and here I mean especially business theorists and economists) set about researching and theorising the world of global business.

No doubt some academic readers of this book will not like my line of argument, particularly my suggestion that there are serious gaps and conceptual weaknesses in how academic work on transnational business is carried out. And undoubtedly, critical readers will be able to find the limitations that exist – as they could in any study – in my own research and theorising. There is always more literature that could have been included and better sources of data than the ones used. Yet no matter where you fall in the debate over the strengths and weaknesses of quantitative versus qualitative methods, or whichever superior data sources you are aware of over those used in this book, my challenge to the dominant way of researching transnational corporations is grounded in the clear dissatisfaction I found amongst senior business people with the nature of academic theory. Such dissatisfaction is hard to ignore. Generalized theories of globalization, 'scientific' models of corporate form, quantifiable industry-trends and descriptive theory – all in their way are the cause of this gap between academic discourse and business practice. The research in this book as a consequence, its limitations notwithstanding, is a deliberate attempt to make a different kind of theoretical contribution to the volumes of papers produced in business and management journals. I hope this will generate some constructive debate with those who feel secure in the dominant disciplinary paradigms of business studies and other academic fields.

The arguments and ideas forwarded in this book have been several years in the making and could not have been developed without the help and support of a whole range of people. What began life as a doctoral thesis has continued to grow and evolve long after I thought it would be over. In that respect, I owe a great deal to Linda McDowell who has played an enduring advisory role in the formation of my ideas, along with Andrew Leyshon, Nigel Thrift, Ron Martin, Harriet Bulkeley, Liz Watson and Rich Harris in Birkbeck. I must also thank all the business people who gave up time in their busy schedules to talk to me and Tessa Hilder for her painstaking proofing. In particular, the practicalities of transatlantic research wouldn't have been possible without Brian Larkman in London and Patti Hoffman, Rit Agarwala and Frank Ballabio in New York. Finally, I would like to acknowledge the invaluable advice and constructive criticism of the anonymous referee involved in the publication process.

London, October 2002

1
'Globalization Theory' and the Complexity of Global Business

> Globalization is a complex set of processes, not a single one. And these operate in a contradictory or oppositional fashion.
>
> (Giddens 1999: 13)

Rather than beginning with the premise, as so many globalization theorists, critics and media commentators appear to do, that globalization represents a single phenomenon *out there* in the world to be explained and theorized (or even resisted), this book is concerned with the material practices of 'doing' business at the transnational or global scale in order to explore what the globalization of business activity actually consists of. It does this though the presentation of detailed empirical research into two of the most supposedly 'globalized' of advanced service industries (Bryson & Daniels 1998; Sassen 2001): investment banking and management consultancy. In examining the transnational nature of business activity in these sectors, the aim is to show how 'generalized' globalization theory is simply not up to the job of effectively theorizing contemporary transnational business, and how it may well be dangerously misguiding for business practitioners as a way of thinking about the world economy at present. The key argument is that a generalized approach to understanding 'globalization' is misconceived and often unhelpful because the concept is too amorphous and broad to permit meaningful theories to be based around it. Consequently, the insights developed from the research also have implications for academics, business managers, policymakers and even those who are seeking to resist the changes that globalization is seen to represent. Before I can begin to present this research, however, the basis for this theoretical critique requires some elaboration.

Explicit theories of globalization in general are comparatively recent developments. Although the word was coined during the 1960s when similar expressions such as 'global village' were added to the vocabulary (McCluhan 1962), it is only since the mid-1980s, however, that theorists have begun to construct globalization in theoretical terms, referring to it in a wider process-based (Harvey 1996, 2000a; Eade 1997; Gill 1997) or systemic sense (Sklair 1992; Barrett 1997; Jervis 1997). Despite its novelty as a concept, the component processes that social scientists see as producing globalization as not themselves entirely new. If globalization is understood in a broad sense as the integration of society/economy/polity (Scholte 2000), then many forms of integrative processes are argued to have been present for a considerable period through human history (Wallerstein 1979, 1984; Giddens 1984, 1990; Axford 1995). Thus, in many ways the globalization literature of the last decade or so also represents the latest development in a longer standing debate concerning the integration of human societies (Hopkins 2000).[1]

That said, the term globalization is argued to warrant utility because it arguably corresponds to something 'new' (Leyshon 1995; Castells 1996). According to many, there has been a qualitative shift in the nature of societal integration in the last few decades (Harvey 1989; Giddens 1990; Mittelman 1997) – a shift which defines a current 'period' or 'phase' of globalization and which has seen for the first time the development of truly global forms of economic, social, political and cultural organization (Giddens 1999; Held *et al* 1999). In short, globalization warrants a new kind of theorizing about the world because the changes that have occurred in recent decades and are continuing to occur are largely unprecedented, if not entirely in their nature, then certainly in their degree and extent (Giddens 1990).

This intellectual argument – that globalization represents a novel and pervasive source of change in early twenty-first century world society – has risen to prominence within the academic social sciences over the last fifteen years. Whilst much attention has focused on the economic dimensions to globalization – the international trading system (Chen 1998), global finance (Daniels 1998; Strange 1998a), transnational firms (Corley 1989; Dunning 1997; Doremus *et al* 1998) and regulatory structures (Herring & Litan 1995; Arup & Soloway 2002; Majury 2002) – globalization as a concept in the academic world has now pervaded many other debates. Almost all social science disciplines are now heavily embedded in researching, explaining and theorising the multifarious contexts to which globalization has been applied theoretically. Whether it is sociology, economics, management or international relations – even anthropology – all disciplinary fields of the social sciences show a growing level of attention to globalization as an idea (Waters 1995; Spybey 1996; Clark 1997, 1999).

Yet globalization as this generalized umbrella idea, as a broad *concept*, is problematic (Kofman & Youngs 1996). The main reason for this is that 'globalization theory' as a field of knowledge and a way of understanding the world – whether that be the nature of society or transnational business activity – is constrained above all by the impossibility of unifying all the different phenomena that globalization as word or concept seeks to bring together under one theoretical framework (Mittelman 2000). Academic thinkers, politicians and business gurus have thus often been too quick to leap onto the bandwagon of globalization theory without paying enough attention to the deep-rooted difficulties that developing a 'grand theory' of globalization presents (Rosenberg 2001).

The possibility of developing a general theory of globalization relies on the implicit assumption that there is a 'core' phenomenon, or set of phenomena, that can be equated to globalization. In effect, this is the 'transferable' abstract process or phenomenon at the heart of globalization as a concept that must be identifiable in every context to which globalization can be applied. For example, in their influential book, David Held and his co-authors define this core phenomenon as the 'widening, deepening and speeding up of worldwide interconnectedness in all aspects of contemporary social life' (Held *et al* 1999: 2). Other leading theorists have made similar arguments. Anthony Giddens, for example, defines globalization at root as 'the reordering of time and distance in social life' (Giddens 1990: 528) and Ulrich Beck sums up globalization at root as 'denoting the processes through which sovereign nation-states are criss-crossed and undermined by transnational actors with varying prospects of power, orientations, identities and networks' (Beck 1999: 11).

However, this tendency to search for a single abstract phenomenon at the root of globalization is being increasingly challenged. Earlier criticisms that such definitions are too generalized (Mittelman 1997) or ambiguous (Leyshon 1997) have developed into a more coherent scepticism within academic thought about the virtue of fitting everything into one theoretical framework on globalization (Mittelman 2000; Rosenberg 2001). It is not that globalization as a concept cannot be defined in these very broad terms, but that doing so is more of a theoretical hindrance than a help. The very general definition of globalization used by Held *et al* and in their 'transformationalist school' – globalization as the widening, deepening and speeding up of worldwide interconnectedness – only works as a theoretical generalization because it is *so* broad as to almost be a self-evident truism. Such an ontological approach can only generate limited theoretical understanding because it is reliant upon defining globalization in a manner that captures virtually *every change* occurring in today's society.

Of course, this stumbling block is often acknowledged and countered by those seeking to theorize globalization (Waters 1995). The common response is to try to overcome the generalist nature of globalization as a single concept by adding further 'sub-concepts' – a more specialized layer of more specific concepts onto the broad foundations of globalization theory. For example, Held *et al* propose that 'globalization is always and everywhere defined by four spatio-temporal aspects' (intensity, extensity, velocity, impact). In this way, generalized globalization theory can become more sensitive to the diverse array of issues that it is intended to help theorize. Also common in the literature, almost to the degree of now being an accepted framework for dividing up the debate, is to refer to economic, political, cultural and other sub-forms of globalization (Holton 1998; Lechner & Boli 2000). Unfortunately, as Rosenberg (2001) points out, the real problem may be with the conceptual foundations of the idea itself.

Contributions such as that of Held *et al* (1999) are clearly helpful in identifying similarities in how different aspects of social life are changing at the moment. Yet the problem is that academic theorists – in trying to develop a generalized approach to theorizing globalization – are faced with the impossibility of reducing what they are trying to theorize in practice (globalization in an applied case) to even a few abstractions. Instead, when it comes to theories of globalization, new sub-concepts are proliferating rapidly. Various globalization theories are populating academic thought with a plethora of new (or reconfigured) abstract concepts in an attempt to contain the monstrously broad scope of globalization as an idea. When it comes to even developing a satisfactory theory of a substantial tract of globalization's realm of application as a concept – global business activity for example – what tends to emerge is a complex web of abstractions, with struggling globalization theorists hastily having to concede that many 'intersect with others' (Scott 1997; Castells 2000). All this proliferation of jargon is about permitting globalization in general to be viewed 'as a process, as a condition, or as a specific kind of political project' (Harvey 2000a: 54) in one overarching framework. It is not only the novice to academic theories of globalization who might be forgiven for becoming overwhelmed and confused by the growing number of new concepts in circulation around such generalized globalization theories; business practitioners I have interviewed during my research, along with my own students, regularly express bewilderment at the volume of 'jargon', as it tends to get termed, emerging from the globalization literature.

I am not seeking here to pass judgment on the relative success or otherwise of *each* of the numerous academic analyses of globalization. The utility of different theories of globalization varies hugely according to the specific topic being researched and theorized. Rather I want to question the merit of approaching this problematic concept of globalization in such a way in the first place. My suggestion is that generalized globalization theories are ultimately misconceived and unhelpful because globalization as a concept is too amorphous and broad to permit meaningful theories to be based around it. Those who worry that the word has become meaningless are right in doing so (Strange 1998b; Modelski 2000), not because it has become so but because it is a hopeless basis around which to start theorizing the changes in the world today in the first place. The emerging schools of thought on globalization are seeking to build theoretical frameworks that are trying to capture almost every contemporary change in society under the wing of this concept. In so doing, this kind of approach is undermining the value of globalization as a concept that represents anything more than the most general of descriptions. It is no foundation for a general theory of anything.

The view taken in this book is therefore different from much of the globalization literature. The implication of the research into business-service companies presented in the following chapters is that adopting a generalized theoretical stance on globalization is problematic for anyone seeking to act in a highly complex and rapidly changing world. For the practitioner trying to build an understanding of what is changing in – to take the example most relevant to this book – the world of business, the long list of various abstract concepts deployed in globalization theories are neither easily usable in terms of how they relate to each other nor immediately relevant to the kind of questions that people with more of an agenda for action than the theorists might have. It is not that it is impossible to build a general theoretical framework but rather that this emerging paradigm for understanding globalization is unhelpful for those seeking to deal with, act upon or formulate policy in an integrating world. Furthermore, it is diverting attention from the important task of developing better (and more specifically targeted) theories of that changing world.

Understanding globalization – the business practitioners

> But globalization is a myth; it never really occurred anyway . . . the vast majority of manufacturing and service activity is organized regionally, not globally.
>
> (Rugman 2001: 1)

Academic thinkers, business gurus, policy advisors and others have thus been instrumental in producing a growing field of generalized globalization theory in recent years, but the power of these discourses is actualized only when it becomes incorporated in the actions of those who make decisions about global business activity or policy. Generalized globalization theory therefore represents a potentially influential discourse far beyond academic discussions. The research into business transnationalization in management consultancy and investment banking provided strong evidence in this respect. It suggested that there are strong similarities between the view of globalization being developed by academic globalization theories and the ways in which senior business practitioners in these business-service transnational corporations (TNCs) understand globalization in the context of their firms. The way in which globalization is understood by business practitioners, therefore, is the key issue that the rest of this introductory chapter will consider. These insights into the understanding of globalization amongst senior business people provide the basis for the examination of practices that follows in subsequent chapters.

The study around which the arguments of this book are based intended from the outset to approach research into the nature of transnational business in a different manner from the norm for management theorists or economists. These disciplines tend to focus on quantifying, measuring and modelling at the industry- or country-scale (for example, Johanson & Vahlne 1977; Casson 1991; Cantwell 1995). Although this study used many of the same methodological techniques of data collection, the difference lies in the manner of constructing theory and the assumptions about what kind of theory should be developed. Rather than seeking to quantify or model transnational business at the industry or country-wide scale, with the objective of theorizing common aspects of features, the research aimed to explore in depth the complexity of changes occurring within individual firms before trying to draw out any wider commonalities. Furthermore, the study did not aim to construct a definitive generalized theory of what is happening in management consultancy or investment banking as sectors but rather sought to identify the nature of differences between companies. All this emphasis on a difference in approach corresponds to an attempt to develop a more sophisticated understanding of the complexity of transnational business than a generalized, model-based approach permits.[2] I will return to this issue of how my approach to theory-building differed from the norm amongst management theorists in greater detail in the next chapter. For the moment, however, I will provide an outline of the two categories of methods.

First, over a three-year period between 1998 and 2001, I conducted over 75 semi-structured interviews with (mainly senior) management consultants and investment bankers in major offices of their firms. All the respondents were based (although not exclusively located) in one of two urban centres – London or New York – and were interviewed for the most part in their workplace. The respondents worked, however, for a variety of firms originating from the US, Europe and Asia and so were not necessarily living and working in either of the two cities in the long term. In general, the interviews lasted between 45 and 90 minutes and were taped and transcribed. A number of respondents were also interviewed a second time as part of the study. The interviews followed an open structure insofar as I adhered to a topic guide in terms of what was discussed, but both I and individual respondents were free to concentrate on aspects of my research that they felt most informed about or that were most significant (Healey & Rawlinson 1993; Hert & Imber 1995). A comprehensive list of all the interview respondents in the study are provided according to urban base in Tables 1.1 and 1.2. For reasons of confidentiality, the specific names of individuals and the companies worked for have been withheld (Thomas 1995). Respondents are thus identified by their position in the business-service TNC and the national origin of that company.

Second, the hundreds of thousands of words of interview transcript material was supported, expanded and investigated through a range of other information resources: company annual reports, websites, internal publications, journalistic commentary and industry statistics. These secondary sources of data tend to often be the first rather than the second source of data for much that is written on TNCs and economic globalization. Whilst obviously important for establishing wider trends within companies and industries, they represent quite deliberately just one part of the array of information resources used to compile the arguments of the study. Whilst it is not possible to name specific companies in relation to specific interview respondents, Tables 1.3 and 1.4 show the top twenty largest investment banks[3] and top twenty management consultancy firms[4] in the world, indicating which TNCs had respondents included in the study.

Table 1.1 Interview Respondents (Senior Management) in London

Interview	Company	Position
1	UKBank2	Managing Director, Equities & New Issues
2	EuroBank2	Managing Director, Head of Human Resources (Europe)
3	UKBank1	Director, Capital Markets
4	UKBank2	Director, Global Head of Money Markets
5	UKBank1	Director, Head of Training
6	UKProfAssoc1	Chief Executive
7	USBank1	Director, Corporate Finance
8	EuroBank1	Executive Director, Global Fixed Income, Currencies and Derivatives
9	USBank1	Director, UK & European Bond Sales
10	USConsultancy1	Managing Partner, Financial Institutions
11	USConsultancy2	Managing Partner
12	USConsultancy3	Partner
13	UKBank2	Director, Human Resources
14	EuroBank3	Director, UK Corporate Finance
15	EuroBank2	Managing Director, Money Markets
16	EuroBank4	Managing Director
17	USConsultancy1	General Manager
18	USConsutlancy3	Managing Partner
19	USBank2	Senior Associate, Corporate Finance
20	USConsultancy4	Senior Partner
21	EuroBank4	Director
22	USBank3	Managing Director
23	JapanBank3	Managing Director, Equity
24	JapanBank1	General Manager
25	USConsultancy2	Partner, Retail Services
26	UKBank1	Executive Director, Corporate Finance
27	USConsultancy4	Partner
28	UKConsultancy1	Managing Director
29	JapanBank1	Director, Equity Research

A further 14 interviews were conducted with employees below a senior managerial level, pursuing certain key issues lower down the organization.

In methodological terms, therefore, this study places much greater emphasis on qualitative methods of data collection (c.f. Crabtree & Miller 1999; Silverman 2000) in contrast to the dominance of more quantitative approaches used by many management theorists and economists. In-depth interviews allowed a detailed exploration of the changing nature of transnational business within individual firms and made use of interviewees as key informants (Walford 1994; Newman & Benz 1998) who knew a great deal about what is happening in practice.[5]

Table 1.2 Interview Respondents (Senior Management) in New York

Interview	Company	Position
1	EuroBank1	Director
2	USBank1	Senior Manager, Operations
3	USConsultancy2	Partner, Financial Institutions
4	USConsultancy3	Partner, Japanese Clients
5	USConsultancy5	Partner, Pharmaceuticals
6	USConsultancy1	Partner, US Finance
7	JapanBank1	Senior Business Analyst
8	USBank4	Director
9	USBank1	Managing Director (Board), Corporate Head of Human Resources
10	JapanBank2	General Manager
11	JapanBank3	Chief Economist, Research Division (Senior Vice-President)
12	JapanBank2	Director, US Corporate Finance
13	USConsultancy7	Partner
14	USBank5	Managing Director, Human Resources
15	JapanBank1	Senior Manager, Human Resources
16	USConsultancy2	Partner
17	USConsultancy3	Managing Partner
18	UKBank2	Director, US Investments
19	USBank2	Senior Manager, Operations
20	EuroBank4	Director
21	USBank3	Manager, Equity
22	USConsultancy4	Partner, Retail
23	USBank2	Executive Director, Human Resources
24	USBank5	Managing Director, Capital Markets
25	USBank4	Director, Equity
27	USConsultancy8	Senior Consultant, Financial Services
28	EuroBank3	Managing Director, US Capital Markets

A further eight interviews were conducted with employees below a senior managerial level.

In that sense, my *purposive sampling* strategy (Denzin & Lincoln 1998) was based on the significance of knowledge held by individuals to the study. This is the basis for the theoretical insights I draw out. In that sense, my research agenda had no use for the questionnaire surveys or tick-box summaries often used in other disciplines. In my view, such methodologies are often inappropriate research strategies to use in trying to theorize complex social activities such as business dealings, management practices or corporate culture. They contribute to the production of precisely the kind of generalized theories of transnational business and globalization I am seeking to counter. Whilst, therefore,

Table 1.3   Top Twenty Global Investment Banks (ranked by revenue, 2000)

Rank	Bank
1	**Deutsche Bank**
2	**JP Morgan Chase**
3	**Credit Suisse**
4	**Bank of America**
5	BNP Paribas
6	**Mitzuho Holdings**
7	**HSBC Holdings**
8	**UBS Warburg**
9	Fortis
10	**ABN AMRO**
11	Credit Agricole
12	Hypo Vereinsbank
13	Santander Central
14	**Royal Bank of Scotland**
15	Wells Fargo
16	Bank of Tokyo-Mitsubishi
17	**Bank One Corp**
18	**Barclays**
19	Sumitomo Bank
20	First Union Corp

Bold denotes a firm with respondents in the study.
Source: Fortune Global 500, 2000; Fortune Magazine, 2000.

I broadly adopted an approach that can be described as favouring *methodological pluralism* (Williams 2002) that combines aspects of both quantitative and qualitative techniques (Brannen 1992; Neuman 2000), in terms of researching how business practitioners understand and theorize ideas such as globalization, I argue that a heavily qualitative approach has to be central.

From both the interview transcripts and other written corporate material, I identified shared threads of understanding with regard to globalization amongst the respondents. Whilst clearly not exhaustive, the research provides an illustration of the way in which generalized understandings of globalization as a concept permeate the way in which senior management consultants and investment bankers think. By analyzing this material, I identified at least four key themes in this regard. These common themes inform and legitimize the decisions and practices that key business people undertake in relation to this general

Table 1.4 Top Twenty Global Management/Strategy Consultancies (ranked by employee numbers)

1	**Accenture**
2	CSC[1]
3	**Cap Gemini/Ernst & Young**
4	**Price Waterhouse Coopers**
5	**KPMG Consulting**
6	William M Mercer
7	Hewitt Associates
8	**Deloite Consulting**
9	**Andersen[2]**
10	Towers Perrin
11	AMS
12	Booz Allen Hamilton
13	**McKinsey & Company**
14	Watson Wyatt
15	AT Kearney
16	PA Consulting
17	Cambridge Technology
18	**Boston Consulting**
19	Arthur D Little
20	**Bain & Company**

[1] CSC is an IT firm but is involved heavily in consultancy related to management issues.

[2] At the time of writing, Andersen is unlikely to survive as a global firm after its involvement in the Enron affair. Indications suggest it will break up and be bought/merge into other consultancy firms.

Bold denotes a bank with respondents included in the study.

Source: Authors' survey of corporate websites and industry directories.

idea of globalization within the specific context of their own and other people's companies.

First, amongst both management consultants and investment bankers globalization – as a generalized concept – is understood to refer to a set of phenomena or processes that are assumed to be inevitable and natural. Globalization is the ongoing product of an anticipated course of history. Social scientists have a word for this – teleology – meaning the notion that history progresses and follows an identifiable path. When the business managers I interviewed use the term globalization, or refer to 'the global', they understand it as a phenomenon that has happened in the past, is happening now and will continue to happen in the future. I've taken an extract from an internal publication in one company that illustrates this well:

For years, companies have paid homage to a distant ideal called 'globalization'. Today, it's arrived – with a vengeance. Some thoughts on how to ride the global tidal-wave . . . "Globalization" has been a prime buzzword in American business since the heady days of President Kennedy's New Frontier. Yet it is only now becoming a fact of corporate life.

(Extract from an unpublished internal report, USConsultancy1)

Consultants conveyed the implicit argument, to quote a senior partner in a US firm, that 'it's no use fighting globalization because you are just fighting the course of history' (Senior Partner, Financial Institutions, US-Consultancy3, London). Globalization is thus framed as being the inevitable outcome of longstanding historical trends which senior managers saw their firms as needing to 'keep up with'. For example, a number of respondents referred to 'stages' of globalization. Take the comments of one senior consultant in New York who told me what he thought was happening to American firms bought up by Japanese TNCs:

> Then the last thing it is probably the finance, the money. Companies never release control of the money, the CFO[6] retains control of that. The Japanese auditors in Japan are often reluctant to release it to an American-based CEO.[7] It is a symbolic American CEO because the finance is still controlled by the Japanese even for the overseas company. But if you see that the people have no strange feelings working for Americans or Japanese or vice versa. And that is the ultimate stage of globalization I think.
>
> (Partner, USConsultancy4, New York)

He refers implicitly to the end point of the contemporary globalization process: the 'ultimate stage' where the truly global corporation emerges (Doremus *et al* 1998; Sklair 1998; Mourdoukoutas 1999) as the world economic organizational paradigm.

This represents a second major theme in thinking about globalization amongst senior business practitioners: organizational globality is in general a desirable goal. Globalization, conceived as an abstract process, is 'progressive' and represents a more 'advanced' form of business activity[8] and as such requires a concomitant 'globalized' form for TNCs is therefore a natural parallel shift in the form of business organizations (Deloitte & Touche 1998):

> Being a more global firm has a range of positive attributes for us. I mean, for example, there's often a strong sense that having a more global attitude in the way they go about things is a big advantage. And

the ability to operate seamlessly across different countries, with one approach, one attitude to our clients. Wherever they hire [US-Consultancy2] they know what they're getting.

(Senior Partner, USConsultancy2, London)

Organizational globality is thus perceived to be a competitive advantage, and major organizational restructuring in the largest global companies is being driven and legitimized within this way of thinking (or discourse) on globalization. Such changes have profound impacts on the operations of companies, on profitability, on employment and so on:

Becoming more global as an organization is a big task, and it means uprooting some longstanding ideas about how you do business internationally ... [it] requires changing mindsets, all the way to the top: management, strategy, finance ... a whole new way of structuring things to make the way we do business more advanced.

(Senior Partner, UKConsultancy4, London)

In effect these globalization 'discourses' are central to the long-term strategies of major companies. There is, therefore, much at stake here if the theoretical framework being drawn upon by key decision-makers has serious limitations.

However, the legitimacy and power of the necessity of shifting corporate structures towards organizational globalness amongst the management consultants and senior investment bankers I talked to is reinforced by a third strand to their shared understanding of what globalization 'is'. Many senior business practitioners expressed the view that there was no alternative to the radical restructuring involved in creating more globalized business organizations because globalization represented an irresistible force that individual companies are relatively powerless to resist. For example:

Okay, in the world of consulting I saw bar charts four years ago when we as a firm were talking about globalization. We said, "here are the big players for consulting [USConsultancy1] and a couple of others. These are the big firms and there are the firms in the middle like us and others. And either we should aim to become very big or we should just become a boutique." But in the middle, if you look at the projections over time, these two bars expand and the guys in the middle get crushed. And I think to some extent, that is not a bad model for the banking industry as I see it. For most industries in fact . . .

(Partner, Financial Institutions, USConsultancy3, New York)

Yet senior consultants and bankers recognized that there are serious issues and problems in implementing organizational globalization in practice. Producing a more globalized corporate organization is more difficult than the rhetoric of globalization found in management theory books suggests:

> I think that is true but there is a conflict at present between the economists' view of the world which is actually pushing towards more and more of a global perspective and a managerial perspective which is struggling to handle that complexity, and in fact it is often failing. And banking is a great example. Where currently we see around the globe these multi-product, multi-country, multi-customer segment financial services institutions being developed. Erm . . . but they are not being well-managed and as a result our view is that shareholder value is being destroyed. And look at the German banks . . . I think in 5 to 10 years time they will be looking back at some of the mistakes they have been making recently – moves they have been making which they will then perceive as mistakes – in the same way as a lot of the industrial conglomerates look back today.
>
> (Executive Director, Global Fixed Income, EuroBank2, London)

This response reflects a prevalent message communicated by business managers when talking about the 'difficulties' and actual material practices linked to globalization. Transnational business-service companies – supposedly the most globalized of *all* industries – are finding the process of becoming 'truly global corporations' at best difficult, and a better description would often be 'traumatic' (Director, Capital Markets, EuroBank5, London). However, this experienced reality was not interpreted as a problem by the companies. They just hadn't got it right yet (Partner, USConsultancy2, London) or were not fully down the global path yet (Senior Manager, USBank3, New York). The poor performance of globalized activities was never scrutinized as perhaps reflecting a problem with managers' understanding of what globalization 'is'.

The irresistibility of globalization flows into a fourth characteristic of the shared understanding I found amongst senior business practitioners: the idea that globalization is an external reality out there in the world. The literature on globalization theory and management studies has helped to create the view amongst business managers that this abstract thing called globalization is implicitly something a company has to respond to:

> Globalization is the reality that everyone in business now has to face up to. Some don't like it, some relish it, but ... well, I guess in the consultancy or banking business – like any other – they are trying to deal with that. Because if you don't address it, if you were to ignore what's going on in the world outside this office building, then you're not going to last very long I can tell you ...
>
> (Partner, Japanese Financial Institutions, USConsultancy1,
> New York)

Two elements to this externalization of globalization were widely cited: globalized clients and globalized markets. Taking the former first, the existence of 'globalized clients' is understood as an externalized agent of change requiring firms to globalize their own operations. Management consultancy itself, for example, is in this discourse an industry that is 'being pulled' to globalize and in which consultancy firms are passive respondents to this process:

> Consultants are neither leaders nor followers ... with regard to what is going on with globalization. I think we have a tendency to meet the challenges that our clients present to us in their efforts to globalize. I wouldn't suggest that we globalize to pull our clients, it is more a push situation.
>
> (Senior Partner, UKConsultancy2, London)

Similarly, senior consultants also explained how in their advisory work for other large TNCs, the key issue in terms of organizational restructuring is often the need to adjust corporate form so that the corporation in question can better serve the needs of clients:

> And usually the larger projects – particularly in the world I operate which is Wall Street – those clients are always global. It could be ... designing the systems architecture for foreign exchange trading for a client. Now that by its nature will be global because they trade foreign exchange all around world.
>
> (Partner, Financial Institutions, USConsultancy4, New York)

And the fact is that clients desire that globalization so you have got to have open communication to deal with the clients.

> (Partner, USConsultancy1, London)

The concomitant external aspect of globalization, running hand-in-hand with the globalized nature of clients, is the globalized nature of markets. Whether individual companies or corporate strategists like it or not, within these business-service industries, global markets are a 'reality'. For example:

> Well, among the globalization fishes there is no doubt . . . we see the spread of the market environment and – if you like – the challenge to national autonomy is creating global markets not only across the Atlantic but increasingly across the Pacific.
>
> (Partner, US Finance, USConsultancy3, New York)

Senior consultants, themselves influential producers of thought on globalization amongst business practitioners more generally, perceive globalization as a reality to a large extent beyond their individual sphere of influence. It is something that has to be 'dealt with', again understood in a similar worldview as the academic theorists who preach globalization theory. The question I would, and did, raise with these people is to what extent is this generalized understanding of the external 'big' nature of globalization relevant to their day-to-day business activities. Whilst, of course, the existence of increasingly integrated global markets and clients with a 'global presence' must be crucial to business success in banking and consultancy, the specifics of these business realities proved more complicated than the theoretical perspectives being adopted by interviewees to deal with them. For example, several senior consultants admitted that whilst some of their clients were increasingly 'globally present' and looking for a standardized global approach to their business, other important clients were not and effectively bucked the 'more global' trend (Senior Partner, USConsultancy1, New York). Furthermore, the existence of global markets varied considerably depending upon which industry you were talking about, and worse, often which sector of which industry you were dealing with.

What these acknowledgements reveal is that the nature of current trends in these industries and others in the world economy are diverse and complicated phenomena. In utilizing a shared generalized understanding of globalization in tackling this diversity and complexity, therefore, business practitioners run the dangerous risk of failing to sufficiently understand what is occurring. Amongst the business practitioners I spoke with, there was an appreciation of the discrepancy between globalization theory, based upon whatever source, and the needs and practices of 'doing' real business:

There's a lot been written, I know...colleagues of mine are up to their ears in books on global business this, global business that. And I know all you academic people are churning this stuff out. It's a bit mad if you don't mind me saying...[a lot] of it seems off-target when it comes to what the world of business is really doing...

(Partner, USConsultancy4, New York)

Yet, as the preceding discussion outlines, management consultants and senior bankers in general continue to subscribe to a shared general understanding of globalization that presents contradictions and limitations on their ability to run transnational business. General theories of globalization, as exemplified by the academic literature discussed earlier in this chapter, play an important part in shaping senior managerial understandings of what globalization 'is' and how it should shape business practice and strategy. Each of the respective common threads to business practitioners' views of globalization reflect pervasive elements of academic generalized theories, which forms a powerful basis for decisions and action within transnational firms. In that sense, therefore, the relationship between the burgeoning academic literature on globalization and senior business people warrants much closer scrutiny than it is currently receiving since the two spheres of activity are clearly and increasingly intertwined. The *academicization* of business practices, manifest in the growing requirement by TNCs for more and more of their employees to take MBAs and other business qualifications (Thrift 2000) can only serve to consolidate this relationship further. A critical engagement with 'what' exactly business managers are learning on MBAs and other academic courses of study – in this case in relation to globalization – is thus a crucially important wider agenda for those concerned in the future development of transnational business (see Green & Ruhleder 1995). However, the focus in this book will be on problematizing general understandings of globalization in relation to the complex reality of transnational business.

In the end is the practice

Globalization theory in both its managerial and academic versions is a seductive discourse in that it appears to provide a bigger reality, beyond individual decision-makers and organizations, that necessitates and legitimates a whole string of corporate strategies. In today's world, globalization as a generalized phenomenon is widely hailed as the 'most important force of the twenty-first century' (Bauman 1998) but many commentators are referring to very different phenomena. This introductory chapter has illustrated how business understandings of what globalization 'is' are being informed by an exploding academic literature in the social sciences that is more and more moving in the direction of adopting a comprehensive and integrated theoretical approach towards globalization. The concept has shifted from being a buzzword used in a whole variety of different contexts that were relatively insulated from each other to being the flagship of a 'big' theory of the world which business practitioners, like everyone else, apparently would be foolish to ignore.

The interview extracts quoted in the discussion so far certainly bear witness to the dramatic impact that ideas about globalization are having on transnational firms. Management consultancy firms and investment banks, manifest in the rhetoric being deployed in recent years by their most senior staff, are keen to be seen to embrace the challenges that globalization presents and to be at the forefront of the dramatic changes it requires of business (see Deutsche 1997; Deloitte & Touche 2000). These companies, as subsequent chapters will go on to explore in depth, are embracing radical and demanding programmes of organizational restructuring and reconfiguring as part of their response and strategies with regard to globalization. Furthermore, both sectors, as key business-service industries, play a central and influential part in advising and assisting other TNCs in many different sectors in adapting to a world of globalization. Management consultants in particular have found much business in the boom of the 1990s around the issue of *organizational globalization*, and early indications suggest this is continuing, albeit in an increasingly 'rationalized' version in the downturn of the 00s (Deloitte & Touche 2002; Morgan Chase 2002). Even a cursory glance at the advertising pitch of the websites of these companies reveals that despite the arrival of a global economic downturn, globalization as an issue occupies the core of their advisory business.[9]

If the initial evidence presented in this chapter indicates that the understandings that senior consultants and bankers have of globalization is heavily reliant on wider general theories of globalization, then the much wider argument of this book is that this situation is fraught with potential contradictions and pitfalls. General globalization theory is built on soft ground because it relies on a whole of array of abstractions that assume there is a core 'thing' to which globalization in general can be reduced. The research presented through the following chapters will show how, certainly in the case of transnational business, this is not the case. Generalized globalization theories can only be of limited use to anyone who wishes to seriously engage from a policy or practice perspective with the issues of societal integration that they are used to help describe and explain.

The remainder of this book elaborates these arguments from a series of different perspectives on the nature of contemporary management consultancy and investment banking business. In the next chapter, I present a detailed analysis of how transnational corporations are understood in theoretical terms, calling into question many of the assumptions made in the conventional social science and management studies literature. This discussion develops my overall argument by problematizing relationship between generalized globalization theory and the literature's understanding of TNCs as definable and delimitable units of business action in the world economy. In calling for a new kind of theoretical approach towards understanding TNCs, the chapter suggests that business strategists and policy-makers will find it more useful to pay much greater attention to the nature of social practices that actually constitute what a TNC 'is'.

Chapter 3 takes up this agenda from the perspective of the organization. It draws heavily on research into the nature of management consultancy firms and investment banks as transnational organizations. This focus on the organizational scale thus explores in depth the processes of restructuring and change that have been implemented by senior management in leading firms in these industries over the last few years. It thus examines such issues as office locations, divisional structures and managerial hierarchies. In particular, it puts under scrutiny the arguments deployed by management strategists in attempts to create truly 'global corporations' in terms of corporate structure. Many leading investment banks and consultancy firms are involved in organizational restructuring with this goal in mind, and in the case of the consultancy firms, this is one of the advisory functions they can and do perform for clients. The chapter questions the way in which dramatic corporate restructuring is informed by wider understandings of globalization and argues that senior business managers should remain focused on the specific core issues affecting their own business sector, rather than paying too much heed to anyone preaching 'big' globalization theory.

Chapter 4 moves down a scale of analysis to examine the role of individuals in actually 'doing' transnational business in investment banking and consultancy. It examines the social practices that constitute the activity of business within and between transnational corporations, and in particular argues that direct social interaction between business people will remain a crucial and central feature of global business for the foreseeable future. In the context of the business-service industries researched, this argument is developed through a discussion of the role of personal contacts in acquiring and retaining the client basis upon which even the largest banks and consultancies rely for most of their business. In that sense, the chapter gets beyond 'black box' analyses of transnational firms and argues that any sophisticated theory of global business needs to address the central importance of interpersonal relationships in today's world economy.

Continuing this line of analysis from a slightly different tack, Chapter 5 complements the discussion of interpersonal relations in transnational business by discussing the issue of global corporate culture. The idea that TNCs should seek to develop a common global corporate culture has recently begun to be discussed within the management studies literature (Trompenaars 1993; Flood *et al* 1995; Harvey *et al* 1999) and an increasing number of TNCs in a variety of industries present at least the image of intent in this regard. Drawing on the interviews with senior bankers and consultants, the chapter thus assesses what practices, logics and strategies are being deployed by companies to help engender a common corporate culture at the global scale. It argues, however, that the very idea of a common global corporate culture is problematic and in reality a contradictory objective for many companies to pursue. The suggestion made is that many of the arguments made for the benefits of setting out to develop a unique global culture in TNCs are founded in generalized globalization theory and have to date taken little account of the difficulty and complexity of such a stated goal. In that sense, that chapter develops another 'cut' at criticizing the utility of globalization theory for business practitioners.

In the last chapter, the overall implications of the study for the management consultancy and investment banking sectors are drawn together. I identify what ramifications the research has for business practitioners who are currently working in these industries and point to the issues that they need to think carefully about in globalizing their organizations. Finally, the book concludes with recommendations of how the complex changes being captured in globalization theory and theories of the transnational firm might be better theorized and researched in the future.

2
Rethinking the Transnational Firm

> I think the balance is between, as someone once said, thinking globally and acting locally ... business is not simply global or local. What aspects of your business are local and what aspects are global, well, you need to think about them locally and act globally. And that inevitably leads you into a somewhat *complex* [my emphasis] matrix, structures and ways of thinking – that is the essentially real challenge.
>
> (Managing Partner [Europe], USConsultancy3, London)

Despite the vast academic literature that has developed over the last 30 years, the terminology used with regard to multinational firms (MNCs) or 'transnational firms' (TNCs) is hardly clear. Many academic writers and researchers still refer to 'MNCs' or 'multinational enterprises' (MNEs), never mentioning the term 'transnational firm'. For example, Held *et al* (1999) – the influential globalization theorists referred to in the last chapter – refer only to MNCs as a generic term for the world's largest private companies. The book, like many others (Hu 1992; Dunning 1993a; Dicken 1998), charts the historical rise of multinational business enterprises from the nineteenth century and earlier, moving on to consider how MNCs are responsible for the globalization of production in the world economy. Such an academic line of analysis is now well rehearsed (North 1985; Wilkins 1991; Jones 1992) and it is not my intention to reiterate the history of the MNC again here. What is more important to the argument of this book, is the question of what an MNC or TNC is, and whether all such organizations can be easily discussed and theorized so as a category in the contemporary world. The argument of this chapter is that TNCs cannot be clumped together as one category (and increasingly so). To understand why this is the case, and to find a path through the various, apparently overlapping, definitions of these business organizations, it is first necessary to differentiate these three terms: the MNC or MNE, the TNC and the global corporation.

The oldest term is, of course, the multinational company or enterprise (MNC or MNE). Within the social science literature, despite some debate as to when it is first relevant to refer to MNCs, these kinds of firms date back in a more or less equivalent organizational form to the latter part of the nineteenth century (Dassbach 1989). Multinational companies are generally defined as business enterprises that have productive operations in more than one nation-state (Cohen *et al* 1979). In the nineteenth century, those business enterprises that were involved in overseas activity were concentrated in the primary and extractive sectors (Wilkins 1994) and it is only in the interwar period in the earlier part of the twentieth century that foreign production becomes generally evident in manufacturing industries (Jones 1996). In the 1920s and 1930s, however, the scale and extent of these early MNCs' international operations was very limited in comparison to what has happened in the global economy since the end of the Second World War (Lipson 1985). The interwar years are important though because they saw the emergence of MNCs whose organizational form and approach to overseas production corresponds for the first time to that adopted by contemporary TNCs (Hymer 1976). Where earlier MNCs and concomitant flows of foreign direct investment (FDI) were concentrated in primary and extractive industries, the (primarily US) firms that undertook overseas production in the 1920s and 1930s operated in major manufacturing sectors – automobiles, electrical consumer goods and pharmaceuticals (Dunning 1988). For example, it is during these decades that companies like Ford, Hoover and Electrolux sought to move out of the domestic US economy and build factories and plants in Europe (Langworth 1987). In that sense, this period represents the beginning of multinational production in the world economy.

The MNC as a business organization has really only made its presence felt since the 1950s. In the immediate post-war decades, US firms reinstigated the project of internationalizing their businesses on the back of the political dominance gained in the West by the US at the end of the war (Griffin 1996). The 1950s and 1960s saw US manufacturing firms investing heavily in production plants in Europe and elsewhere, eager to expand their operations beyond the US domestic economy (Jones & Schroter 1993; Vatter & Walker 1996). The MNCs of this era fit the common popular understanding of what a multinational firm 'is' and how it is set-up. Companies like Ford or General Motors remained initially heavily dependent on their home economies which constituted the majority of their markets (Dunning 1988). In multinationalizing their operations, management control functions remained strongly concentrated in the origin economy with overseas production co-ordinated, certainly from a strategic perspective, from head offices in the home economy. The production operations themselves, at least, began life as relatively discreet undertakings from home economy production (Dunning 1993b). Thus, for example, car manufacturers such as Ford invested in European production where almost all of the components of the cars manufactured were made by new Ford-owned factories in the country concerned. Car manufacturers often achieved this in European economies by buying out existing domestic car firms or component supplier – General Motors purchased Vauxhall (UK) and Opel (West Germany) – but in terms of the organization of production, many of the MNCs of the 1950s and 1960s set-up the entire production operation in a new nation-state and market.

Within business studies, this kind of approach to multinational production (although a generalization) is reflected in the classic 'area-based' business model for an MNC as an organization (c.f. Wilkins 1974; Hymer 1976). Figure 2.1 shows this in a stylized form.[1]

Core managerial and strategic functions, along with research and development, remain largely concentrated in the home origin economy of the MNC whilst a series of separate and smaller overseas branch operations correspond to the company's activities in overseas markets. This business model was proposed as a generalization about the nature and form of the world's largest business organizations during the immediate post-war decades, certainly within the manufacturing sector, but since

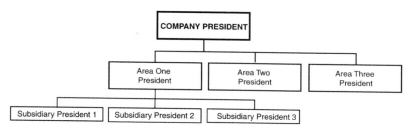

Figure 2.1 Classic Area-based Model of the Multinational Corporation (after Franko 1976)
Source: Franko (1976).

the 1970s a number of important shifts in the nature and form of MNCs have led to a reconceptualization amongst business theorists and social scientists (for example, Lall 1983; Hertner & Jones 1986; Eden & Potter 1993). It is due to these changes in the nature of MNCs as international organizations themselves that the term transnational corporation (TNC) has come into use. For the sake of brevity, I want to characterize the important general changes that MNCs have undergone along at least five themes.

Firstly, since the 1970s the number and size of MNCs/TNCs have increased dramatically. By the year 2000, there were more than 60 000 such corporations with over 800 000 affiliates abroad (UNCTAD 2001). Compared to earlier decades, the MNC or TNC has thus become a much more important generic player in the world economy. The share of total manufacturing output held by TNCs in all the largest advanced economies has increased dramatically (OECD 1996) and levels of foreign direct investment (FDI) continued to increase dramatically throughout the 1990s reaching a record $1.3 trillion in 2000 (UNCTAD 2001). Furthermore, contemporary TNCs are much larger than ever before. In 2000, the largest 25 TNCs in the global economy accounted for 12, 16 and 15 per cent of the total foreign assets, sales and employment of the world's 60 000 plus TNCs (UNCTAD 2001).

Second, the number of 'origin' economies of MNCs/TNCs has also been greatly diversified. Compared to the 1950s and 1960s when most of the world's largest business enterprises originated from the US, by the 1980s – as expressed in *Fortune* magazine's Global 100 – the ranks of the world's largest corporations included many European and Japanese companies. In the 1990s, a growing number of companies from what had been formerly known as the Newly Industrializing Countries (NICs) had joined this list: South Korea, Singapore, Malaysia and Taiwan (Lim & Teoh 1986; Kozul-Wright & Rowthorn 1998; Yeung 2002). Companies such as Lucky Goldstar (LG), Daewoo and Samsung – to name a few – are now amongst the top global players in their respective markets, the Asian Economic Crisis of the late 1990s notwithstanding (Sklair 1998). Furthermore, at the start of the twenty-first century, a small but growing number of the larger MNCs started out in states formerly considered to be part of the developing world – India, Chile, Brazil, Argentina (Heenan & Keegan 1979; Lall 1983; Khan 1986). In that sense, the MNC as an organizational form for business activity has long since ceased to be the reserve of a few large US firms and increasingly represents the dominant form of business enterprise across the globe.

Third, the largest manufacturing firms now operate at a global scale with much less importance for their national origin markets. Furthermore, within the major manufacturing sectors (automobiles, electronics, textiles, engineering) many commentators point to the existence and increasing importance of what are termed 'global production networks' (Taplin & Winterton 1997; Cheng & Kierzkowski 2001). Manufacturing production, in contrast to the discreet multiple national operations of the 1950s and 1960s, is increasingly organized by MNCs (or TNCs) across a network of production facilities in many different countries around the globe. Firms such as Toyota or IBM, for example, manufacture different components for their respective products in different countries with assembly of the final product occurring often elsewhere again. This often involves the use of complex subcontractor linkages with firms across the planet (Dyer 2000). Amongst academic theorists, this has been dubbed as the emergence of 'the global factory' (Grunwald & Flam 1985; Kamel 1991) where in its most extreme form, a car produced in the UK might have components manufactured in upwards of twenty other countries before it is exported to another European state. Even smaller TNCs, however, are increasingly organizing production through global networks of subsidiaries or affiliates (Bell 1995; Dyer 1996). In that sense, the geography of manufacturing production has radically altered to the degree that it becomes hard to define a single country where a given product was made, and it is also increasingly meaningless to refer to 'foreign' production in a global economy where in many key industries much manufacturing occurs in several countries.

Fourth, since the 1970s the classic organizational model of the MNC shown in Figure 2.1 has become much less applicable to the world's largest companies and in many cases it no longer fits the form of these business organizations. If manufacturing production increasingly takes place 'across' rather than 'within' multiple states, then the corporations responsible for this production have also transnationalized themselves in organizational terms. The shift in terminology from MNC to TNC is thus grounded in internal changes in the structure, organization and management of the largest corporations that have moved away from the multi-state framework (Gang 1992). By the 1980s, theorists of business organizations were widely discussing the 'matrix management model' where the matrix is formed by an intersection of functional and geographical organizational structures (Bresnen 1990; Rowe 1992). This model has been widely adopted as corporations have tried to globalize their organizational firm (shown in Figure 2.2) and sought to achieve

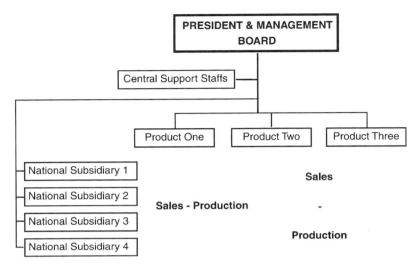

Figure 2.2   Matrix Model of Global Organizational Form

'the precarious balancing act' between geographical and functional structures in the TNC (Dunning 1993b: 220).

However, the implementation and effectiveness of matrix management has continued to be debated with no clear consensus on a single organizational model for the TNC (Doz & Prahalad 1991). What has been important has been the continuation of the process of dispersal of different corporate functions in many TNCs. Within manufacturing firms, it is not just production itself that has been split down at the level of components between many states, but also other aspects of the company's operation (Pitelis 1993). Core functions such as managerial control, marketing, research and development – to name a few – no longer remain the cherished privilege of the home origin economy but have themselves been decentralized across firms' transnational operations in many countries (Bartlett & Ghosal 1989; Pearce 1990). Thus, for example, companies such as Nissan or Microsoft have invested heavily in key research and development facilities in the US and Europe respectively. Figure 2.3 shows a stylized model of transnational organizational structure as might be applicable to a transnational car manufacturer. The key difference overall falls on the shift in emphasis in the way that the firm is structured – some or all divisions of the company are increasingly organized around functional rather than geographical (national or regional) lines. Management theorists argued that this represented a key

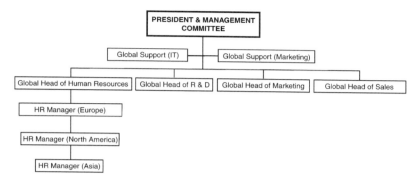

Figure 2.3 Model of Transnational Organizational Form (Manufacturing Firm)
Source: Various: Franko (1976): Interviews (Partner USConsultancy4, from a hand-drawn-
diagram).

trend in the organizational form of MNCs as far back as the early 1970s
(for example, Stopford & Wells 1972; Franko 1976), but the relevance of
this shift to more and more industries and companies that is significant
(Pauly & Reich 1997).

Fifth, the final major theme of change is the emergence and growing
importance of service-sector TNCs (Howells & Wood 1993) which have
pursued very different strategies of transnational organizational development from either the classic MNC model or contemporary manufacturing
TNCs (Knight 1999). In the 1990s, more and more companies in all
kinds of service-sector industries became transnational in the scale, scope
and outlook of their operations. Where earlier post-war MNCs were
concentrated almost exclusively in the primary extractive and manufacturing sectors, the contemporary global population of TNCs includes
both consumer-service firms (food, beverages, hospitality, retail) and
producer services (accountancy, banking, advertising, law, media, management consultancy) (Friedland 1992). More important than the emergence of international firms in these sectors *per se* however, is the
implications that the transnationalization of business in these industries
has for understanding and defining the TNC as a category.

In this respect, researchers in management studies have identified
what is termed the 'born-global' phenomenon amongst small firms in
a number of economies (Knight & Cavusgil 1996; Madsen & Servais
1997). In essence, often operating in high-tech and – most importantly
to this study – 'knowledge-intensive' service industries, these small
firms are set-up from start-up to operate at the global scale (Bell *et al*
2001). Although not an industry discussed specifically in the literature,

the 'born-global' argument is highly relevant to many small management consultancy firms. Thus, corporations in service industries have not so much moved away from the classic MNC organizational model shown in Figure 2.1, but rather many never had that kind of organizational form in the first place. To take a further service-sector example, large consumer-service companies such as the fast-food chains (McDonalds, Burger King, Kentucky Fried Chicken) have transnationalized their businesses using a very different organizational formula from that of manufacturing companies. Unconstrained by the necessity of substantial production plants physically making large or complex products, these corporations have pursued a mixture of franchise-based outlets combined with a centralized transnational approach to quality-control, advertising and marketing (Ahoroni *et al* 2000). Such an organizational structure bears little in common with classic post-war MNC models but represents a very different kind of model for transnational organizational form when compared to manufacturing TNCs – a stylized representation of the corporate form of these kind of fast-food TNCs is shown in Figure 2.4. In that sense, therefore, the arrival of service-sector TNCs in the global economy further erodes the usefulness of the classic MNC model as a theoretical base for understanding corporations operating in more than one country, and also complicates the idea of the TNC as a generalizeable category.

The contemporary concept of a transnational firm is thus much more complex than the earlier idea of a multinational company. Whilst in some cases it could be argued that for some firms the classic MNC model is still very applicable, these five major shifts in the nature of international business suggest that contemporary corporations are better referred to generically as TNCs. However, the debate around nomenclature does not stop there because within the business studies literature, and increasingly in the media, many of the largest TNCs are being described as 'global corporations' (Greider 1997; Doremus *et al* 1998). For some the 'global corporation' is taken as no more than a generalized synonym for the TNCs with the most geographically extensive production operations (Gray 1998; Holton 1998), but for other commentators within business studies, this idea of truly 'global corporations' represents the ultimate goal of the kinds of shifts I have described here in the shift towards more a transnational form in MNCs (Fukuyama 1993; Ohmae 1995). In that sense very few, if any, of today's largest TNCs have yet reached this state. To some extent, therefore, the difference between a transnational or global corporation might be considered semantic. However, the next section examines how the

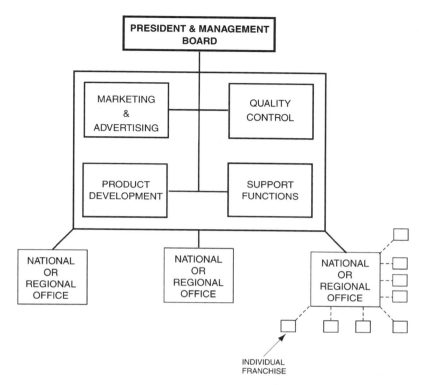

Figure 2.4   Model of Transnational Organizational Form (Consumer Services)

academic debate over the nature of TNCs is lacking in important respects.

The myths and realities of the 'global corporation'

In the last five years or so, it has become the vogue for TNCs in all kinds of business sectors, manufacturing and services, to market and present themselves as global corporations. Being 'global' has now become so well established as a desirable goal for any successful company that the rhetoric of management fads seems to have already moved on from the simple question of corporate globality to considering what kind of global company TNCs should seek to become. Even the most cursory time spent surfing the websites of major TNCs reveals that at the start of the twenty-first century there is hardly a TNC in existence that does not at some point mention its 'globalness' or 'global strategy' in its corporate publications and marketing material. Being global, at least in some general if undefined manner, has become an accepted requirement of good business practice for managers in large corporations. As one Executive Director who oversaw a large US investment bank's corporate finance business told me, 'if you're not global head of something these days, you're nobody' (Executive Director, EuroBank2, London) – he was referring to the managers he dealt with in the TNCs that represented most of his clients. Both employees and firms themselves have come to see the need to be global in their outlook, operations and image.

The key question that needs addressing, however, is to what extent this new rhetoric of globality is justified as a description of new kinds of organizational form in the largest TNCs. Or is the idea of the 'global corporation' more hyperbole and myth than business reality? The subsequent chapters will address this issue in some considerable depth within the management consultancy and investment banking sectors, but before this analysis some broader discussion of the debate surrounding the idea of the global corporation is required. This section lays out the criteria by which the term 'global corporation' might be justified and assesses what evidence has been presented amongst social scientists in this regard. It also discusses the logics and arguments that lie behind the rhetoric being developed and adopted by senior business managers to justify the emergence of this new kind of business enterprise.

Firstly, then, how might a 'global corporation' be usefully defined? The unsubstantiated and 'loose' use of the concept as a simple synonym for the largest TNCs is wholly unsatisfactory. The *hyperglobalist* perspective of some globalization theorists (after Held *et al* 1999) tends to use the term in this manner as a generalized description of very large TNCs in order to emphasize the increasing integration of global economic activity at the international scale. The 'global corporation' within academic writing, therefore, often represents compatible rhetoric to those who share a belief in the virtues of accelerating and strengthening economic globalization. In contrast, I want to suggest that a definition based on the nature of the organization itself is more useful. A global corporation – if such an entity exists – is better defined as a business organization whose productive activities are so dispersed around the globe that no specific nation or region is significantly more important to the company than another. Of course, 'significantly more important' becomes the crux of the issue and there can be no universally agreed refinement to that – different TNCs have very different geographies of production. The point, however, is that the global corporation – to be a concept worth differentiating from TNCs in general – suggests a new degree of 'beyond nationalness' (Ruigrok & Tulder 1995).

Within the social sciences, the more critical globalization theorists have been quick to embroil this discussion in their wider debates about the impact of globalization in general on nation-states and national sovereignty. Held *et al* (1999) effectively dismiss the idea of a 'global corporation' on the grounds that the concept rests on the assumption that the largest TNCs have become 'deterritorialized' (Giddens 1990) from national economies and national/regional contexts. Amongst economists and other business theorists, research has quite quickly discredited such a claim on the (rather obvious) grounds that TNCs are deeply embedded in local, regional and national environments – whether that be through component supplier linkages, labour markets or market access (Dicken 1998; Doremus *et al* 1998; Yeung 2000). The 'global corporation' is thus argued to be a misnomer because, quite rightly, TNCs are heavily involved in the political, economic and social contexts of the many territories they operate in.

This debate misses the point though – certainly from the point of view of the business practitioners I spoke to – about what a global corporation is or is not. The criteria that are most important in establishing whether something new has happened to TNCs in the last few years should not be concerned with the nature of the external relationships in different contexts but rather with internal changes in the transnational organization. In considering the evolution of the MNC into TNC, I have so far argued that, as a generalization, the term TNC is increasingly more appropriate to describe large business enterprises in the global economy because of the way in which these organizations have changed in extent and form. Today's TNCs are very different in terms of how internal functions and operations are set-up from those of the 1960s (Bharat 1997; Devinney *et al* 2000). This in turn is reflected in a different international organizational structure in terms of functional divisions within the TNC as an organization that increasingly spans political-territorial boundaries rather than replicating them within the business organization (Raines & Brown 2001). The essence of this argument is illustrated in Figure 2.3 by contrasting the model of transnational organizational form with what would represent a new model for corporate globality.

The criteria I want to suggest are best used to assess the validity of both the idea of a global corporation and its appropriateness as a description of any given firm are therefore grounded on identifying a further degree of internal organizational change that increasingly decouples (but not deterritorializes) organizational structures, practices, operations and functions from state political boundaries. A global corporation is thus one whose *organizational form* has ceased to be significantly influenced by external geographical boundaries but rather is geared to allowing the company to compete globally most effectively. It is worth reiterating again, however, that these internal shifts in organizational form do not mean that geography, territory or external political institutions and boundaries become irrelevant or even less important to the firm's successful operation (Davidson & De la Torre 1989). On the contrary, it is likely that as a firm becomes more 'global', the growing numbers of different political and institutional contexts the company operates in will mean these issues absorb more of the corporation's resources. But globality also means that any given national or even regional context specifically becomes less important to how the business organization as a whole is organized and structured. The necessity of dealing with increasing numbers of different national contexts in increasingly complex ways leads the business organization to deprioritize any one geographical consideration in its organizational form.

This is the definitional criterion applied to the idea of the global corporation through the rest of this book. The argument is that the reality (or otherwise) of 'global corporations' rests with the nature of the business organizations operating in today's world and not with wider structural shifts in the geography of production, trade, investment or any other broadly quantifiable indicator. In that sense, therefore, a large part of the existing discussion of TNCs in relation to wider 'generalized' globalization theory is limited and unhelpful. Where it has been more salient and useful is in the realm of management studies and organizational sociology where the focus has long been on questions of what goes on within the largest TNCs in the global economy (for example, Barnet & Cavanagh 1995; Nohria & Ghoshal 1997). Therefore, in assessing the evidence for corporate globality in line with my definitional criteria, it is these disciplinary traditions that I will consider next.

Again, given the substantial literature in existence, I will focus on two recent works by leading theorists within business and management studies. The arguments made in these books reflect a much wider body of research and debate and in that sense are a good indicator of current thinking about the 'globalness' or otherwise of TNCs. In that regard, both works are quite clearly aimed at redressing the *hyperglobalist* tendencies of much business rhetoric and globalization theory with their titles – '*The Myth of the Global Corporation*' (Doremus *et al* 1998) and '*The End of Globalization*' (Rugman 2001). The arguments made by both share common ground in offering a critique of the idea that most TNCs even operate, let alone are structured, at the global level. In that sense, therefore, the research these authors present casts considerable doubt on the prevalence of the kind of shift in organizational form illustrated in Figure 2.3. I identified five major common threads that these critiques of the concept of 'corporate globality' develop between them.

Firstly, Doremus *et al* (1998) argue that the idea of the global corporation is in reality no more than a myth from an organizational perspective. They focus first on the 'high order' functions of TNCs, examining the nature of corporate governance and managerial control. They argue that if the largest TNCs are becoming more global as organizations then it is to be expected that the regimes of corporate governance (the basic patterns of control within the organization) along with the sources of long-term finance that such companies utilize will be becoming more similar. In comparing US, German and Japanese TNCs, they find enduring diversity in the way in which the largest TNCs which originated from these national contexts are both governed and financed. For example, for US firms individual shareholders continued to have little voice in managerial decisions taken by the board whereas in Germany stakeholders may exert more managerial influence in the corporate governance process. A similar argument is also made by Alan Rugman in his book.

Second, Doremus *et al* also point to what they see as continuing diversity between TNCs originated from different countries in approach, funding and implementation of investment and innovation. Again, contrary to the view expressed elsewhere in the business studies literature (Fukuyama 1993; Barnet & Cavanagh 1995), they argue that any view of converging corporate behaviour across the industrialized world is misplaced. Their research provides evidence of very different and distinct institutional environments shaping the strategies of TNCs between the US, Germany, the UK and Japan (see also Coleman 1996; Cerny 1998).

This links to a third theme refuting the notion of the global corporation according to Doremus *et al* – the continued variable geography of research and development (R & D) between large TNCs in all sectors. Both Doremus *et al* and Rugman (2001) make the point that even the largest TNCs adopt highly regionalized, if not localized, approaches towards R & D with this high-order function continuing to be concentrated on disproportionately in origin economies. In the shift of organizational form from a transnational to global model, this would be expected to be an indicator of the declining significance of any one (and especially the origin) country.

Fourth, Doremus *et al* argue that another of the supposed key indicators of corporate globality – the level of cross-border intrafirm trade between affiliated units of TNCs – varies considerably depending on what sector the TNC operates in and where it originated. In general, they point to the fact that US firms invest abroad in ways that tend to create much less intrafirm trade than German, Japanese or British originating TNCs and thus argue that TNCs from different national bases are pursuing very different global production strategies.

Finally, both Doremus *et al* and Rugman place great emphasis on the evidence they find for the considerable regional concentration of TNC activities. In short, if TNCs no longer are highly dependant on national markets and national production operations, then many companies are still very much reliant on regional markets rather than global ones. Many firms within the EU, for example, continue to operate and trade far more proportionately in Europe than they do globally. The idea, therefore, that such TNCs are global corporations is seen to be an exaggeration based on the persistence of regional bias and volumes of trade and revenue concentrated in those regions (Hirst & Thompson 1999).

Overall, therefore, these authors between them present a case against the careless use of the term 'global corporation'. In so doing they echo the direction taken by a substantial body of work within management studies journals.[2] Yet, whilst their contribution is undoubtedly valuable and an important critique – not least in counteracting the extreme claims of the *hyperglobalists* – they do not fully invalidate the concept of the global corporation. The argument I want to make is that the limitations of these attempts to discredit the global corporation as an idea have more to do with the terms rather than the substance of the rebuttal. In identifying general trends between TNCs in different sectors and with similar national origins, Doremus *et al* rightly add another layer of understanding to the complexity and diversity of global business enterprise amongst TNCs. What this does not do, however, is directly address that question about the increasingly pervasive shift in organizational form within these organizations. Finding evidence of the continued importance of national institutional contexts or the way in which research and development is organized by TNCs from a certain country in general does not refute the validity of the notion that these TNCs are shifting towards greater organizational globality. Likewise, arguing from a sector-wide viewpoint against the general relevance of the term 'global corporation' fails to acknowledge both the key importance of the few largest firms in the global economy (UNCTAD 2001) and the evidence these 'leading' corporate globalizers might offer in respect of the future development of TNCs.

Consequently, it would be helpful to change the terms of the debate around the concept of the 'global corporation'. To some extent, the nomenclature of MNC, TNC or global corporations relies on differences that are defined and determined on generic classifications of the global population of over 60 000 large firms with operations in more than one nation-state. How these diverse and varied group of business organizations are determined to be multinational, transnational or global thus rests often on measures which vary enormously between individual firms, firms in different business sectors and originating countries – conceptual definitions in that sense always rest on relatively arbitrary definitions of what constitutes 'transnationalness' or 'globalness' at the collective level. For that reason, in order to understand the changing nature of contemporary TNCs, it is important to conduct research and theorize change within these organizations that goes beyond the generalized model approach illustrated in Figures 2.1, 2.2 and 2.3. Most of the literature to date on globalization and TNCs from a social science perspective is grounded in research, as with Doremus *et al* and Rugman, that focuses on groups of companies which are in reality operating in very different markets, institutional contexts and have very different forms of businesses. More attention needs to be focused on individual organizations and groups of similar firms in the same sector and different kinds of (qualitative) data are needed to explore these changes.

Overall, my suggestion is that the critique of the 'global corporation' being deployed by theorists like Doremus *et al* (1998) and Rugman (2001) is not sufficient to justify discarding the concept itself. More importantly, this kind of research is only going part of the way when it comes to providing more detailed understanding of what changes are occurring amongst the key business enterprises in the global economy. What is needed is an in-depth analysis of what changes individual TNCs are undergoing, along with the managerial logics and strategies being implemented in attempts at organizational globalization. Management studies as a discipline has long researched and debated many of these issues about the nature of transnational firms, and this work provides an important basis to many of my arguments about *organizational globalization*. Yet this discipline also continues to operate within a quantitative and generalist research paradigm that rarely explores the nature of business globalization within specific TNCs or groups of firms. My contention, therefore, is that a different methodological and conceptual approach is required if organizational globalization is to be better understood.

Inside the transnational firm

The experiences of conducting research into TNCs in the investment banking and management consultancy sectors highlighted the strength of adopting a more interdisciplinary framework to theorizing how TNCs operate and function in today's world. In seeking to overcome disciplinary narrowness, I drew upon the research traditions of several social science disciplines to examine what solidified into four key conceptual aspects of these advanced service-sector TNCs. All four concepts produce a theoretical insight that is more focused on the organizational scale rather than exclusively on quantifiable 'external' measures of TNC activity.

The first of these concepts is *organizational form* – the institutional structure of TNCs in terms of how companies are set-up along divisional and geographical lines. Management theory has, of course, always been concerned with the strategic and technical issues surrounding how to structure corporate organizations, and in the era of increasing numbers of TNCs, this has naturally become increasingly concerned with how to structure transnational business organizations (Morrison *et al* 1991; Ghoshal & Westney 1993; Nohria & Ghoshal 1997). However, in contrast to the often (but not always) generalist approach of much of the management literature, there is considerable diversity in the organizational forms of contemporary TNCs, related to factors such as industrial sector, corporate size, corporate and managerial culture and business strategy. Management theory and organizational sociology provide, for example, general theoretical models of how transnational firms should be structured as organizations (Kogut & Zander 1993; Hedlund 1994; O'Donnell 2000), which form part of MBA courses. Yet in order to understand the future development of specific TNCs, organizational form needs to be understood in the wider context of any given firms' activities (Holmström & Roberts 1998) and not just from the logistical 'how-to-do-it' perspective of much management theory.

Secondly, and related, the management and business studies literature are concerned with the nature of *managerial structures* within firms, and in that sense increasingly within transnational firms (for example, Richards 2000; Sethi & Thompson 2000). Again, however, this tends to be primarily from a logistical and implementative perspective rather than through a critical engagement with the nature of power and control in TNCs. In order to understand the activities of TNCs in the global economy more effectively, there is a need to engage theoretically with the way in which internal decisions are made and implemented along with the effect that those managerial activities have on the TNCs' operations (Papadakis *et al* 1998) – aside from pure quantitative indicators of 'competitiveness' (Porter 1990; Grant 1991; Keltner 1995). For example, the key foreign direct investment decisions made by TNCs which are becoming increasing important to states and other firms are clearly shaped by the ability of TNCs to effectively construct adequate systems of control within the transnational organization. Without engaging theoretically with these transnational managerial structures, only a limited understanding of the development of TNCs' global production or investment patterns is likely to be achievable.

This leads to the third key conceptual area to my framework for rethinking how TNCs are to be theorized. This is concerned with the role of *interpersonal relations* as employees in TNCs 'do' transnational business. Within several social science disciplines, there has been a growing interest in the social nature of economic activity over the last decade with research being conducted into the nature of interpersonal relations between employees within firms (Thrift 2000). The 'new economic sociology' argues that in contrast to classical approaches to economic theory, economic activity needs to be understood as being 'embedded' in social relations (Granovetter & Swedberg 1994; Ingham 1996). However, in line with the arguments of some management theorists (Harvey *et al* 1999; Brock *et al* 2000) and others (Yeung 2002), in re-examining how TNCs are theorized, I take these arguments further by arguing that an understanding of the nature of social relations at the transnational scale needs to be central to future theories of TNCs. As firms become larger, more globally extensive and complex – and in the current era where many argue that information and knowledge are becoming more central to business activity and success itself (Archibugi & Michie 1995; Castells 1996) – engaging with the social relations that constitute transnational business activity both within TNCs and between their employees and other firms or organizations needs to be at the centre of any theoretical framework. Management theory has gone some way in this regard in trying to theorize the nature and importance of interpersonal relations in TNCs generally, but such studies have so far stopped short of in-depth analyses within specific firms and sectors. Rather, the existing management theory in this area tends to rely on wider-ranging quantitative surveys that produce models intended to guide business practitioners (for example, Harrison 1994; Murtha *et al* 1998; O'Donnell 2000). In arguing for the significance of *interpersonal relations*, I am suggesting that this theory needs to get much deeper into the complexity of this issue than the management studies approach has so far pursued.

The fourth and final concept that arose from my research experience is captured in the term *transnational corporate culture*. Interest in corporate culture is argued by some commentators to be little more than a recent management 'fad' (Geneen & Bowers 1999) and it has indeed generated a considerable volume of literature amongst business gurus and management theorists. However, a growing body of academic writing has begun to take the question of corporate organizational culture more seriously, assessing what kinds of behaviours correspond to identifiable corporate cultural facets and exploring the impacts that different kinds of corporate culture might have on the success or otherwise of firms (Trompenaars 1993; Brock *et al* 2000). What has received little or no attention, though, is the question of corporate culture within TNCs – does such a thing as global corporate culture(s) exist? In understanding the future development of TNCs, this concept represents a basis for theorizing how collective social relations interact with organizational histories in TNCs, how accepted methods for conducting transnational business are evolving and the way in which wider cultural norms are dealt with and are significant in the workplace. Thinking about transnational corporate culture also enables an investigation of how transnational organizations are bound together and made coherent by shared cultural values and behavioural norms – all kinds of theoretical issues that figure little in existing theorizations of economic globalization.

Conclusion: rethinking the transnational firm

Across the social sciences, the literature concerned with TNCs makes much of external wider changes taking places in terms of the information technology revolution that has greatly facilitated the transnationalization of business activity (Castells 1996) or the shifting supra national political and institutional structure that has aided firms in their transnational business strategies (Held *et al* 1999; Langhorne 2001). However, whilst being clearly important, the role of such changes can be over-prioritized in explanations and theories of contemporary global economy. Considerable empirical research has propagated an acceptance of a standard script concerning the globalization of business without paying sufficient attention to the details of how individual firms in specific sectors are actually becoming more transnational (or otherwise). Broad quantitative data on, for example, the rapidly increasing proportion of world trade that now is accounted for by different parts of the same TNC 'trading' internationally with each other has appeared to provide ample support for the pervasive claims of the centrality of TNCs to globalization in general. Likewise, many academic commentators rely on aggregate numerical data quantifying, for example, the growing numbers of TNCs, their operational locations around the globe, global sales and total global employees. Whilst this kind of data does provide some insight into the significance of TNCs in today's world, my suggestion is that it offers only a very limited picture of the key actors in the global economy. Furthermore, reliance on this kind of research data is likely to produce misleading theoretical claims about the role of TNCs in economic globalization whilst also serving to reinforce the problematic generalized theoretical approach to globalization I adopted in the last chapter.

Consequently, there is a need for an ongoing theoretical and conceptual 'rethink' as to how TNCs are researched and understood. In theorizing transnational investment banking and management consultancy firms around the four concepts outlined in this chapter, the goal is to produce a much more sophisticated understanding of the complexity of transnational business activity in today's world. TNCs in all sectors are growing in number, size and organizational sophistication. They employ more and more people in more and more different locations around the globe, and as these business organizations grow in complexity, the kinds of theoretical insights that can be drawn from existing theoretical approaches to economic globalization – grounded in generalized globalization theory – are limited. It is only by taking an interdisciplinary theoretical approach which seeks to get inside the 'black box' of the TNC in specific industries and contexts that any meaningful understanding of how firms are likely to evolve and develop in the contemporary global economy will emerge. There is still a place for broader quantitative analyses of the TNC as a generic category, but future research increasingly needs to address the specifics of corporate organization in more detail by exploring the processes of change from within companies. This does, of course, present some methodological challenges for both academics and business theorists who will need to spend more time talking to business practitioners themselves rather than relying on numerical data produced by the transnational corporate machinery.

The next three chapters offer evidence of the advantages to such an approach as they examine the transnational management consultancy and investment banking industries through the conceptual framework

I have outlined. Chapter 3 therefore now turns to examine the first two concepts in this approach – transnational organizational form and managerial structures – in constructing a theoretical understanding of what is occurring in these advanced business-service industry sectors.

3
Global Investment Banking and Management Consultancy

> When I joined *UKBank3*, it was only a couple of thousand people in a dozen countries – that was eight years ago. Now we have over eight thousand in something like seventy-five locations across forty different countries.
>
> (Director, Human Resources, UKBank3, London)

For academics and business people alike, the globalization of business seems to be quite easily 'proved' by the large and growing number of physical locations in which contemporary TNCs have offices. Whenever I asked a senior management consultant or investment banker about the issue of 'globalization' in general, their first inclination was, like the Director quoted above, to tell me about the sheer number of offices their respective companies had in different cities around the globe. 'Globalization' in both these industries is strongly associated with the physicality of having a building and staff in multiple, strategic locations around the world. And such locations tended to be in urban centres in different countries where these service companies currently are undertaking (or planning to undertake) business activity (Jenkens 1996). Likewise, in the academic social sciences, the key importance placed on 'global' and 'globalizing' cities is largely founded on empirical research concerned with the numbers, spread and locations of corporate head offices (for example, Brotchie *et al* 1995; Lo & Yeung 1998; Beaverstock *et al* 2001; Sassen 2001).

Unfortunately, this kind of data on office locations has generated too simplistic a theoretical story of business transnationalization.[1] Quantitative studies of office locations alone cannot develop much theoretical leverage in understanding the nature of business transnationalization because such theories are restricted to a weak assertion of a company's *presence* in multiple national economies – and I am not even sure that they adequately theorize that. The problem is that knowledge of a company's *'presence'* in a certain location explains nothing about the nature of its business activities. This chapter therefore begins by examining research into broad trends of organizational change in both business-service industries, arguing that common to both management consultancy firms and investment banks is a trend of shifting organizational structure away from a geographical- towards a function-based model of the TNC. Although this shift in organizational form is by no means a coherent or uniform process of change occurring either between firms or industries, it does represent a general process of organizational globalization occurring within TNCs in these industries. The research found evidence of this shift in respect of three aspects of the TNC as a business organization: office location, business division structures and corporate financial structure. I consider each in turn.

Changing patterns of office location

At the industry-wide level, little attention has been paid to management consultancy in the context of the wider globalization debate within the social sciences and amongst business commentators, perhaps as a consequence of its relatively recent emergence as a growing business sector in advanced industrial economies (Czerniawska 2001). The literature that deals with this industry specifically within the social sciences – such as it is – is concentrated almost exclusively within management studies (for example, Bloomfield & Daniela 1995; Clark 1995; Sturdy 1997; Fincham 1999). Across the rest of the academic debate around globalization, management consultancy tends otherwise to be lumped together with other 'advanced business services' that are argued to be important to contemporary globalization and today's accompanying 'informational economy' (Daniels & Moulaert 1991; Castells 1996; Ferguson 2002). Investment banking has, on the other hand, fared rather better – at least in terms of social scientific research and the clearer centrality of large investment banks in the continuing development of the global economy (Smith & Walter 1997). Especially since the later 1980s when deregulation (Helleiner 1994) and information/ communication technologies led to the accelerated integration of global financial markets, investment banks have become the object of academic interest as key players in the wider processes of globalization (Henwood 1997; Thrift & Leyshon 1997; Martin 1998). In fact, investment banking as a sector has been argued by many academics and business commentators to represent one of the 'most globalized' of all business sectors because of the high degree of integration achievable in finance with advances in IT (O'Brien 1991; Martin 1994; Hutton 1995; Liaw 1999).

However, when taken together there are a number of common trends of physical organizational restructuring – manifest in office location patterns – that can be detected in the management consultancy and investment banking industries in recent years. The first of these trends is that in both industries, the pattern of head-office location appears to have continued to centralize (Sassen 1994; Llewelyn-Davies 1997). Table 3.1 shows the head-office locations of the global top twenty investment banks and Table 3.2 shows the head-office locations of the top twenty management consultancy[2] firms. These companies continue to have a strong locational preference for cities regarded as being at or

Table 3.1   Head Office Locations of Leading Investment Banks

Rank	Bank*	Head Office Location
1	**Deutsche Bank**	Frankfurt (Germany)
2	**JP Morgan Chase**	New York (US)
3	**Credit Suisse**	Zurich (Switzerland)
4	**Bank of America**	New York (US)
5	BNP Paribas	Paris (France)
6	**Mitzuho Holdings**	Tokyo (Japan)
7	**HSBC Holdings**	London (UK)
8	**UBS Warburg**	London (UK)/Zurich (Switzerland)
9	Fortis	Brussels (Belgium)/Amsterdam (The Netherlands)
10	**ABN AMRO**	London (UK)
11	Credit Agricole	Paris (France)
12	Hypo Vereinsbank	Frankfurt (Germany)
13	Santander Central	Madrid (Spain)
14	**Royal Bank of Scotland**	London (UK)
15	Wells Fargo	Chicago (US)
16	Bank of Tokyo-Mitsubishi	Tokyo (Japan)
17	**Bank One Corp**	New York (US)
18	**Barclays**	London (UK)
19	Sumitomo Bank	Tokyo (Japan)
20	First Union Corp	New York (US)

* The banks are ranked by revenue, but whilst most are both commercial and savings banks, the data does not permit the separation of commercial and savings activities.
Bold denotes a company where senior managers were interviewed.
Source: Fortune Global 500 (2000), Fortune Magazine (2000).

Table 3.2 Head Office Locations of Leading Management Consultancies*

1	Accenture	Chicago (US)
2	CSC[1]	Los Angeles (US)
3	Cap Gemini/Ernst & Young	London (UK)/New York (US)
4	Price Waterhouse Coopers	London (UK)/New York (US)
5	KPMG Consulting	London (UK)/New York (US)/ Amsterdam (The Netherlands)
6	William M Mercer	New York (US)
7	Hewitt Associates	Chicago (US)
8	Deloite Consulting	New York (US)
9	Andersen[2]	Chicago (US)
10	Towers Perrin	New York (US)
11	AMS	Fairfax, Virg. (US)
12	Booz Allen Hamilton	London (UK)
13	McKinsey & Company	Boston (USA)
14	Watson Wyatt	Washington, DC (US)
15	AT Kearney	Chicago (US)
16	PA Consulting	London (UK)
17	Cambridge Technology	Cambridge, Mass. (US)
18	Boston Consulting	Boston (US)
19	Arthur D Little	Cambridge, Mass. (US)
20	Bain & Company	Boston (US)

[1] CSC is an IT firm but is involved heavily in consultancy related to management issues.

[2] At the time of writing, Andersen is unlikely to survive as a global firm after its involvement in the Enron affair. Indications suggest it will break up and be bought/merge into other consultancy firms.

* This table is as comprehensive as key data source permit but due to the ill-defined nature of the 'management consultancy' sector, some firms have been omitted which do undertake similar business-service activity as part of their operations.

Bold denotes a company where senior managers were interviewed.

near the top of the 'global urban hierarchy' (Beauregard 1989; Short & Kim 1999; Beaverstock *et al* 2001).

The second trend, as other studies in the early 1990s indicated for these industries (Knight & Gappert 1989; Sassen 1991; Daniels 1993), is that in the last five years these business-service TNCs have expanded into a growing number of cities around the globe. It was widely indicated by senior managers interviewed in both industries that growing 'global presence' is a common shift with companies continuing to expand the number of countries with operations, business cycle fluctuations notwithstanding:

> Throughout the last decade we have been opening new offices. Cautiously, at times, I'd say ... But a steady increase in numbers of cities where we have people.
>
> (Managing Director, EuroBank1, London)

We are growing globally, yes. We've opened two new offices over the last year – both in Asia. And that process will continue. Undoubtedly. That's the wider pattern in consultancy, and also in accountancy, financial services . . .

(Managing Partner, USConsultancy3, London)

This is reflected in survey data on country operations, although there is some evidence that this expansion has been tempered in both industries by the global economic slowdown of the 00s (JP Morgan Chase 2001; PWC 2001). Tables 3.3 and 3.4 show the locational presence of the top 20 firms in each industry in different countries (by region) around the globe in 2002. In general, there are three points I want to draw attention to that arise from this data. First, within both industries there is a high degree of transnationality insofar as presence in countries is an indicator. Almost all these business-service companies have multiple offices in the three major triad regions and in many cases the largest firms

Table 3.3 Country Presence (by region) of Leading Investment Banks

Firm	Countries	Americas	Europe	Asia	Other
BNP Paribas	86	18	26	14	28
HSBC Holdings	81	13	23	19	26
Deutsche Bank	74	12	26	15	21
ABN AMRO	67	12	29	16	10
Fortis	65	n/a	n/a	n/a	n/a
Barclays	62	22	23	6	11
Credit Agricole	60	12	17	17	14
JP Morgan Chase	55	12	17	11	15
UBS	50	14	15	9	13
Bank of Tokyo-Mitsubishi	44	10	12	14	8
Santander Central	42	18	12	4	8
Hypo Vereinsbank	40	4	25	8	3
Bank of America	38	7	11	10	10
Credit Suisse	37	8	16	11	2
Sumitomo Bank	28	3	6	13	6
First Union Corp	28	8	5	10	5
Mizuho Holdings	23	4	5	12	3
Wells Fargo	13	8	1	3	2
Royal Bank of Scotland	12	2	5	4	1
Bank One Corp	11	3	2	5	1

Table 3.4   Country Presence (by region) of Leading Management Consultancies

Firm	Countries	Americas	Europe	Asia	Other
Price Waterhouse Coopers	138	31	41	15	61
Andersen	84	17	30	13	24
KPMG Consulting	62	15	34	5	8
Accenture	47	7	22	11	7
McKinsey & Co	44	8	21	11	4
William M Mercer	40	16	12	8	6
AT Kearney	38	6	20	9	3
Hewitt Associates	37	9	16	6	6
Hay Group	35	7	19	6	3
Deloitte Consulting	34	6	15	10	3
Booz Allen & Hamilton	32	9	12	6	5
Arthur D Little	32	5	15	5	7
Cap Gemini/Ernst & Young	31	3	18	7	3
Watson Wyatt	29	6	11	10	2
Towers Perrin	23	6	9	5	3
CSC	22	3	14	3	2
PA Consulting	19	2	10	4	3
Cambridge Technology	18	6	9	2	1
Bain & Co	18	4	7	5	2
AMS	13	1	11	0	1

operate branch offices in upwards of 40 countries. Second, many of these banks and consultancies still display a clear regional bias to their business with many more offices in the region nearest to their origin economy. European or Japanese investment banks tend to have greater country-presence in Europe and Asia respectively, and amongst the consultancy firms the dominance of an origin region is especially apparent amongst the smaller companies. Third, when compared to many manufacturing TNCs, the size of the companies measured in terms of employees is relatively small given their degree of global presence. The largest manufacturing TNCs employ many hundreds of thousands whereas only a handful of the largest business-service firms have in excess of 100 000 employees globally. The consultancy firms are also on average smaller companies than the banks, even though they generally maintain a presence in a comparable number of countries.

This last point represents the third common trend: at the industry-wide level business services, transnationalization of the business is not just restricted to the larger companies. Contrary to the image of global

TNCs as 'Fortune 500' sized companies,[3] smaller management consultancies in particular have a growing number of offices outside their originating region. A Partner in one such small consultancy described this:

> I am trying to give you a sense of our global spread. Today we have twenty-five offices around the world in nineteen countries. For the first time in 1998, more than half our business came from outside North America which is a psychologically important milestone – having been founded originally in Boston. We have to date thirteen hundred consulting staff – about 2000 staff in total. So we are not a small operation . . .
> (Managing Partner, USConsultancy3, London)

The same trend is occurring in the investment banking sector, although 'to a lesser extent' (General Manager, JapanBank2, New York) as banks are, in the opinions of many senior managers, more able to compete globally if they have a larger capital base[4]:

> We have offices in 67 countries. Corporate Finance offices are originating business in 40 offices, and we have securities operations which have significant operations (a greater than 5% market share) in ten countries in Asia. We have securities operations in 14 countries in Asia.
> (Managing Director, Equities and New Issues, EuroBank1)

From the industry-wide data on office locations, therefore, both these industries appear to be undergoing dynamic changes which are more or less in line with the generalized globalization arguments found in the existing literature: that business-service firms are 'globalizing' and spreading their operations throughout the global economy through an interlinked network of offices in a 'globalized city network' (Sassen 2001).

However, when I suggested such an argument to senior business managers, a range of issues emerged which considerably complicate and problematize this simplistic notion. First, managers in both transnational banks and consultancies told me that their firms tend to have a 'multi-layered hierarchy' of offices. Centralization and 'office significance' correspond to at least several locational layers of importance in the organizational structure. Take one of the major European investment banks, for example:

We have our headquarters in Zurich, a retail division in Switzerland with about 6000 people, and we also have group management in Zurich as well with about 3000 people. The largest and most important centre outside Switzerland is London with 3000, then New York 2000, Singapore, Hong Kong each have 500, Tokyo about 500 to 600. Then our next largest is Frankfurt with 300 on the investment banking side, 400 on the investment management side, Luxembourg 200. Then there are a lot of smaller offices under these... so some are more important offices, yes.

> (Managing Director, Head of Human Resources [Europe],
> EuroBank4, London)

A similar story was told by a manager in one of the biggest global consultancy firms:

Well, like any business we have a chief executive globally. He has a small team of people, one of them is responsible for the service line development, one of them is responsible for the industry program, and one for planning. But that is quite a small group. And the global control is split into three regions. And then after that control flows down through the different office hierarchies.

> (Partner, USConsultancy1, London)

The implication of this is that beyond the head-office, different offices vary considerably in size and importance in relation to business activity.[5] Many firms have what was described as a 'regional-layering' to their physical location structure:

We've got an office in New York, one in London, one in Madrid and Frankfurt... so there's one in the North American time zone, three in the European, and five in the Asia-Pacific time zone in Singapore, Hong Kong, Tokyo, Sidney and Seoul. Sidney and Seoul we've publicly said we're pulling out of..er..so we will only have three units in Asia-Pacific in due course, and you know, units in Europe are under review. So there is a consolidation process...

> (Global Head of Money Markets, UKBank2, London)

As far as *EuroBank5* bank is concerned, the world sort of revolves around Frankfurt, London, New York, and to a lesser extent Toronto, Sydney, Singapore... but the three major places... the major hubs are the first three. As far as regionalization – just to take Europe as an idea – we have what is called the hub and spoke concept so that Frankfurt and London are hubs, and in the spokes are Madrid, Paris, Milan, Brussels, Amsterdam, Prague, Lisbon. So on the regional basis and to some extent copied on the global scale we have these main centres which are responsible for trading and then sales. And then the other satellites which are very much sales orientated.

(Managing Director, Money Markets, EuroBank5, London)

Yet although business managers definitely saw their companies as having 'another tier of key offices' (Managing Partner, USConsultancy6, London) below the head office, this does not neatly correspond to any urban hierarchy that urban theory has proposed (Hall 1984; King 1990; Brotchie *et al* 1995). Different firms have different office locations which are important and between different firms, the locations of the significant 'second tier' offices is not easily generalizable. The same cities are important in given regions, of course, but which specific centres are locations for second-tier offices depends upon where the company originates, its historical development in the world economy, where its current major markets are, and 'what strengths the business has' (Senior Analyst, EuroBank2, New York). For example, in one investment bank, the more significant 'second-tier' offices are located across Asia because the bank is very active in the securities markets in that region:

Although we operate out of nearly 90 countries, like other banks our... Asia shall we say is the most important region for this part of the business, particularly based on securities where we have a strong presence... so that means there are several big offices there – Kuala Lumpur or Singapore – which for other firms may not be so important.

(Senior Manager, Capital Markets, USBank3)

Yet in another bank, of comparable size but whose market strengths are quite different, second-tier offices are in quite different locations:

Our main strengths are in blue-chip clients. We don't tend to deal with the smaller companies. Most of our business originates with existing clients – most of our revenue base that is – all of whom tend to be major corporations. And that is where we focus our energy, reflected in the major branches: New York of course, but then

Chicago, Los Angeles, Miami. In Europe we have big offices in all the
main centres: London, Paris, Frankfurt, Zurich.

(Senior Manager, Global Head of Operations, USBank1, New York)
[abbreviated]

Whilst several senior managers told me that their companies have
been opening new offices in recent years, my third point is that many
of these offices are small and 'relatively unimportant' (Managing
Director, Money Markets, EuroBank3, London) locations for business
activity. The study suggests it is rare for one of the large investment
banks to set-up a new, second-tier regional office, as I was told by the
same man I have just quoted. At the time of the interview he was
responsible for new office creation in one of the largest US investment
banks:

Q: So how many offices are you going to open?

A: About ten. Over the next two years.

Q: So in the past decade, *USBank1* hasn't opened new offices?

A: Very few. I mean, there are offices where you have literally a room
and a secretary. We have opened those. But a full branch? The last
full branch we did was Mexico, you know, about 10 years ago. Maybe
less – seven years ago. And Johannesburg which just went live in the
fall. So it is very unusual for us.

(Senior Manager, Global Head of Operations, USBank1, New York)

Documenting the opening of new offices, therefore, does not necessarily constitute an extension and deepening of the company's business.
The absolute number of office locations that a firm operates in is not a
particularly useful indicator of business transnationalization. Most
of the offices that USBank1 are to open are not 'full branches' – they
are not key locations with substantial numbers of staff. Rather, they are
small offices which are little more than outlets for contracts in countries
that are peripheral to the major activities of the bank:

R: Most of these new offices are of course small-scale. Half a dozen
people who will seek business, find opportunities, and so on.

Q: So they don't represent a lot of business then?

R: No, no. It is more the desire to have a presence. We may have a big client with some operation there ...

(Senior Manager, Operations, USBank1, New York)

Such a situation was reflected widely among the business managers interviewed. Although office location patterns at the start of the new century loosely follow the trends documented by previous research, a closer examination suggests a more complicated and diverse picture. To properly understand transnational business activity in these TNCs, attention must be turned to what has been occurring within the transnational business organization.

Globalizing internal corporate divisions

There are three dimensions with regard to the changing internal divisional form of management consultancy firms and investment banks that emerge from the research. The first is the issue of divisional reorganization in relation to corporate globalization strategies. Both management consultancy firms and investment banks have undertaken corporate restructuring designed to shift organizational form from a 'geography-based' towards a 'function-based' divisional structure. Often couched in the language of management theory, senior consultants and bankers explained that their firms' divisions had previously been much more structured along geographical lines, thus fitting the classic model of multinational organizational form:

Historically, we had a pretty regional structure, so if you go back four – five years, erm ... we pretty much had a whole executive level, at this level, with a head line here sitting in Zurich, run out of Zurich, run out of Switzerland. And then you had regional structures around the globe, so you had an organization in London which pretty much replicated the overall structure. We had a chief executive, kind of, in every division, and in trading and sales, we had a thing called functional advisors. So you had a number of these people pretty much as Heads of this, our businesses advising the Head on this. The power pretty much, like, was within the region so you had Europe which at that point was run out Zurich. You had North America, you had East Asia, you had Japan, and that was ... so you had much more regional structure and regional guys. The product itself was only the second layer ...

(Executive Director, Global Fixed Income, Currencies and
Derivatives, EuroBank4, London)

Prior to internal restructuring, the 'London head office's internal structure' had 'replicated the geographical divisional structure of the organization across the globe' (Executive Director, Global Fixed Income, Currencies and Derivatives, EuroBank4, London). This bank's business activities were therefore organized on a regional basis with the actual 'products'[6] being less significant determinants of organizational structure. As this Director went on to explain, this regional divisional framework has been radically reorganized in recent years:

> Now with globalization we've tried to change this, now the product is much stronger than the regional structure, so for us, hence Peter...[Director, Global Head of Corporate Finance] wants this... he is the guy who calls the shots around the globe. He tells the guy in Singapore we want to do it this way, we want to hire this guy, we want to fire that guy. Erm...the same is true for North America, Japan, and in Switzerland.
>
> (Executive Director, Global Fixed Income, Currencies and Derivatives, EuroBank3, London)

The new divisional structure he is describing is illustrated in Figure 3.1. This is based on a diagram drawn by the Director in the interview and on a corporate report's representation. At the time of the study, these

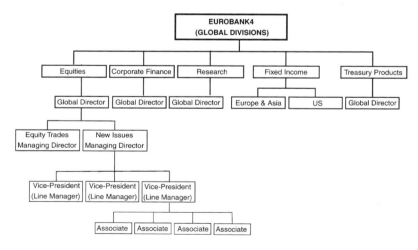

Figure 3.1 Global Organizational Structure in EuroBank4
Source: Hand Drawn Diagram & Corporate Report supplied by Executive Director, Global Fixed Income, Currencies and Derivatives, EuroBank4.

service TNCs were in the middle of, or embarking upon, a dramatic (and traumatic) shift of organizational structure away from geographical lines. The research suggests, therefore, that these business-service firms are undergoing similar kinds of shifts in organizational form that management theorists have long identified as occurring in the largest manufacturing (and other industry) TNCs (Robock & Simons 1989; Dunning 1993b). As in other industries, the study suggested that banks and consultancy firms alike are seeking to abandon their emphasis on a geographical organizational structure in favour of a functional or product-centred form:

> We have just re-organized into an organization which is giving us some internal issues. It is based around three major components. The first is what we call 'global markets'. And we have six major industries which are 'global markets'. First there is 'Products' which is our manufacturing-related stuff and you can guess what is in that. 'Resources' which is again fairly obvious and 'Financial Services', 'Government' and 'Communications'. In fact it is five. There was another one 'Healthcare'. . . . And they basically serve clients: get work, carry out work, ensure work is of good-quality – all the client-facing stuff in the marketplace. The second major leg of the organization is called 'Competencies'. Now these are again organized globally and we have four major competencies: strategy, technology, process – which is knowledge of all the different business processes – and something called change management.
>
> (Senior Partner, USConsultancy2, London)

However, this goes beyond the formation of a 'geography-product matrix' (Knight 1977; Rowe 1992) as discussed in the management studies literature. The respondent made this point as he continued his outline of USConsultancy2's new organizational form:

> . . . the result of this organization is that everybody in the firm has a particular competency in one of those four. They normally work in a particular industry and so it is a sort of matrix organization, but a product-product one, not product-geography as it used to be – if you see what I mean. The third leg of the organization is called 'global services' and that is there to provide all the infrastructure that we need to run the place world-wide. And again we are running that globally not locally. So we are now about to move from this building into a new building in a couple of years time and that is or being

organized not by a local team here in London, but by this global services organization. So what we have done is to move, literally in the last six months, to trying to get to a truly global organization.

(Senior Partner, USConsultancy2, London)

The general view of respondents, especially those working in the large banks or consultancy firms, is that the geographic element of organizational structure is being strongly deprioritized relative to the function or product aspect (Figure 3.2). For those talking in terms of geographic-product matrices, 'the product element' in the way senior managers theorized their firms – and thus in divisional structure – is becoming dominant.

When I started, the geographies dominated, absolutely dominated. Now the products have a lot more say. If you ask the geographies about it, they will say the products now dominate.

(Managing Director, Equities and New Issues, EuroBank2, London)

This Director, like many of the managers I interviewed, regarded this divisional restructuring process as corresponding to a shift from an 'international' to a 'global' firm:

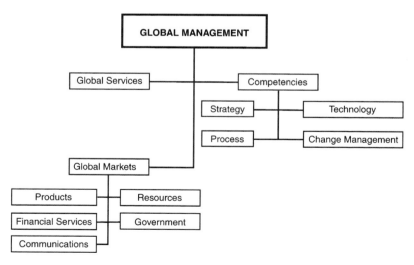

Figure 3.2   Global Organizational Structure in USConsultancy2
Source: Senior Partner, USConsultancy2, USConsultancy (1996).

I'd say it [the company's business] is becoming more global. I mean, the example is that we have always been an international company, okay? But we had a US operation, a European operation, we had an Asian operation. We had an Asian Head, a Head of Europe ... you know, everyone did their own business and processed their own business. Singapore did that business and processed their own business. What you are now seeing is the globalization of the entire business so that if we are doing, if we are trading foreign exchange, if we are selling Eurobonds, if we are dealing in whatever forms of derivatives, we have the global organization for each of those products. The products are organized globally, so is the processing – so that is generating revenue for the organization globally. I would say that this is particularly over the last three or four years. Not regionally, okay? We were a regionally based organization before. Now we are a global organization with, let's say, we have all our Equities group is organized globally. There is an equities team in Europe, an equities team in Asia, and they report to the Head of Equities who may also have a relationship with the management committee in Europe but the prime driver is not location, the prime driver is the global product business. Okay? And the same with our investment banking. We have ... we are now a global investment banking business. And so on ... and also on the processing side it used to be the case that what was done in France was processed in France. That is not the case anymore.

(Managing Director [Board], USBank1, New York)

In this sense, USConsultancy2 is reorganizing its corporate structure along 'global' product lines in much the same way as USBank1 – a fact confirmed by an internal policy report in that firm discussing how USConsultancy2 is aiming to 'become the first truly global consultancy firm' (USConsultancy2 1998). When compared to investment banking, the 'products' are different, but the divisional changes are similar. What such comments show is that in these business-service industries there is a strong impetus for transnational companies to move towards organizing their business divisions along 'globalized' product lines. Rather than understanding, organizing and managing business activities around the globe from a regional or national perspective, the objective of this divisional restructuring is to deal and trade in the same products around the globe. What 'globalized' means in this context, therefore, is a standardization of both products and business practices at the global scale.

'Globalization' for senior business managers – from a divisional struc- tures point of view at least – is consequently concerned with removing geographical boundaries in terms of the way business is administrated, supported and managed (c.f. Ashkenas *et al* 1995). Many of the managers I discussed this with often cited the idea of 'the truly global firm' (Partner, USConsultancy2, London) which, when further examined, proved to be a common reference to 'the globalization of the organization' (Senior Manager, USBank1, London) – a goal which internal divisional restruc- turing sought to achieve through a reconfiguration of business activities on 'global' functional lines rather than regional geographic lines. Yet any firm's restructuring sits in the wider context of the industry as a whole (Sanchez 1999). The research suggests that the restructuring of banks and consultancies both at the firm and industry level is following a pattern dictated by the world market for business services (that is, mostly transnational manufacturing enterprises) which is, in turn, a factor directly bound into the advantages presented by economies of scale and scope in capitalist firms (Altenbas & Molyneux 1993; Maskin & Xu 1997; Jackson 1998).

This issue of industry-wide trends and forces is the second dimension of divisional restructuring. When I asked who are the main 'clients' of a bank or consultany firm, respondents generally said that the bulk of their business was with 'major Fortune 500 corporations' (Partner, USConsultancy4, New York). Although management consultants are hired by banks and other service firms, much of the 'big business'[7] is with transnational manufacturing or extractive companies:

> We concentrate on trying to attract and hold onto contracts with the major players – the Toyotas, the Exxon's of this world... most of our most important clients are the big global players in their industry... because they are the people with the real money to spend.
> (Senior Partner, USConsultancy4, New York)

Major manufacturing and extractive TNCs are their major clients, and these companies – when deciding which bank or consultancy firm to give their contracts to – increasingly want firms which 'could meet their global needs' (Partner, USConsultancy6, London). Respondents were largely of the opinion that it was the larger, more transnational business- service firms who could best meet those needs:

> Yes, being bigger is better if you're in these service businesses – that's the philosophy everyone's going for anyway... and I think you

could say that of management consultancy firms or accountants as well as banks. Look at *USConsultancy3*. Everyone wants to follow them. The advantages are clear from a cost-cutting or a scale economy viewpoint... but on top of that, it's the ability to serve your market. These guys are bidding after big global contracts, you know: for the big names. And these big names want global service. They want service guys who can do what they need anywhere, anytime. And so the days of the local specialist are gone...

(Chief Executive, Professional Organization2, London)

Almost everybody I spoke to saw this as a reason for the continuing, and even accelerating, transnationalization and oligopolization of the global investment banking and consultancy industries.[8] That is to say, in both industries the perspective of senior managers and directors is that the firms with the largest global market share and the largest operations are growing bigger and that smaller companies are either being swallowed up as larger companies expand through mergers and acquisitions, or are attempting to survive in niche markets:

There is kind of merger mania. So everybody thinks they need to go in the same direction. And we will only find out in five or six years from now, whether this makes sense. And to some degree the whole thing will come back a little bit. Erm... what's clearly true, and that's kind of pushing it a little bit into the direction – the whole thing is kind of expensive.

(UK Head of Corporate Finance, EuroBank4, London)

The consultancy industry is globalizing just like banking, accountancy, whatever. There are the big players – half a dozen maybe – who want to get bigger. There's maybe not the same merger thing going on like with banks like *EuroBank3* or *USBank1*, but it's the same kind of thing...

(Partner, USConsultancy2, New York)

The evidence of such activities is apparent in the string of mergers and take-overs, particularly in investment banking over the last five years (Washington Post 1998; Financial Times 1999). Even as I was conducting the first phase of interviews in late 1998 and 1999, four of the banks were involved in mergers. One of the consultancy firms became the subject of a hostile take-over bid only a week after I had been there

(Financial Times 1999). At the industry level then, managers perceived 'a race to global market share' (Partner, USConsultancy1, London):

> What's you're seeing is mergers to try and grab global market share ... everyone' s scared of being squeezed out. ...
>
> (Director, USBank5, New York)

This merger trend has continued in the global economic downturn of the 00s (The Guardian 2000, 2001). The underlying logic behind this industry movement appears, therefore, to be effectively centred on economies of scale and scope in a client market, where most of the large contracts (and thus increasingly more of the potential revenue) come from very large TNCs. Business-service firms can cut prices by reducing IT, administration and support operation costs whilst also offering a more comprehensive 'global presence' to potential clients:

> You see, the client doesn't really care whether he [sic] talks to the guy in Singapore or London, or New York. He [sic] wants the best price. And the organization which can provide him [sic] with the best price, is the organization that gets the deal. So you have to make sure that you can organize yourselves to satisfy those requirements. At the same time you have to try to do it as efficiently as possible. If you do it globally, you can actually do this for a really small group of people. If I would do the same thing locally, I would have the need for at least double the people – so I might need a hundred people here – because in each instance I'd need a full infrastructure here, a full infrastructure there, and a full infrastructure there [*indicates several continents on sketch map*]. Plus a layer that can talk to all the guys to make sure that communication works. So if I actually take away stuff, and say "no-no, you don't have a head of marketing. Your head of marketing sits in London." I've pretty much got a more efficient way to get things done.
>
> (Executive Director, Global Fixed Income, Currencies and Derivatives, EuroBank2, London)

It is these scale and scope economies which are the goal of divisional restructuring away from a geographically based framework. Apart from, perhaps, the more obvious advantages of having a larger capital base[9] and efficiency gains from support functions being rationalized and centralized, the attractiveness of being able to offer a client a wide range of different functions in any location appears to be most important for many firms. Senior managers, especially in the dominant large TNCs, regularly cited the idea of becoming a 'one-stop-shop' for their clients: providing, in the case of investment banking, a complete financial package which might include elements of equities, foreign-exchange, complex derivatives and so on:

> When you are relatively small, you can either say, "Okay, I just focus on a couple products," – which is increasingly difficult because the clients don't care what products you have, they just want the service. What kind of product behind the service they don't really care. If you limit yourself, and say, "I only do fixed income bonds", they don't care either. Because I might need a bond, I might need equity, I might need perhaps a combination of the two. I want it to be convertible. And short-term I would like to swap this and that with what I already have; long-term I would like to do this and that. So I would rather go to one shop that has all those things and not just one. Because it might be a bit cheaper but the client doesn't care, because it's not like you're going to the supermarket where you know what the product is. You want a combination of products. So you go to the guy who has the whole thing.
>
> (Managing Director, Equities, EuroBank2, London)

In the past, product specialism amongst firms has certainly been a key feature of the investment banking industry. Certain companies (and certain urban locations) were known for being market leaders in, for example, Bonds or Foreign Exchange (Cerny 1994). However, transnationalization corresponds in part to an effort by the large transnational banks to capture more of the market by being the only company a transnational client need deal with. As one manager explained, the competitive advantage from this accrues as clients become involved in larger and larger investments where it is easier for them to contract one larger bank than ten[10]:

> The big clients simply find it easier to deal with one firm who they trust and who can provide the range of services you need in a modern deal...it's about being able to deliver a complete service, [rather] than the client running around trying to tender everything separately...
>
> (Managing Director, UK Head of Corporate Finance, EuroBank3, London)

A similar argument was made in relation to the 'products' that consultancy firms are selling: large firms are better able to offer the diversity of experienced consultants who can deal with the increasingly complex problems faced by, for example, a transnational manufacturing client operating in thirty different tax or legal environments.

However, the third dimension to the research into divisional form is that there are limitations to the number of generalizations that can be made about organizational globalization in this respect. Not all of the banks or management consultancies in the study are globalizing their internal organizational structures on the basis of needing to achieve greater economies of scale and scope. The strategies and theories concerning restructuring amongst the senior managers are by no means coherent or uniform. As one consultant explained to me, 'there are an enormous range of reasons why management will seek to restructure' a company (Partner, US Finance, USConsultancy3, New York), ranging from the harsh realities of the market to internal political and logistical issues specific to a given industry (or even company). For example, the need to break down organizational stagnation and inefficiency prevails to some extent in senior managers' theories of the need for organizational change:

> It is hard to overcome all tension between the geographical and functional. And one of the ways to think about it in the larger organizations that might be nonsense, but part of me suspects probably makes sense, is every three to five years to break the structure and shift the primary dimension to something else. Then a few years later you shift it back to the way it was – because there is an old line in Silicon Valley which is that, "if it ain't broke, break it." Because somebody else will break it for you. And it shakes things out and it gives people a chance to rethink what they are doing.
>
> (Director, USConsultancy5, New York)

Furthermore, even in those firms where dramatic divisional restructuring towards 'global product orientation' is occurring, managers told me there are considerable difficulties, inconsistencies and contradictions inherent in such changes. Respondents in large companies admitted that divisional restructuring along these lines 'could prove an expensive gamble' (Managing Director, UK Head of Corporate Finance, EuroBank2, London) while often in smaller firms, the geography-to-product shift is more unstable than management rhetoric portrays:

Erm... so it comes back to this picture, for those businesses we are much more reluctant to kind of go full-blown global, so this is much more regional still. What we have here is kind of a scaled-down version. We say we have global guys in charge, and call these globally-managed businesses, but in terms of the set-up, these are pretty much regional businesses. Erm... so here we have still various building blocks... erm... it's not always as clear as the management manuals make out.

(Director, Capital Markets, UKBank2, London)

And even in the large companies, 'global' product orientation produces difficult and unfeasible organizational realities:

He [Senior Director] would say, "I want a global organization, I want to do this". So I then went and said, "There are two ways; one-way is we just kill all those guys, forget about them, and do this globally." This is not feasible because at the moment we have that regional structure so it is a gradual process to get there. So then he [Senior Director] asks me what's a good way to kind of make sure that we have all the right elements in place within the existing structure. And at this stage we're definitely still working on it...

(Executive Director, Global Fixed Income, Currencies and Derivatives, EuroBank1, London)

Another banker explained how the ease of product-line globalization depends on which of the bank's products is being dealt with:

ForEx[11] is a very good example because they are already used to those changes working 24 hours a day. So mentally they are much more prepared to do this. But the real challenge is... for other products this is not so easy... the whole local infrastructure you have is focused on locational requirements. So if you have an accounting guy here in the US, he goes home at five-thirty, and he doesn't think of his counterpart in Europe. So the front [office] US pass whatever they have on to their European guys here but you to have to make sure that Europe is ready for this and it works. And often this is a problem.

(UK Head of Corporate Finance, EuroBank3, London)

Similarly, another manager explained how in investment banking it is not just the differences between products, but also the difference in the national markets and institutional environments they are traded in:

If one of those guys has to talk to the government bond trader in New York, it's already different, or Japanese bonds, or whatever. So on the outside you think this is all same stuff, the same product – this is just like a different flavour – but all the technicalities and the little details are different. So this makes it much more difficult to globalize any of these businesses than a relatively new business like derivatives.

(Senior Manager, JapanBank3, New York)

A further difficulty in terms of implementation is that employees are often less than receptive to a 'global' product-based divisional framework that requires them to be highly flexible in terms of where they work. One of the consultancy firms heavily embroiled in restructuring was, at the time of my interviews there, experiencing a considerable rate of employee-loss as a consequence of the upheaval:

So that is our new structure [product-based divisions]; it is just bedding down. To be frank, it is creating havoc because a lot of Europeans say, "Well, I am a Partner in the Italian practice and I, first and foremost, feel Italian. Although I work in financial services I have no more in common with the guy doing financial services in New York that the man in the moon. And if I can't find work with *USConsultancy3* in financial services in Italy then I am quite happy to go and work in a utility company rather than be picked up and put on a financial services job in Oslo.

(Managing Partner, Public Utilities, USConsultancy3)

Certainly, for some of the companies in the study, the shift to a product line was regarded as 'more a pipe-dream than a reality at the moment' (Partner, Japanese Institutions, USConsultancy2, New York). In that sense, many senior managers described their current divisional framework as a persistent 'geography-product matrix'[12] where global product-orientation is incomplete, leaving the existing structure more than a little unclear. This lack of clear divisional definition itself appeared to be leading to all sorts of difficulties for transnational service firms. The following responses were typical of many when I asked about the problems that the practicalities of persistent divisional matrices create:

In a matrix you will always have tension. The matrix leads inevitably to that tension because you have two lines of thought. The issue is how well you divide the roles, the responsibilities. In our bank the responsibilities are for the divisions, so the functional business side is responsible for the result and the product, and the regions – the line side – is responsible for the cost and the customer. But we have customers on a regional basis . . . it is this division of responsibilities that should actually reduce the tension, but personalities sometimes get in the way.

(Managing Director, Equities and New Issues, EuroBank3, London)

The problem I have is that people working here in London for me in Capital Markets report to me, but to the extent they are in Hong Kong or New York, they have dual reporting rights. They report to me as a product Head, on a geographic head they report either to the head of investment banking or to a country head in a geographic location where they are themselves at the top of an organization.

(Director, Capital Markets, UKBank2, London)

Thus there can be no consensus on even the necessary benefits endowed on business-service firms by becoming larger and larger to gain economies of scale and scope. A number of managers in the smaller firms – perhaps not surprisingly – and also in consultancy firms commentating on both industries more generally, suggested that smaller consultancies and banks could succeed transnationally by specializing and becoming niche market occupants:

Yes, I do think it is possible for the niche players to survive. I mean, I'm sure if you go to *UKBank1* in London they'll say that. Or *UKBank3*. They provide a good service, and they have a client base who know they can do what they want. But all I'd say is – I think in the longer term – there is always this issue of cost cutting hanging over them . . . look what happened to *USBank7* or *USBank8*[13] . . . but no-one can say what will happen.

(Senior Manager, Global Head of Operations, USBank1, New York)

To summarize, therefore, in both investment banking and management consultancy the research suggests that over the last five years there has been a trend towards shifting organizational form away from national and regional configurations towards a 'global corporation' model. However, these changes represent a reconfiguration rather than a move towards greater centralization of organizational form at the global scale and the processes of organizational restructuring are far from uniform across and between firms and industries.

The equivalent need to globalize financial structures

Both management consultants and bankers were often quick to assert the significance of organizational financial structures[14] in relation to corporate globalization. Yet the study suggests – to use the words of one director – that 'financial structures are the last things to change' because senior managers in firms that are transnationalizing their business activities are 'scared to death about losing control of the thing that matters most – that is the money' (Director, USBank6, New York). Despite this reluctance to reorganize or globalize financial structures, however, for divisional restructuring towards a product-based organizational form to succeed, major changes to financial arrangements ranging from capital provision to employee remuneration need to be made. Three main issues emerge.

First, in both industries the highly skilled specialist employees need to be paid in a way that allows a 'global perspective on products' (Executive Director, Global Fixed Income, EuroBank3, London). That is to say, if USConsultancy1 wanted to be able to take one of their hundred thousand or so consultants world wide[15] – a specialist in electricity industry privatization, for example – and send them anywhere where a client required, then this consultant has to be paid on a global standard. Instigating product-based divisional structures requires a structure of standardized remuneration so that, as in the older geographically organized multinational companies, well-paid consultants in the US regional division, for example, will not resist being sent to the South American regional division where pay is lower. A number of the companies in the study addressed this matter directly with a system that adjusted remuneration to the relative cost of living in different countries:

So for the Americans in the US then they get obviously a hundred cents on the dollar. In Switzerland they get about a hundred and fifty cents on the dollar, in India they get 35–40 cents on the dollar. So we, as you say, coefficient adjust so that you don't have the guy in India being paid exactly the same as the guy in New York. So we use that coefficient adjustment to equalize the real economic equivalence between the countries.

(Managing Partner, Public Utilities, USConsultancy1, London)

Second, and relatedly, with regard to the remuneration of senior management and partners in these business-service TNCs, the companies' profit structures have commonly been shifted to a non-geographical basis.

In several of the consultancy firms, profits are not split according to geographical origin, but are centrally distributed throughout the firm. In some cases, transnationalization simply builds on long-standing profit-sharing financial structures:

> A definition of globality is to share profit between everybody in the firm across all disciplines over the last 40 years. And the way we do that, is we express our profit in dollars. We put all those dollars in a big pot and we share them out across the different countries on what we call a coefficient basis.
>
> (Managing Partner, USConsultancy3, London)

But in many firms, this 'global profit-sharing' structure is something perceived as being a necessary element of restructuring away from national or regional-based financial structures:

> From the beginning, the view has been all Partners eat off the same plate. And if you think of it as a matrix of industry specialization, geographical focus or residence and also the scale of transaction or complexity – from early stage start-up to large skill turnaround or buyout – everything is shared by everyone. You see, if you are one percent interested in the firm wherever the investment is made, whatever kind of investment, whatever industry it is in, then you take a more serious global view. So in that way we have now gone global; we do not have the challenge of making it integrated globally.
>
> (Managing Partner, USConsultancy6, London)

The reasons for these financial changes relate to the wider issues of better competing in a transnational market-place for business services where clients are tendering for contracts which may span multiple national or regional divisions in a geographically organized corporation. As one partner in one of the largest consultancy firms explained, the process of presenting an attractive tender to a transnational client is not aided by a financial profit structure where different divisional heads are fighting internally to 'get the contract on their geographically based books':

> We have a global partnership. We have a global pot. So to some extent the mindset has become global. In *USConsultancy3*[16] you have a separate profit pot for Europe. So they are international. They have

the same schools[17] and whatever...but they will talk about decisions, about who gets called in and about who gets positions in front of a global client – it is ugly. Those barriers reduce the play. We recently did a project with a bank which has a global service requirement. The other two firms showed up squabbling and kicking. And interestingly enough, those two firms were organized where each country had its own sort of partnership and its profits. And we got the deal and they did not. So the challenge is to ask them why we did and why they didn't. And the assumption is that they do not have an open partnership whereas to us it does not make any difference where the Partner comes from, he's there to serve the client. We share the profits. We make the same amount of money and so that has motivated our Partners to do very different things and difference pays off. To operate globally and manage your business globally, you need those kind of people.

(Partner, US Finance, USConsultancy1, New York)

In this sense, financial profit structures within service TNCs are subject to a similar and related strategic discourse as the divisional structure of these firms. Both banks and consultancies are shifting their financial architecture towards a non-geographically dependent structure so that their internal organization does not hinder global competition for contracts with client TNCs.

However, and third, the processes of financial restructuring are again potentially problematic. Amongst senior managers, perhaps not surprisingly, there was considerable resistance to the transnational product-based model of financial organization. It might make the firm more attractive to transnational clients if regional divisional directors aren't squabbling over the way the contract will be divided between them, but the strategic solution to this issue entails removing geographical control and letting product-based divisional managers make company-wide contract and investment decisions. This was seen by many managers as a risky strategy:

Oh yes, you encounter risks alright. Your product Head in New York relies on his guys in Chicago or Sidney or Paris. If you run products globally, you also have the risk of losing money if the local knowledge is not there...it's a question of balance.

(Partner, USConsultancy5, London)

Senior managers suggested that such a process of financial restructuring presents their TNCs with difficult control and management issues and this may explain the continuing reluctance in companies to push forward with this aspect of organizational globalization:

> There are issues about how money is flowing internally...it's difficult to really make that global while the rest of the organization is fighting it out in their own bit of the market...our division Heads want to be close to their own financing decisions, not forced into things by guys three thousand miles away...
>
> (UK Head of Corporate Finance, USBank4, London)

Thus, as with the shift in divisional structures this reconfiguration of internal financial form does not simplistically correspond to a process of centralization. A move away from a geographically based financial structure does not necessarily constitute a concentration of control or functionality in a global head office. Rather, as the next section explores, the reorganization of transnational organizational structures is leading to a concomitant reconfiguration of power and management which amounts to pressures towards dispersal rather than centralization.

Power and control in the transnational corporation

Organizational globalization is producing a dramatic reconfiguration of the way in which managerial power is exercised, implemented and distributed with investment banking and management consultancy. An abandonment, or at least drift away, from the old multinational model of corporate form requires a significant redesign of management hierarchies that firms in the study are struggling to varying degrees to construct. Some senior managers I interviewed told me that, rhetoric aside, 'global management' (Clarke & Clegg 1998) is more management rhetoric than reality – achieving effective and satisfactory structures of global control in these TNCs might appear in this light to be wishful thinking. However, there can be no doubt that the stakes in this regard are high. Investment bankers are only too aware of what ineffective global control systems can do: both the collapse of Barings Bank in 1995 and of Long Term Capital Markets in 1998 have been widely explained to a large extent in terms of management failures (Tickell 1996; Leeson 1997; Lowenstein 2001). Most worryingly, in the Barings case in particular, the lack of managerial knowledge in the London head office allowed Leeson 'the rogue trader' to undertake disastrous trading in southeast Asia. One might say, therefore, that Baring's over-zealous attempts at organizational globalization ended in a catastrophic outcome.

Consequently, since 1995 the banking industry has become increasingly fixed on questions of global management and highly cautious of globalizing managerial structures.[18] Further recent examples of losses incurred by unregulated trading in distant branch offices, such as those incurred by Allied Irish Bank in 2001, only serve to reinforce that suspicion (Kane 2002). The second part of this chapter suggests, however, that there are strong organizational logics driving the need for the reconfiguration of managerial and control structures in TNCs that banks and consultancy firms are finding hard to resist. There are three main points in this regard.

First, strategic and managerial power in these transnational service firms is increasingly constituted through a number of levels of the management hierarchy at a transnational scale. Strategic control is spread through the organization in a way which does not necessitate the 'centre' being heavily involved in individual business decisions. Senior managers located in head offices do, of course, have enormous potential power but this power is normally diffused through the transnational management hierarchy. For example, in many of the banks and consultancy firms I interviewed in, I was told that overall 'global corporate strategy' was set by (beneath board level) 'global management committees':

> Every year, a budget is put together, which is reviewed by the Management Committee . . . but at a strategic level, that management committee will talk about various decisions, but in the business management perspective it is decentralized down to the front-line products and the geographies.
>
> (Managing Director, Equities and New Issues, UKBank1, London)

> We have a group of Partners in each of the major sectors of the business who meet regularly to talk about where that part of the business is going . . . and how successful this has been . . . erm . . . and they feed ideas back to other Partners who are courting new business. So our general strategy is informed by these meetings between the people close to the business . . .
>
> (Senior Partner, USConsultancy4, New York)

In this sense, financial power is negotiated and wielded by senior management from a centralized perspective. Yet, as this Director explains, the market context of investment banking is such that there is no written strategy for the company. Global corporate strategy is a negotiated and fluid phenomenon that emerges, in the words of another manager, 'from a continual process of discussion at our monthly committee meetings' (Managing Director, Global Head of Financial Markets, UKBank3, London). The financial power that senior management wields, therefore, is mediated through the information and knowledge that line managers can provide:

> So global strategy is all very well, but it's really the guys with their ears to the ground who know what you should be doing. Certainly in a global firm. I can't know how the Japanese market is going medium term – or not more than partially, any case. I'd need Jo Bloggs who sits in Tokyo... and he can certainly change strategy, yes. So it's a two way thing to some extent...
>
> (Director, Capital Markets, EuroBank4, London)

The exercise of strategic power is, therefore, something which arises through the managerial network – 'global corporate control' is a more diffuse activity than simple centralized management structure run out of the London, Tokyo or New York head-office. Head-offices are thus the physical base for senior management but managerial decision-making is a practice that is effectively shared across a network of managers located across the firm's transnational office network. One Managing Director explained it in this way:

> Essentially individual centres act very much on their own initiative. We encourage quite a high degree of autonomy in the different centres, encouraging local management to use their local skills optimally. And that's proved very successful... it requires a good degree of understanding and co-operation between the global management team. In fact, philosophically I think the company is quite keen not to create rigid lines of responsibility amongst that team...
>
> (Managing Director, Global Head of Money Markets, UKBank2, London)

Senior managers in head offices are the people who, at the end of the day, make a decision, but there is a considerable degree of influence held by junior managers who are actively engaged in business activity. In that sense, contrary to the image of centralized power somehow 'held' in transnational head offices, strategic power is diffused through a transnational network of managerial actors.

Second, where senior managers do exercise 'centralized' power in these transnational firms, it tends to be at the 'global scale' – to use an expression that was common amongst respondents. They may not directly intervene in the day-to-day running of businesses by line managers in a given country or region, but their interventative power becomes apparent at the level of transnational corporate strategy:

> Our world-wide managing director ... may get involved to arbitrate or because he sees something in any particular country which that particular country cannot see because he has the overview. There was a situation last month like that ... So he was able to add value, to bring global perspective and as a result, we have put additional resources onto that.
>
> (Managing Partner, USConsultancy3, London)

The key element of 'central' power is the role of 'transnational overview'. This senior manager has power in terms of dictating what 'the wider picture' is beyond a given national context, and he is also the mediator who resolves conflicts that arise lower down in the managerial hierarchy.

Such a 'mediating' role for senior managers, in the view of many respondents in both investment banks and consultancy firms, is important in trying to align 'local' business dealings with a firm's wider 'global objectives' (Partner, USConsultancy4, London) or 'strategy' overall. Senior managers based in head offices or regional key branch offices thus wield executive power in terms of deciding whether specific business activities and deals or areas of the business 'fit the company's wider goals and objectives in the global marketplace' (Managing Director, Corporate Finance, USBank3, New York). In that sense, strategic decision-making is a composite process of negotiation between informed 'local' managers and social actors, and 'global' senior managers who assess whether specific parts of the business are sufficiently compatible and acceptable to the firm as a whole:

> Probably two thirds of my time is making sure each deal is either originated, being done, controlled to a standard that we feel comfortable with, that this deal or that deal fits into our wider strategy. On the other hand, it's also making sure that its not Coca-Cola, that the guys have initiative, that they feel they can develop a product, trying with a light hand to make sure those permanencies are there. Too much interference upsets the balance, you see and you can't

always right them if things aren't working because it's too
sensitive . . . think local, reach global – is what I have to do.

(Director, Capital Markets, UKBank4, London)

This Director sees his role therefore as ensuring some degree of standardization whilst also permitting the 'local' managerial independence necessary to compete in different markets around the globe. The practical
side of this function in terms of managerial 'practice' is that senior
managers in both business-service sectors, rather than wielding power
from the global city head office, spent an (often substantial) amount of
time travelling. The practice of managerial control, whilst supported by
information technologies, relies heavily on direct social contact between
managers at different levels:

That's really what being a senior guy is all about. I spend most of my
time on business trips. On a plane somewhere to have a meeting of
regional heads, or meeting the man in Sidney who's running a
project we're doing at the moment in Australia. Or my counter-part in
Los Angeles. You see . . . well, there's no IT system in the world that
will change that. IT – email, video-conferencing, teleconferencing
whatever – only helps you keep up to date. A lot of decisions are
never made over the phone . . .

(Senior Business Analyst, JapanBank2, New York)

As another Managing Director went on to emphasize, whilst IT assists
the process of control, key decisions rely on senior managers flying out
to branch office locations several times a year or more regularly than
that. In the social science literature, the centrality of social relations as a
factor behind the agglomeration of activity in global cities is widely
cited, but my argument in the light of this research, is that it is overly
reductionist to regard head offices as the location of managerial power.

Third, the implication of this is that global managerial control *must
necessarily* be 'diffuse' in these advanced business-service firms. The
reason for this is what Clark & O'Connor (1995) have termed the
'knowledge-density' of the products that these firms 'produce'
(Abrahamson 1996; Fincham 1999). A managing partner in one of the
consultancy firms described this very well:

What we are as a firm if you cut through all the crap [sic], is basically
a huge knowledge engine. We absorb knowledge, spread its across
50,000 people and then take it to market anywhere in the

world ... and it is a management responsibility for trying to make this knowledge-engine's geographical structure operate in a unified way across different geographies ... but no, I wouldn't be involved in the specifics. That's the role of the line managers on the ground.

(Managing Partner, Public Utilities, USConsultancy2, London)

Both investment banks and management consultancies trade in knowledge and their products are highly 'information-dense'. This has consequences for power in these transnational organizations, because this reliance on information-dense products – a given consultants' knowledge of a sector in South Asia, for example – *necessitates* that strategic control cannot be too centralized in the head office. A senior manager sitting in London or New York cannot take too strong a role in specific business deals around the globe because they do not have (or it is unlikely that they will have) sufficient knowledge of any given deal. The consequence is that middle management is relatively empowered compared to a conventional management hierarchy model, because it is the managers around the world who are 'on the ground', who are the ones who must be relied upon substantially to make strategically crucial decisions:

It's the guys [sic] in the branch offices who really know what's happening. They are the ones who have their ears to the ground, if you like. Who know what the markets are doing, who know the local political circumstances, who hear the rumours and know the people involved and so on. And that really is invaluable ... and it's why you can't do too much from New York or London or somewhere like that. Because you just don't know enough about what's going on in all those local centres ...

(Director, Capital Markets, UKBank4, London)

Individual Partners and even MCs [management consultants] who are dealing with clients, who are providing the service ... they have a lot of autonomy to follow a certain line of argument or take certain decisions ... Making sure that process doesn't get out of sync with what the rest of the company is doing – that's the trick.

(Senior Partner, USConsultancy1, New York)

As this last quotation describes, the knowledge-based nature of the products in investment banking and management consultancy dictates that managerial control cannot be too centralized. No senior manager can be that interventative in the specifics of a given deal because he or she simply cannot know enough about the deal's specific circumstances to make a well-enough informed decision. Command and control therefore, in these business-service industries at least, is by its nature a negotiated, complex and diffuse process that arises through a network of (admittedly differently empowered) scattered social actors. Where service-sector products are knowledge-based in this way, senior managers operating from head office locations are better understood as heading a network of people who have different inputs and a share of influence in the decision-making process.

In summary, the formation and operation of management hierarchies of course differs between specific firms but at the industry-wide level, the research suggests that the organizational restructuring banks and consultancies have been undertaking produces a different structure of power and control in these TNCs. Organizational globalization necessarily leads to a more diffuse managerial control structure where key decisions are shared (if unevenly) between more actors who are scattered throughout the firm's global locations. The research reveals that the primary reason for this diffusion of control functions is that, in these information-centred businesses, senior managers cannot know enough about specific deals from head-office locations on a day-to-day basis. Whilst they obviously retain ultimate decision-making power, senior managers in these service TNCs are having to rely more and more on the information and judgement of more junior management in different locations. The impact of organizational globalization on power and control mechanisms has and continues to present serious problems for TNCs in both industries and particularly in banking – most notably in the fact that failures in (transnational) managerial control have been attributed as key factors in recent banking collapses, including Barings' Bank in 1995 (Tickell 1996; Leeson 1997) and Long Term Capital Markets in 1998 (Lowenstein 2001). Thus, organizational globalization for TNCs in these sectors poses some potentially disastrous risks.

Global communication: information technology and international travel

Like that apocryphal story about the HR guy who finds his seminar room has been booked out by someone. He calls them up internally, says 'Look, I'm sorry but you really can't have this room. I need it, and I booked it out first...' The guy on the other end of the phone says, 'Do you know who I am? I'm the MD of Global Training!' To

which the HR guy replies, 'Oh, do you know who I am?' 'No', replies
the MD. 'Good' says the HR guy ... and hangs up!
(Senior Associate, UK and European Bond Sales, USBank1, London)

Information and communications technology has often been placed at
the centre of the globalization debate (O'Brien 1991; Martin 1994;
Cerny 1997), particularly with reference to business-service industries
such as banking and management consultancy (Daniels & Moulaert
1991; Howells & Michie 1997; Kim 1999). Both academics and business
commentators have argued that new forms of telecommunications,
computer-systems, screen-based trading systems and IT, in general,
have been a driving force to contemporary processes of economic and
financial globalization in the last twenty years. Such a perspective is
perhaps typified by Manuel Castell's argument that we now live in an
'informational' society and economy where contemporary communications and information technologies have radically altered all aspects of
life (Castells 1989, 1996).

However, the third phase to my argument in this chapter is that the
enthusiasm of globalization theorists and others for placing new
information technologies at the centre of their globalization theses
needs to be tempered. Economic and business globalization is not
'driven' by IT nor is IT in any simplistic way a 'cause' of globalization
(Santangelo 2001). Whilst the prevalence and importance of IT and
other communication technologies to the transnationalization of business
activity is undeniable and evident from numerous studies documenting
the level to which TNCs are involved in the production, support and
consumption of such technologies (Bloomfield 1997; Talalay *et al* 1997;
Braudo & Macintosh 1999), IT is better understood as a facilitating
mediator of business transnationalization and organizational globalization rather than a driving force. As the anecdotal excerpt quoted above
exemplifies, communications technology is inextricably bound into the
social nature of business organizations, and that applies even more to
global business. Yet technical communications systems cannot be
understood outside of the context of the social practices that constitute
their functioning as a part of business transnationalization (see also
Winfield 1991; Scarbrough & Corbett 1992; Chaffey 1999). In that
sense, I now turn to part of my research into banking and management
consultancy concerned with how communication – in all its forms –
plays a crucial and central role in determining the success or otherwise
of processes of organizational globalization within these industries.
I consider first the use made of information technologies in these

business-service sector TNCs before examining other more direct forms of global communication in the form of international face-to-face business meetings.

The role of information technologies

Within the investment banks and management consultancy firms information technologies are crucial and central to the successful operation of transnational business. In the workplaces of these firms, at the start of the twenty-first century, the prevalence of information technology is immediately evident. Investment banking has perhaps been more widely studied for the dramatic impact that computerized trading systems has had on financial markets: as is widely recorded, currencies, shares, bonds and a whole range of 'new'[19] financial products have since the mid-1980s been traded on globally integrated computer systems that permit the almost instantaneous actualization of trading transactions (Cerny 1997). However, information technology in the form of desktop PCs, internal telephone systems, video-conferencing, e-mail, and real-time televisual office links – to name but a few – is a central feature of working life in consultancy firms as well as in banks. Many of the office buildings themselves have been designed increasingly as 'smart buildings' (Streitz *et al* 1999; Travi 2001) with integrated IT structures incorporated into the construction of the physical environment (service ducts for cable, fibre-optic local area networks and so on).

The research suggests, in general, at least three principal functions for information technologies that are shared by firms in both sectors. First, information technologies are crucial to the organizational coherence of these TNCs because it facilitates business support functions. IT systems in the shape of computerized trading systems, databases and computerized modelling and so on provide support functions for the activity of doing business. Quite clearly, investment banks now rely heavily on such systems for their core trading activities in capital markets and currency trading, let alone the almost complete reliance on computerized models to guide activities in derivatives businesses:

> That [derivatives] is of course highly technical ... [we] employ specialist technical staff who develop complex computer models and systems of analysis which feed into the structuring our of products, our activities in various markets and so on ...
>
> (UK Head of Money Markets, UKBank3, London)

However, as one senior consultant explained, IT systems play an equally central – if less obvious – part in facilitating the business of doing management consultancy:

> You need systems, you know, databases, you need work products, you need all this kind of stuff along with the ability to bring that together anywhere in the world. For example: sophisticated directories of who you have within your firm and also who the key people are on the outside – people who you can bring to bear. So a lot of this whole knowledge management translates down to best practices, people, methodologies, how you can capture all that and bring it to bear. And all of that relies to quite an extent on how good your IT is.
>
> (Partner, Financial Institutions, USConsultancy3, New York)

Second, information technologies are becoming increasingly central to business-related research and the collection and/or circulation of information (Bradley *et al* 1993). In these 'information-dense' industries where knowledge is the commodity that often either constitutes a product (for example, contracting an experienced consultancy to reorganize your salary structure) or is the source of a competitive edge (for example, knowledge of a company's recent performance when trading in its shares), information technologies are at the centre of research activities (Howells & Michie 1997):

> Well, the Web has made things a lot easier. You can do research all over the world on the Web. We don't really have industry contacts overseas because it would be too costly and really it would not make much sense. But that is the whole idea with the merger. Say you are an industry analyst in the United States and you see a certain trend appearing and you want to know, 'Is this going to occur someplace else, or is it occurring, or has it occurred?' ... the Web has definitely made the job easier in that way.
>
> (Senior Analyst, EuroBank2, New York)

Senior managers also suggested that IT systems are extremely important in 'generating information flows' (Partner, Financial Institutions, USConsultancy3, New York) within their firms. Key actors in office locations around the globe can be brought together to exchange information about each other's activities, so that one part of the transnational organization could find out what the other was doing or thinking:

The other information comes from internal research. We have this – this is a bit of globalization for you – will have a meeting every morning. I mean, we have conference calls all the bloody [sic] time. At least two a day, and there is one every morning at 7:15 a.m. when we get in. And you have traders on the line from all the offices Tokyo, Singapore, Hong Kong, the European offices – Paris, Frankfurt, London and also Sydney as well sometimes. They will have another conference call later in the day when New York gets in.

(Senior Associate, UK and European Bond Sales, USBank1, London)

So although there's good, close communication between the units, the Asia-Pacific FX traders will talk to but act independently of the London traders, who again will talk to but act independently of the New York traders. There's close communication erm .. between the centres, both physically by conversation and meetings which take place two or three times a year, and also electronically. We're all linked up to the same system. Messages are passed around the globe continually, both on the market, on customer activity and you know commentary and opinion is shared. So there's quite a lot of interaction between units of Foreign Exchange.

(Global Head of Money Markets, UKBank1, London)

As both these respondents explain, information and knowledge flow is crucial to the coherent operation of transnational trading activities. Effectively, both investment banks and consultancy firms make money through dealing in and generating information, a considerable proportion of which is located, created and mediated through information technologies.

The third key function is the way in which IT enables managerial control to be exercised in the global context (Currie 1995). IT systems – particularly technologies such as video-conferencing and direct 'video links' – are an important part of a senior manager's ability to control the operations of the division:

We're incredibly IT conscious and I think the big development of our business that has enabled us to grow this capital markets business has been IT. I mean the ability to communicate with 25 offices on a daily basis is absolutely impossible ... you know in Asia. However, once you know the people, they send you an email requesting something, you can delegate it to people to work on a solution, review it, and get it back out to them during a single working day. IT has hugely increased our productivity, and our ability to use these specialist skills in many locations, so that we can now take a telecomms specialist or a convertibles specialist and move him [sic] around ... I mean his [sic] skill base is available to everybody. Video-conferencing I use a lot. It hasn't yet had any impact on clients in winning business, but the ability to manage a business, to have committee meetings globally with my people, I have a video-conference facility both in this office, but more importantly on the trading floor. We stand up and talk to our Hong Kong office.

(Director, Capital Markets, UKBank2, London)

In that sense, information technologies are an undeniably central aspect to organizational globalization within banking and consultancy. However, both senior consultants and bankers painted a picture of IT within their firms that runs in contradiction to the view of IT often constructed by globalization theorists. Most important to this argument is the point that, as many senior managers told me, 'IT is not a driver of globalization itself' (Director, Human Resources, EuroBank1, London). Investment banking and management consultancy are not being forced into transnationalization by changing IT:

It [information technology] is not the determining element. It is an enabler. For example, our system was down for two days last week. Saturday, I came in just to see if my PC was working. Today, I had a hundred and fifty messages in my email account. Just to give you a sense of the volume. Particularly when you are running a global business. Technology does assist you in communication enormously. If I want to talk to somebody in Australia, the human window is quite small. So email allows that to be easy.

(Managing Partner, Financial Institutions, USConsultancy3,
London)

The reason for this is that the role of IT in actually 'doing' global business remains secondary to questions of competitiveness, competence and markets. Rather myopically, the globalization theory literature often implicitly, if not explicitly makes the assumption that IT is behind the globalization of business services and especially banking (Ohmae 1995; Castells 1996; Carrington *et al* 1997). Whilst it is certainly true that contemporary IT has enabled global financial market integration and the development of new products and new volumes of trading, the assumption itself is crude in that this study suggests that both investment banking and management consultancy – when it comes down to whether or not these TNCs succeed in 'globalizing' their operations – remains heavily dependent on social relations.

Information technologies have provided the possibility for organizational globalization. What ultimately determines whether investment banks and management consultancies succeed as TNCs is their global competitiveness which in these service industries rests with the nature of their employees. The next chapter addresses this issue in depth but for the moment, I want to end my analysis of communication in these TNCs by proposing that IT should be understood as a medium for enabling and transmitting these crucial interpersonal business relationships. IT is the facilitating medium for the social relations of business, but it is no substitute for them:

> The answer is, I currently find there is no substitute for meeting a person. Once you've met a person, you can cut down the meetings hugely. You probably only need to see them once a year. I think in our environment you probably need to see a client two to three times a year, but what you can do is cut that down to once a year and have two to three video conferences.
>
> (Director, Capital Markets, UKBank2, London)

In that sense, 'IT systems are not some magic answer to all the problems of globalization' (Director, [Board], USBank1, New York). Rather, they are 'only as good as the ability of your staff to use them' (Chief Economist, Research Division, JapanBank4, New York). For example, one consultant gave me his view of the role of e-mail in the TNC:

> Communicating – email is absolutely essential. But other people may have told you this: the value of email is in direct proportion to the extent to which the people at either end know each other. Because its bandwidth is relatively small and it is really important that you know what the other person needs, you have a shared context for reading.
>
> (Director, Financial Institutions, USConsultancy4, New York)

The value of IT based communication, in this context, is determined by the nature of social relations that underlie electronic communication. That is to say, good communication is achieved when the parties involved already know each other well because the communicators have a relationship of understanding that does not rely on the IT medium. When I asked them about the use of the telephone, I received a similar response:

> People don't think about the telephone...but telephone manner, culture...whatever you call it...is very important. Certainly you would say it is a much better form of communication if you know the person on the end of the line...
>
> (Partner, USConsultancy3, New York)

Furthermore, many of the management consultants explained that information technologies are not standardized, inflexible aspects of doing business which firms impose on their organizational structures. Rather, IT systems are features of transnational business services that evolve (Harrington 1991) and are developed to the requirements of individual firms (Legge *et al* 1991) in a way that reflects, for example, the culture of video-conferencing practices in a specific corporate environment. As one Director explained:

> Oh, I have always used teleconferencing, video-conferencing...all that stuff a lot. Ever since it first was possible. But I don't think it's...erm..it's not a case of this IT was suddenly there and then everything worked fine. Teleconferencing was a bright idea in the 70s or whenever and it took them ten years to sort it. Videoconferencing is still new, and you tailor this kind of thing to your firm and your business requirements. We had an IT man who virtually invented a new system from the stuff available because we wanted to meet with maybe a dozen people at each end, and the system we already had...you could only meet with six or so. So it's something you shape to your needs I think...
>
> (Managing Director, UK Head of Corporate Finance, EuroBank1,
> London)

In the light of these arguments, the research therefore revealed that the relationship of IT to the TNC needs to be understood in a different manner to the globalization theorists' causal theoretical construction. They represent an important element of communication within TNCs and play an important part in organizational globalization. However, in investment banking and management consultancy, the idea that IT has superseded direct social contact in the contemporary TNC is a much-exaggerated argument as the continued significance of international business meetings bears witness.

The continued key function of international business meetings

The nature of communication in transnational consultancy and banking is such that not only are IT-based forms of communication 'no substitute' for social interaction, but also in fact they take a secondary role in the key organizational control functions which they are often associated with. The argument has thus come full circle insofar as part of the reason why these TNCs do not exhibit the degree of command and control centralization proposed in the office location-led globalization literature, is that information technologies do not have the impact on key control functions that many theorists suggest. The implication is simple: it is not possible to centralize command and control functions in corporate head offices in any straightforward way because IT-based communication is not a sufficiently reliable medium of control. One consultant explained why this is the case:

> If you have worked together with people, you can do it in shorthand. You can communicate well and then you also have to know when you have to increase the bandwidth. The telephone has much more bandwidth than email because you can really hear a tone of voice and video has more bandwidth again. But the reason that you always have to be prepared to jump on a plane is that there are conversations where – and somebody used this phrase to me 25 years ago and I have never forgotten it – "you have to be able to smell the sweat." And that you can only do face-to-face. That is a challenge but it is also one that if it is met, frankly, it creates a fundamentally different kind of work-place.
>
> (Director, Financial Institutions, USConsultancy4, New York)

As a growing literature on the sociology of business interaction points out (for example, Zukin & DiMaggio 1990; Thrift & Olds 1996), face-to-face contact is crucial in terms of effective communication and generating trust between different actors in a business dealing. Almost all of the senior managers I spoke with said that IT was, to paraphrase the words of one, 'only an aid to the process of global management' (Senior Manager, Operations, USBank1, New York). In fact, one senior consultant reflected the work experiences of many when he said:

> That's really what being a senior guy is all about. I spend most of my time on business trips. On a plane somewhere to have a meeting of regional heads, or meeting the man in Sidney who's running a project we're doing at the moment in Australia. Or my counter-part

in Los Angeles. You see...well, there's no IT system in the world that will change that. IT – email, video-conferencing, teleconferencing whatever – only helps you keep up to date. A lot of decisions are never made over the phone...

(Senior Partner, USConsultancy4, New York)

Within these transnational business-service firms at least, IT has to be understood as taking a secondary role in terms of the constitution of managerial command and control activities. Key decisions are made by the decision-makers physically meeting up together in an office somewhere in the world. Most of the divisional heads in the companies I studied share a common work pattern in this regard: they regularly attend international meetings where strategy and main control functions are performed:

I see my counterparts at least twice a year...er...unless there is some special project. That's the formalized global meeting. I mean, I'm responsible out of London as a regional Head of Human Resources to manage things in the region. So next week I have actually my regional workshop where I meet with the location managers for two days in Frankfurt...but in terms of the personal relationship, video-conferencing helps, but it doesn't replace it fully. Part of the main function of these meetings, these conferences, is always the networking. Because in a structure like this, the networking – the individual network is the key to success. You have to build the network if you manage cross boundaries, cross-borders.
(Managing Director, Human Resources [Europe], EuroBank1, London)

The whole global FX management team will meet 2 or 3 times a year, the global money markets team will meet a couple of times a year. Erm...but the executive committee in North America will meet monthly if not more frequently than that, and those meetings may coincide with an executive meeting in London.

(Partner, Japanese Clients, USConsultancy3, New York)

A substantial fraction of senior managers in the study, as a consequence of the need for face-to-face contact, spend a lot of time travelling between different parts of the transnational office network:

In my previous role I used to take 200 plane flights a year – that would be travelling 80 or 90 percent of the time. And I can tell you what globalization involves in terms of that sort of role. I now have as an agreement with my fellow partners that I will do much less travelling and I am now based in London. But I still nip over to New York four or five times a year – much much less travelling.

(Partner, USConsultancy2, London)

Another example, we have been working with one of the big banks in South Africa on their investment banking group which we started about 18 months ago and which we are now reasonably responsible for. Which means I go to South Africa at least three times a year and I went probably 20 times last year.

(Managing Partner, USConsultancy6, London)

This is not just a question of major strategic meetings. Many divisional managers regarded communication through the environment of social contact that an international business meeting produced as a normal, routine part of their managerial practices. In this sense, the existing globalization literature over-states the significance of IT systems with regard to the constitution of managerial power in the TNC. IT has enabled a substantial growth and qualitative shift in informational flows, but I was told again and again that managerial control is exercised through personal contact:

It's a project we are running on a global basis. Things we want to work together: policy issues, procedural issues. I mean as tasks need to be spread out, you need to sit together – sit down physically in an office and beat it out sometimes – because it may not work in all the locations. You've got to know where the frictions are in terms of what is known, what is available, what is possible on the legal side. I would say it's developing new initiatives, if you want to move in certain directions, these issues concern everyone. And also it's the cost performance on top of that.

(Managing Director, Corporate Finance, EuroBank3, London)

Finally, most of my respondents did not foresee that new forms of IT would change the significance of personal managerial contact in the near future. It was not a case where 'rapid advances in IT are going to somehow make me meeting my guys obsolete' (Managing Director, UK Head of Corporate Finance, EuroBank3, London). IT systems would have to become a lot more like social contact than they were at the moment for managerial control to significantly move away from a social contact basis:

> It all helps. You know, you just have to get used to using the phone and the video conferencing. I don't think anybody particularly likes it. Some people like the phone but you still have to travel. And you know, have frequent gatherings, get togethers, and preferably rotate people around so they know what it is like. I don't think anyone has got that one yet and I can't see that changing. No matter how good the IT.
>
> (Senior Manager, Global Head of Operations, USBank1, New York)

> Face-to-face meetings will always remain very important. I don't know maybe video-conferencing comes closer and face-to-face meetings in the future may not be as important. But if I am trying to learn a new company, there is no better way than to either visit a company or let the company come to me and give a presentation. If you are just listening to other people talk about the company or reading analysts' reports, or reading the annual report, it isn't going to give you nearly the perspective that a face-to-face visit does.
>
> (Managing Director, EuroBank4, London)

It seems unlikely that communication technologies will present a viable substitute for face-to-face business meetings in the near future. In running a global organization, key decisions are still made as a consequence of physical not virtual meetings. As the senior manager I quoted earlier put it, 'you have to be able to smell the sweat'. IT is too poor a medium of communication to engender sufficient degrees of trust and knowledge between people within the organizational hierarchy.

Conclusion

Investment banking and management consultancy as industry sectors provide a strong argument for rethinking how TNCs are theorized in the context of globalization primarily because firms in both these advanced service industries do not fit the standard model of the TNC. The form of corporate transnationalization occurring within management consultancies and investment banks, as examined in this chapter, differs in at least three significant ways from that in manufacturing or extractive industry firms. First, management consultancies and many investment banks have only developed transnational operations relatively recently in comparison to many manufacturing or primary industry companies. Management consultancy as an industry has only really emerged since the late 1960s, and has only employed significant numbers of people since the early 1980s (Daniels 1993). It is true that merchant banking, as it tend to be called,[20] has a long history of overseas trading activity, but until the 1980s many of the increasing numbers of now transnational investment banks were entirely domestically oriented firms (Henwood 1997). Thus, there is a much shorter history – from an organizational perspective – to business transnationalization in both these sectors than in manufacturing or extractive industries.

Second, and furthermore, the *nature of transnationalization* within firms in these industries has been different for manufacturing firms. Many of these companies have effectively moved straight to an organizational form that is *transnational* or *global* rather than multinational in nature, exhibiting different kinds of organizational set-ups from their early domestic market orientation days. This presents a strong contrast to the evolving organizational form of many large manufacturing firms from MNC to TNC in line with management models of internationalization (Johanson & Vahlne 1990; Andersen 1993). Furthermore, these firms cannot be easily fitted to the 'born-global' view of new firm formation discussed by management theorists in the 1990s (McKinsey 1993; Madsen & Servais 1997; Bell *et al* 2001).

Third, the *nature of business activity* in both industries is different to many other TNCs in that as drivers in what Castells (1996) calls the 'informational economy', most of what investment banking and consultancy business consists of is the exchange and sale of information (Alvesson 1995; Abrahamson 1996). Again, this difference in these transnational firms' products is leading to a different form of organizational globalization within these firms, shaped by different business circumstances and conditions than are faced by manufacturing or extractive corporations.

Therefore, although there are certainly common theoretical threads that can be drawn out from an understanding of the processes of organizational globalization occurring within investment banks and management consultancies which can be applied to TNCs in general, these advanced service firms are being shaped by industry-specific factors in their globalization strategies. The discussion showed how the dramatic internal restructuring of these firms in recent years, moving away from a geographical to a product-based structure, is a diverse, contradictory and problematic trend in business services which is intimately linked to the perceived ability of transnational service firms to compete for increasingly 'global' clients. Structurally, such a set of changes is often reflected in financial reorganization in these transnational corporations as well.

The way in which the requirements of managerial control affect and are affected by the logic of organizational restructuring was then examined. New divisional structures have implications for control systems in these transnational firms, and the nature of transnational organizational form is in part shaped by the limitations imposed by control requirements. I also argued there that command and control, contrary to the view of many globalization theorists (for example, Sassen 2001), should not be theorized as being 'centralized' in certain physical locations, nor in the hands of certain senior functionaries in the organization. The research explored how managerial control is necessarily 'diffuse' in form within transnational business-service firms (Jones 2002), and how that that diffusion is directly bound into the nature of the products that consultancies and banks supply to a transnational market. In short, information-rich products impose strong limits on the degree to which it is possible to centralize control.

Finally, in considering how communications, and in particular information technologies, are a constituent part of transnational business services, the key argument developed in this regard is that IT is often regarded in the globalization literature as an abstract, key 'factor' that 'is part of globalization'. In contrast, I have argued that information technologies are intrinsically bound into the social relations of business activity, both in terms of their significance (or lack of it) in business deals and also in the way that information and communication systems have emerged and developed in specific organizational contexts. In the light of my examination of IT in banks and consultancies, I moved to make the further, and more radical argument, that IT should be understood as taking a more secondary role in transnational business integration than the globalization literature makes out. I argued that the social interaction of business activity is still a central and overridingly important feature of whether management consultancies and investment banks are profitable and successful, even at the transnational scale – information technologies are simply an important, facilitating medium through which some elements of global business services are conducted.

Overall, then, the most important argument emerging from this chapter is that to theorize management consultancy and investment banking in a way that permits an understanding of how and why globalization is occurring in these industries, there is a need to explore the interrelations among several different aspects of transnational business activity. This argument has clear relevance to theorizing TNCs more generally. An exclusive focus on geographic location, or financial structures, or organizational power only permits a limited amount to be said both practically and theoretically. Less faith and interest needs to be placed in generalized 'globalization theory' as a guide for academic understanding and corporate policy, and more attention placed on the nature and context of integrative practices. The next chapter takes up this agenda in depth as it turns to examine the inherently *social* nature of management consultancy and investment banking as an activity that senior business managers in these firms lead in the practices of 'doing' business.

4
'Doing' Global Business

Now, all of trading culture is different because it is short-term, it's like, 'we're going to do a deal today' – you know. Okay, maybe the client gets fucked [sic] – so what? There are some more clients tomorrow. For these guys, then, their relationships are clearly not long-term. But then, you know...guess what? This guy finds out how shit [sic] the Bond he owns is – the hundred thousand dollars cheque bond – he's not going to talk to the trader anymore. He's not going to talk to us anymore. Now you might have been able to do that fifteen years ago if you were *USBank7* or somebody, and you couldn't care less about the clients. But not anymore...

(Senior Associate, UK & European Bond Sales, USBank1, London)

Introduction

The popular image of 'global finance' in the new century is of a high-tech, IT-centred world where bankers sit in front of rows and rows of flickering computer screens. Deals are done on computers; money is made or lost in abstract, electronically mediated markets where the only characters to be found are numerical. In popular culture, the explosion of financial service industries in cities like London and New York during the 1980s spawned films such as *Wall Street* (1987) or *The Bonfire of the Vanities* (1988) which portrayed a new world of late twentieth-century finance where millions were being made or lost in speculative trading (see also Hassard & Holliday 1998). In the 1990s, these images were reinforced through popular perceptions of Black Monday (Buiter *et al* 1998), the collapse of Barings Bank (Tickell 1996), collapsing markets in East Asia and Japan (Goldstein 1998; Agenor

1999) and most recently the demise of the US energy giant Enron on the basis of deeply flawed business financing.[1]

To outsiders, this world is often perceived as containing a bewildering array of financial products and incomprehensible new forms of money: junk bonds, debt-for-equity swaps or 'complex derivatives'.[2] Bankers[3] are seen as more-or-less the only people who understand these vast new globally integrated capital markets and, at least in the popular imagination of the last fifteen years, they are often represented as making huge profits through speculation on stock prices and market trends. They inhabit a world where business is perceived as increasingly being concerned with interpreting or analyzing streams of data, where share prices flash across displays at a rapid rate and where global financial markets rule without regulation. The older traditional images of 'gentlemanly finance' (Hutton 1995) in the City of London where business was done in the smoking rooms of gentlemen's clubs on Pall Mall have been swept away by the informational revolution and new actors entering the City (Augar 2001). And even the noisy social interaction of the traditional stock-exchange trading floor has evaporated into office-spaces that are as full of computer-screens as of traders. This is increasingly a world that centres on computers and numbers rather than on people and conversation.

This popular cultural perception of global finance and global cities has distinct echoes in the academic imagination as well (Tickell 1996; Holton 1998). Much of the literature on financial globalization tends to focus on the de-peopling effect of computerization and information technology on financial business (Heetje 1988; O'Brien 1991; Carrington et al 1997; Kim 1999; Lewis 1999). Financial market transnationalization is an increasingly abstract phenomenon from this academic viewpoint. Computerized trading systems reduce the role of human intermediaries, and global finance is argued to be increasingly 'above' the messy, dirty, vulgar world of productive industry, of buying, producing and selling products. Bankers sit in high-rise offices in front of computers, not directly involved with, as traditionally conceived, the 'real economy' where manufacturing industry produces 'things'. This is reinforced by the globalization debate (Fry 1997; Hirst & Thompson 1999; Held et al 1999; Schaberg 1999) which often centres on reams of quantitative data that reveal an ever-increasing volume of financial transactions and capital movements (IMF 2000, 2001). Furthermore, terms such as 'fictitious capital' (Roberts 1994; Harvey 2000b) reinforce this sense of abstraction from social life.

The same point is also applicable to debates over the vulnerability that speculative dealings in new forms of fictitious capital engender for the long-term stability of the global economy (Strange 1996, 1998a; Harvey 2000b). A considerable academic literature regards the integration of global financial markets as a phenomenon that can be effectively understood through the application of modelling centred on the laws of neo-classical economics (Hendershott 1977; Ramanujam & Vines 1989; Hart & Moore 1997). In short, the globalization of finance is often implicitly assumed to be a good example of a 'purer'[4] market where social relations are relatively insignificant and market forces operate relatively unhindered by the intervention of individuals (Gordon 1994). Likewise, the corporate response or government policy response to the perceived and/or real risks of financial globalization (Financial Times 1998) has centred around a mushrooming literature concerned with risk management that again bases its risk assessments largely around numerical and quantitative models (Young & Tippins 2000; King 2000).

However, there are those within economics and other social science disciplines (Thrift & Olds 1996; Leyshon 1997, 1998; McDowell 1997; Thrift 1997) who take a different view – particularly a school of thought known as the 'new economic sociology' (Grahber 1993; Granovetter & Swedberg 1994; Ingham 1996). In recent years, theories of financial globalization as an increasingly *asocial* phenomenon have been countered by those arguing that social relations remain central to transnational financial business (Zukin & DiMaggio 1990; Thrift 1994; McDowell 1997). Building on the work of economic sociologists who have discussed the 'embeddedness' of economic activity in social life (see also Smelser & Swedberg 1993), writers such as Thrift (1994) or Leyshon & Pollard (1997) have examined how (transnational) financial business activity is constituted through social interaction between embodied individuals (McDowell 1997) in a given workplace context. They have emphasized the importance of the development of long-term social relationships in business activity, and in particular the role that trust plays in the successful conduct of business deals (Thrift 1994, 1997; Pryke & Lee 1995). In that sense, the new economic sociology and other academic social scientists have provided a strong critical questioning of the terms of the financial globalization debate.

In this chapter, I develop these arguments in examining the nature of social relations in transnational investment banking and management consultancy. I argue that social relations are a central, crucial and under-theorized feature of transnational business activity – under-theorized to an extent that severely restricts the utility of theories of business transnationalization that fall under globalization theory in general. The interviews with senior managers suggest that the most influential group of factors with regard to the nature, practice and success/failure of transnational business in both consultancy and banking, revolve around the nature of social relations in firms within a transnational context. Thus, in contrast to the implication of financial globalization literature concerned with the speed and volume of capital flows and transactions, I argue that management consultancy and investment banking as transnational business services are, if anything, more, not less, 'socially constituted' than manufacturing activities. A flavour of how this argument unfolds is nicely captured in the colourful extract from an interview with a senior sales associate in the London office of one of the major US investment banks that opens this chapter. As the respondent explains, although finance obviously does incorporate the potential and ability to abstract business relations as the popular image of trading depicts, this is in fact only one aspect (and not an unproblematic one at that!) of the transnational business activities of his company. For this banker, and as I will explore through my case study industries, the social relations of business interactions with clients (and others) are at the centre of his concerns.

In the light of these arguments, the following discussion is divided into four major sections. First, I pick up the 'organization-centred' discussion of transnational business networks in the first chapter where I established that senior managers in investment banks and management consultancies regard transnational contact networks as being 'important' in the abstract. The first part of this chapter unpacks this idea to consider what a 'transnational contact' is in sociological terms, arguing that both 'internal' and 'external' forms of transnational social contact are central to the successful and competitive operation of transnational business-service firms. The second section then explores how consultancies and banks go about encouraging/engendering this crucial form of contact. It assesses the extent to which it is possible at all for firms to actively engender what I term *transnational socialization*. I suggest that although companies invest considerable time and money in this activity, the effectiveness of transnational socialization in facilitating business activity largely depends on the social skills of individual employees.

In the third part of the chapter, the focus is more specifically on the question of what a 'social contact' is and address the question of how trust is engendered. It suggests the concept of a 'contact' is in fact too crude a term for what is, in reality, a far more complex set of social relations. The section thus examines the micro-social nature of client relationships in investment banking and management consultancy, assessing how social contact plays a role in the acquisition of new business and the retention of existing business. As a consequence, I argue client relationships should be understood as constituting transnational business activity, rather than representing a context within which they are somehow 'embedded', and that the question of trust boils down to the relationships between groups of individuals. The final section ends the chapter by taking up this issue of the role of individuals. It examines the significance of informational exchanges of information and the nature of persuasion and negotiation with clients in arguing that in these business-service sectors, at least, certain individual employees are of key significance to the success of the business.

The significance of transnational social contact

> In this industry it doesn't matter where you're trying to do business...local or global, it's a lot about knowing people, building relationships...
>
> (Director, Global Head of Human Resources, USBank1, New York)

As the study progressed in a snowball of interviews spanning the Atlantic, I began to make contact with people in the highest positions in major investment banks and management consultancy firms. On these occasions, the subject material discussed during interviews often tended to be less concerned with the structural nature of their transnational organizations – the divisional forms and management hierarchies I discussed in the preceding chapter – because I had already reached managers lower down the company who had told me at length about these issues. I took the (rarer) opportunity of conversation with the highest-level managers (such as the respondent quoted above who, at the time of writing, is still on the Board of USBank1) to explore the issue of the 'business contact network' that the social science literature (Colombo 1998; Grandori 1999) has become increasingly interested in. It is these interviews that are perhaps the most interesting of all.

Listening to such people assert the crucial significance of trust, contact networks and social relations – individuals who as senior managers take an active and direct part in running, in several instances, one of the fifty largest companies in the world[5] – greatly heightened my appreciation of the importance of social relations in a way which far exceeded its identification as an important 'factor' in numerous academic or management texts (Weinshall 1993; Casson 1995; Child & Heavens 1998). Consequently, as this proved an interesting line of enquiry through the interviewing process, I began to take the assertion of the significance of 'business contact networks' one stage further. I set out to explore – in a qualitative sense at least – exactly how transnational contact networks are important (or not) to the way in which management consultancies and investment banks acquire business. Some of the existing literature in this regard have argued that family-ties or kinship relations are highly significant in investment patterns amongst, for example, the Chinese transnational business community on the Pacific Rim (Yeung 1997; Yeung & Olds 2000). Yet little has been said about whether transnational contacts are more generally important in the everyday functioning of wider transnational business activity.[6]

The argument of this section is that transnational social contacts are not just significant in a few given cases[7] – the Chinese diasporic business community, for example – but that social contact is a central feature of all activity within transnational business-service industries. Management consultancy and investment banking as industries are heavily embroiled in issues of sociality with regard to their constitution and operation, and that sociality should be one of the first objects of research by those seeking to theorize the complexity of transnational business. This arises from the way, in which the competitiveness of transnational investment banks and management consultancy firms is strongly influenced by the nature of transnational social contacts both within and external to the corporate organization. That is to say, if there was one factor through all of my interviews that the top-level management in these business-service firms saw as crucial to business success at the transnational scale, then it was the nature of employee–employee and employee–client social relations.

The first step, therefore, in understanding how management consultancy and investment banking business is constituted through social contact is to explore what a 'transnational contact network' might be in practice. Two different forms of contact network become apparent from the study in this regard, both of which senior managers regarded as important to business activity. The distinction is between transnational contact networks that are 'internal' – those within TNCs – and contact networks that are 'external' – that is, social contact with clients and contemporaries in competing/co-operating firms beyond the corporate structure of the transnational organization.

Consider internal contact networks first. These exist between employees in the same firm and they are crucial to the effective functioning of transnational business organizations and to business success. The functional importance of different employees within a given service TNC is linked to several interrelated 'uses' of 'knowing' people elsewhere in the company. To begin with, if employees have a diasporic network of contacts within their own company, the individual exposed to the business opportunity is more likely to know where to find relevant people with appropriate experience of that type of business in the transnational organization:

> It also means that because I know a lot of people in our U.S. practice, even if the person in question does not have the skills I am looking for, he will know much more about our U.S. practice than I will. And he will certainly have the contact within the U.S. practice so he can pass me onto another node . . . and because he knows me, he will understand what I'm looking for much more quickly.
>
> (Managing Partner, USConsultancy5, London)

The acquisition of new business is therefore 'directly facilitated by networks within the company' that 'enable [the firm] to respond quickly to the enquiry' of a prospective client (Partner, US financial Institutions, USConsultancy2, New York). Such an issue is especially relevant to management consultancy firms where individual or teams of consultants tend to specialize in certain industrial sectors or types of project – for example, privatization of a state sector such as the water industry. Business in such a field will involve lucrative contracts from national governments, but there is relatively little of it: new contracts put out to tender are likely to arise in different national contexts across the globe. That is to say, any government only needs consultancy teams specializing in water privatization for one specific period only – once privatization is complete, there will be no more water privatization contracts in that country. However, future contracts may arise elsewhere – if another national government decides to privatize their water industries (Managing Partner, USConsultancy4, London; paraphrased). In a similar way, as partners in two different consultancy firms described independently, it is crucial for these business-service firms to have employees who know individuals elsewhere in the transnational organization and who have the relevant experience:

> We need what we call 'communities of practice' – which are people who are interested in particular areas; you know, they form

communities on our internal IT network – very much like an Internet discussion group, or something. Most of our people are Internet-enabled and they are into that sort of community or group. And we build, using our technical infrastructure, these different communities across geographies based around industry, technology, whatever the subject might be. So that is certainly one way how people get grouped and form internal relationships: communicating with each other, exchanging ideas, helping us to get business...

(Managing Partner, USConsultancy2, London)

If we come back to the local situation with a UK multinational who calls us up, we then need to – within our own business, our own network – put people together who can meet the needs of that company. So often as we are pitching for business, very often we will call up a team from around the world. And these people obviously tend to know each other quite often, and that is definitely a good thing and something we would encourage because it helps with the knowledge flow.

(Managing Partner, USConsultancy1, London)

However, management consultancy is not unique in this. Senior investment bankers shared a similar view of the significance of internal contact networks within the transnational company. Knowing people elsewhere in the firm is seen to be crucially beneficial in the overall ability of a company to gain new and retain existing business because the organization as a whole functions more effectively in response to the needs, demands and enquiries of clients:

The key to advantage, to being competitive as a company I would say, is knowing your counterparts both in your own and client organizations – feeling comfortable dealing with other people is extremely important in this business. If you know who you are dealing with... not just having a name on a piece of paper but really knowing the person is really important. On the one side, I think the bank profits because it brings back business – it's a trust thing. Its also – if you talk about the cross-selling of products – if you don't know anyone in those locations, it is difficult to sell...you need the contacts...

(Director, Capital Markets, UKBank3, London)

And as several of the senior bankers explained, their firms actively attempted to get physically disparate people together in one place in order to facilitate the development of these internal social networks:

> Part of the key function of these meetings, these conferences, is always the networking. Because in a structure like this, the networking – the individual network is the key to success. You have to build the network as you manage cross boundaries, cross-borders.
>
> (Head of Human Resources [Europe], EuroBank2, London)

These internal networks are linked to the emphasis placed by respondents on building a sense of community in their firms. This extended, in terms of corporate social practices, to 'far more than the occasional trip to Tokyo to meet the Japanese office' (Partner, Japanese clients, USConsultancy3, New York). The study reveals that firms in both service-sector industries expend considerable time, money and energy in attempting to engender a sense of community and identity within the company. As the respondent quoted here explains, a commitment to developing a sense of community and familiarity with contemporaries is expected as an implicit job requirement:

> On the business side, people will know each other in some depth, and certainly we would expect all the people at a certain level to know each other. We'd expect all the Grads or Executives to know each other. We expect all the Directors to know each other. But they don't necessarily, because some of them are very isolated in their own little view. We would expect them to all know each other, and we take steps to try and make sure that happens: appraisal processes, for example, where they all get to meet and talk to each other, find out about other peoples stuff . . . things like that . . . er . . . we'll have organized get-togethers where some of the senior members meet once a quarter.
>
> (Managing Director, Equities and New Issues, UKBank2, London)

Indeed, both consultancies and banks are actively engaged in deliberate activities designed to increase social contact and a sense of community. This will be explored in more depth shortly, but the first point to emphasize is that lack of social contact is seen as a problem. For example, one manager described the inclination of some people in the bank where he worked to remain 'socially isolated' as 'one of the key limiting factors in the effective globalization of our operations' (UK Head of

Corporate Finance, EuroBank4, London). If managers, market-makers or decision-makers in these service TNCs are unable to identify to whom they should be talking in the respective office on a different continent, then the ability of the companies to respond to business opportunities is impaired:

> You normally have a team of bankers and research people across divisions within the company, and now we've merged with UKBank3 that means more and more people around the world... I mean, for bankers it is up to them to take the credit for bringing in the money in the deal, but many times they would never have come across the company without the analysts. More and more the analysts are the ones bringing in the business. So all of us need to work together, know what everyone else is doing, be in contact... because if [you] don't know what the LA office is thinking – who the people concerned are – then you can't serve the client as one operation...
>
> (Senior Analyst, EuroBank2, New York)

And the lack of developed internal social networks was identified by respondents in both sectors as a limit on the ability of their companies to serve [our] clients effectively on a global basis (Partner, USConsultancy3, New York):

> A: Being a global player means having global capability... [pause]
>
> Q: In what sense?
>
> A: Well, for a start you need to get your people talking to each other... as much as possible. Because if your teams don't work one the global level, then how are you going to convince these guys [the clients] that you can help them to achieve that!
>
> (Managing Partner, USConsultancy5, London)

In that sense then, good internal social networks in these TNCs are important for both the firm's internal capability to develop new business opportunities, and for the quality of the service it provides to 'global' clients. Transnational investment banks and management consultancies are, therefore, extremely reliant on internal *transnational socialization* within their organizations. In industries that depend on an individual employee's specialist skills and knowledge, and in 'service-sector markets which are becoming more global in nature'

(Head of Training, UKBank1, London), one of the central problems faced by companies is, how to make sure employees working at the transnational scale are able to accomplish the same degree of communication as they can being in the face-to-face office or urban environment of a given business centre.

However, this issue runs far deeper than the nature and development of internal social networks. To quote one senior manager:

> ... getting our people to know and communicate with each other is just the tip of the iceberg when it comes to globalization ... What you've really got to address is how they relate to clients on the ground ... er ... wherever those clients are. And that's the really hard part.
>
> (Managing Director, Global Fixed Income, EuroBank5, London)

This is the second form of transnational social contact network – the external network. The research shows this is crucial to a firm's global capability in terms of fulfilling two interrelated functions: acquiring and retaining business. With regard to the acquisition of new business, consider how one manager explained how his company achieved this:

> There are probably three main ways that new opportunities will come to us. One is the cold tender which will come to us and a number of others simply because we have a name which is recognized. And I supposed size is also important. Secondly, there are people who come to us because they know us and the third is because we know our clients and so on; the last two are more common: we recognize what is going on in their industry and their particular neck of the woods. We can take ideas to them. And because they know you, they will give you a hearing. And that is where the concept of the client network is important.
>
> (Director, UK Head of Corporate Finance, EuroBank2, London)

The latter two points are quite clearly centred on the relationships that employees within these banks have with potential clients. What is perceived by this Director as important in convincing clients to give their business to his company is knowledge of client needs, trust, negotiation and communication – all of which will be mediated through employee–client social relationships. And even where there is a 'cold tender' scenario, this is not entirely cold in the sense of being an abstracted relation based purely on documents. Being recognized is a consequence of existing social relations. Investment banking, certainly within corporate finance, is an intrinsically social activity – a point well illustrated by the comments of another senior analyst on the function of the international office network of her company:

> All the shoshas[8] have you know international networks. Offices in even very remote areas, it might just be a one man [sic] office but there is a presence there so they are very well networked. They will have on the ground relationships in a lot of countries, even developing countries. The people-presence is the thing . . .
>
> (Senior Business Analyst, JapanBank3, New York)

Global banking and consultancy business needs to be understood, in this light, as being centred on *sociality*. Having even one person in an office with a contact network is the key to getting business. Yet this provokes questions: in what way is this social? Is this a question of formal meetings or less formal social relations? And what aspects of business relations are important?

The first stage in addressing these questions is to examine what exactly social contact within either of these kinds of networks entails. As far as the role of social contact with regard to the acquisition of new business is concerned, investment banks and management consultancies rely to a considerable extent on *individual* employees and the relationships that they have with other *individuals* in client firms. In that sense, acquiring business goes beyond the rather abstract notion of just being 'facilitated' by semi-formal social contact:

> And in terms of how we get the work, you know, we have institutional relationships with . . . we try and characterize it like that. Major firms, and particularly within that, the individuals within consulting groups such as myself. The key guys who, you know, do relationships with people in those firms and find opportunities.
>
> (Partner, US Finance, USConsultancy3, New York)

It is not just a question of 'a few meetings where your people come across as okay' (Managing Director, Head of Human Resources [Europe], EuroBank2, London). Rather the clinching of deals tends to be highly influenced by longer term, and developed, social relations between specialist partners and a representative in the client firm. These are developed, long-standing and 'dense' social relationships:

I know a lot of these people very well, yes. In some cases we have been working together or at least in the same field for years...and a lot of the key business is like that. The top people here know who to deal with in the client...they often have a long history of repeat business. That's where the trust really comes into it...

(Executive Director, Global Fixed Income, Currencies and Derivatives, EuroBank3, London)

This importance of individuals in the process of business acquisition through external contact networks sits within the wider context of the perceived standing of a firm within the relevant business community, manifested and mediated through the social networks of employees. In other words, the reputation of business-service TNCs with their informational products are strongly shaped by a client's opinion of the employees of that company:

Q: So would you ring somebody up if you're beginning a new research project and say, "remember me, I'm doing this."?

A: Yes. It depends on our industry specialists...like we have a large medical client...and so we have lots of doctors who we will call and ask to find out a "hey, do you like this product?", "what do you think about this?" And so on. So it is very important. I mean, what you are trying to do is one come up with a credible reason as to why you should buy a stock and two, trying to give more information than anyone else can give. So that one you make the recommendation and two when the mutual fund wants to buy it, they will go through your company. It is getting noticed. Within the investment community that is really important.-

(Senior Analyst, EuroBank3, New York)

Not surprisingly, it is often older and more senior employees who have the client base that carries a lot of the business – a point made clear as one partner in a consultancy discusses the problems generated by giving key individuals considerable power within his firm:

We are a traditional consulting group where you have partners who have in their own minds, their own little empires and build their client bases; they are selling work and being profitable. But not necessarily bringing other people along with them. So what do we do in the consulting world? We reward team behaviour and we don't reward individual behaviour...it is the same in the world of banking and investment banking. You know, if you can get rid of turf issues, it usually translates down to profit and loss, then you can start working those issues.

(Partner, Financial Institutions, USConsultancy3, New York)

Clearly, therefore, the significance of this external contact network is also in securing repeat work with previous clients. Many senior managers explained that much of their business is 'repeat activity' (Director, Capital Markets, UKBank2, London) where clients return to the same transnational business-service firm on the back of existing social relations from past contact:

A lot of our work is repeat business with large, significant clients. So what we try and do is focus – and this is the approach of the other consultancy firms – is focus now on the large significant clients and do large projects for them. As opposed to having a myriad of clients doing a myriad of different stuff for lots of people – you know, it can be a lot of fun. It appeals to all of us to be able to do different work for different clients in different industries but we have focused in on the larger clients doing one or two projects. And usually the larger projects – particularly in the world I operate which is Wall Street – those clients are always global. It could be...designing the systems architecture for foreign exchange trading for a client.

(Partner, Financial Institutions, USConsutlancy4, New York)

In addition, as another Director in a New York investment bank explained, the significance of 'external' contact networks extends beyond the immediately obvious issue of clients. Whether business is acquired and retained, in his view, also has a lot to do with the multiple arrays of social relations with all the other supporting and related organizations involved in transnational service business. Thus, external relations are also important in influencing the quality of other companies that this firm contracts to provide services:

We have a huge network. A huge network of people who have been executives in companies either previously or are currently invested in. There are some 185 companies in the portfolio and I would say 35 are outside the United States, so a third are outside the United States. A network of lawyers, accountants, consultants that we have worked with over time to know us, who can calibrate us, who have got a feel for the kind of people, the kind of situations that are interesting.

(Director, USBank6, New York)

This indicates how long-term social relations with service-suppliers, as well as clients, are also important to the success of transnational investment banking and management consultancy.

What still needs addressing, however, is how the 'transnational' nature of the case study firms relates to this issue of the sociality of their business activity. If, in business services, as one manager put it succinctly, 'it is the quality of the employee–client relationships that counts' (Senior Partner, Financial Institutions, USConsultancy3, New York) then in what sense should social relations themselves be understood as transnational? Another respondent captured this issue well:

It's actually local networks of business that are important. To a limited extent that there are global networks – but actually it's local. And the reason for that is that consultancy is typically bought not sold. It is very difficult to go into a major company today which you do not know and go and see a chief executive and get access. But to go in and for one thing convince that person that he needs to hire a consultant and that it is you, is actually very difficult to do. What you can do, though, is build up contacts and create a favourable impression such that when they want to hire somebody, they call you up. Now most of that would occur at a local level. So a major UK multinational would call someone here and talk to him about that. Some of that would happen at a global level in terms of the world economic forum happening this weekend in Dallas. We will have some of our senior people there who will meet senior people inevitably who will not be from their own company. And not from their own country. And some contacts will be made and that will constitute a small part of the business.

(Managing Partner, USConsultancy1, London)

This partner regards social contacts largely as existing at (multiple) local scales, with higher-level managerial contact networks being relevant at the global scale. However, the reality is more complicated than this rationale of local and global presents. Overall, the research suggests that transnational socialization is not easily pigeonholed into predetermined scales because scales are too readily equated to notions of territoriality. Local knowledge for the manager quoted above means 'employees in a given office in a given urban centre'. Yet the nature of social contact, communication and information-flow needs to be understood as more than a territorially constituted phenomenon. Consider this through an (inadvertent) explanation of the scale of knowledge and social relations provided by one Director:

Q: So how do the global and local relate in this?

A: It's more the whole picture, if you take my meaning. Having an overview of both. The people in the Singapore office are there to know what is going on in the markets there . . . but it's no use if you don't relate that to the world markets . . . part of my job is to blend the global and the local needs – to evaluate the opportunities in Singapore against the wider market.

Q: So that is your job if you like?

A: Yes, in part. But the people in Singapore do it as well. I have more say, but everyone is hopefully trying to look at the wider picture . . . it's shared . . .

(Director, UKBank3, London [edited])

What this extract demonstrates is that 'local knowledge' of the Singapore market, to take the respondent's example, is not so much knowledge of a set of clients located in Singapore as an understanding of how clients who are based in Singapore relate to the rest of the world's money markets. Such a set of relationships is hard to define in terms of scales because the 'local' is not a bounded arena of business activity. Local knowledge in this sense includes an element of what could be termed global knowledge. Semantic arguments aside, the point is that using a terminology of scale – as many respondents did and as often happens in the management studies literature – is not clear. This demonstrates well the advantage of theorizing *context* rather than just talking about scale.

To summarize thus far, then, both internal and external social contact networks are central to the successful and competitive operation of transnational investment banks and management consultancy firms. The networks of contacts that employees maintain, develop and perpetuate in the transnational context represent the deciding element in whether these business-service firms gain contracts or not. Transnational investment banking and management consultancy should therefore be understood as sectors where *sociality* needs to be placed at the centre of theoretical arguments, rather than being marginalized or ignored as much of the existing literature has tended to do. In order to theorize and assess the future prospects of investment banking or management consultancy firms, research by academics or by firm employees themselves needs to focus on the nature of social contacts within and between firms. This argument is heavily reinforced by the material to be discussed in the next section: the importance transnational business-service firms place on engendering and developing these kinds of contact networks.

Transnational socialization: training and employee movements

> Certainly another global thing is that you do make face-to-face visits... like everyone in our team spends at least two separate one-week periods in the New York office per year. For two reasons: first, to learn some stuff. But mainly, secondly, just to kind of strengthen that bond, see people's faces, shake their hands, go out for drink with them so that next time they are talking to them arguing about allocation, there's a bit more of a personal dimension there rather than just a voice. Because that is the weird thing – is that you will be speaking to someone on the phone for a year and then you will meet them and they look totally different to the way that you imagine. For example, last Friday the whole of the European credit business went out for a shin-dig... to this country house out near Hatfield... Tokyo, New York, Hong Kong flying in basically for dinner on the Friday evening and a bit of a piss-up [sic] afterwards... The next day kind of talks and seminars... but the key thing was to socialize in the evening. And that was just to get a feel of... 'hey, this is the credit team'. So you do just feel comfortable getting on the phone.
>
> (Senior Associate, UK Bonds and European Sales, USBank2, London)

If senior managers regard 'transnational socialization' as crucial to the success and competitiveness of their firms, then companies in both management consultancy and investment banking reflect this valuation through transnational working and training practices. In this section, the emphasis moves to the interviews with Human Resources Directors as they are the key people charged with the task of engendering transnational socialization within investment banks and consultancy firms. Two relatively distinct elements within corporate strategies of engendering transnational socialization are suggested by this research.

The first of these practice-strategies is perhaps the most obvious and direct form of transnational socialization: *transnational training*. When new 'professional'[9] recruits join these firms, they are generally sent on induction and training courses as a cohort. Entry-level training in this manner allowed people joining all areas of the company around the globe to get to know each other, which in terms of internal contact networks, is seen as being advantageous for the company:

> We do make a conscious effort to try to get a group of people to get to know each other before they scatter to the four corners, because the informal network is easily as important as the formal ... and the more people one knows in a different function, then the more healthy it gets. I mean we're talking about almost four thousand people, possibly a bit more ... that's the total today. So it's a big organization and having informal networks is an important part of that.
>
> (Managing Director, Equities and New Issues, UKBank4, London)

New entrants to the transnational organization are therefore 'immediately dropped into an environment where they form relationships with all sorts of people from all divisions and all geographies' (Head of Training, UKBank2, London). This then provides a base where, to quote another Director, 'when they're faced with needing to get some help from the New York office, they're like, "oh, I know so-and-so I'll call them up."' (Director, UK Head of Corporate Finance, EuroBank3, London). For example, *USConsultancy1* sends all new recruits on a three-week induction programme in their 'global training centre' near Chicago:

> So we get these guys together again in Chicago and they go to programmes, lectures for sure, yes. But more than that they meet up, get talking, go out and socialize – we are pretty generous with the expenses as you might imagine. And so you get people building up global relationships ... that 's why we're leading the industry in this shift towards truly global organizations.
>
> (Partner, USConsultancy1, New York)

Many of the US banks have a similar approach to recruitment and training. New recruits in five of the nine US-based firms where I interviewed are all sent to a US centre (generally in New York) for 'basic training':

Everybody goes to the same place – New York – for the same training; no matter where they're from in the world. Part of that, of course, is to get the technical expertise, but probably more important is to build a network. I mean when you are going through the training programme, when your particular class goes through it is 50 to 75 people, it is not only a classroom, it is a lot of social stuff: you get a chance to bond with 50 to 75 people. And those classmates become your soul mates and you stay in touch with them for the rest of your career here whether it is within *USBank3* or outside *USBank3*. So that social aspect is most important.

(Director of Human Resources [Board], USBank3, New York)

Similarly, in one of the major European banks the Director who was responsible for recruitment and training throughout the firm's European operations explained how 'cohort training', in conjunction with several other 'contact media' is seen to be directly aimed at engendering the kind of internal contact networks I have already discussed:

The key instruments are the training programmes you're using: the global training programmes, the regional training programmes... er...the management training which is divisional and happens in the locations on a global basis. And then most of the time we have also training in Switzerland which is actually a fabulous place for that. The central thing is communication which is very important – we use daily news bulletins, staff magazines...and really all sorts of informal meetings. These are all opportunities to create communities. And it's about encouraging people to take the initiative – there is always the name of someone who was responsible for a transaction and who you can contact and talk to...and get to know more people. Then of course the transfer of people to...this is an element of working. Where as the important thing is you create a network where you work and repeat that network to the next step...so you keep that network, and international transfers play a big part in that.

(Managing Director, Head of Human Resources [Europe],
EuroBank2, London)

This type of approach towards training and career development represents a clear, directed attempt at producing transnational socialization of new employees. This is not just a question of occasional training courses where people from different offices around the globe meet, and nor is it restricted to only a few firms. When I asked one head of Human Resources about how prevalent he thought this kind of transnational socialization is across the investment banking industry as a whole he told me:

> Oh, everybody does the same kind of thing. All the major global banks face the same issues: how do you get all these scattered people to talk to each other ... it's no good if your New York office do their own thing and never tell anyone else ... Not if you're competing in a global market place ...
>
> (Director, Human Resources, UKBank2, London)

Thus, in both the transnational banking and consultancy sectors, companies are actively seeking to promote a sense of community through training structures. Furthermore, this does not cease once new professionals have completed their six- or eight-week induction course. Such entry level 'cohort training' is repeated through people's career paths. Senior human resources managers explained how whole strategies of internal promotion, job assessment and subsequent training programmes are geared to continuing this process of engendering internal social contacts. This enables employees from different offices around the globe to form the kind of relationships that enhances the effective undertaking of business:

> We don't recruit nationals necessarily to work in their country of origin. So you use Head Office as a training and then clearing ground for people so that you're beginning to build contacts through a cohort: 'I'm doing business with Italy ... ring so and so, do you remember? Who was on the programme? ... ahh, yeah! ... we trained her. Oh God, she's good, you know?' You're building trust, you're building that sort of relationship again so that you're continually getting flows from regions to head office, from region to region as you move these people around the place ...
>
> (Director, Head of Training, UKBank4, London)

This, then, leads me to the second element of corporate strategies aimed at engendering transnational socialization: 'global movement'. Respondents in both industries consistently stated that what their companies were aiming to create were, as one manager explained, 'transnational workforces ... [that] are as comfortable with hopping between one country and another as with going out for lunch' (Partner,

USConsultancy4, New York). Human resource managers see the nature of professional working practices in both these service TNCs as being dominated by what would have previously been termed 'expatriate placements' that leads to employees with 'truly global contact networks' (Managing Director, Equities and New Issues, UKBank2, London):

> This is a big element of global movement where the important thing is you create a network where you work. Then you move on – get sent back to head office or another office half way round the world. And again you repeat that networking as the next step...but you keep the old network, build on it. And international transfers play a big part in that.
>
> (Managing Director, Head of Human Resources [Europe],
> EuroBank2, London)

However, this 'global movement' needs to be understood as, at the very least, an extension and deepening of traditional conceptions of expatriate work (Beaverstock 1991, 1994). The reason for this is that many respondents suggested that the scale of global movement within their organizations was considerably more than the traditional limited number of mid-managers being located in branch offices around the globe (Wheelan & Hunger 1998; Carrell *et al* 2000). The number of people in 'foreign centres' in both real and percentage terms is substantial and increasing:

> Because at the end in this organization, you know, what you are saying is, "if your client in Kuala Lumpur has a requirement for this service, we will deliver it to you from wherever it is in our organization." We know about the skill, we know the person, they will turn up in Kuala Lumpur and do whatever. That's a huge deal. A huge proposition. If the person is in Kansas City or somewhere, that is a huge deal. So the amount of travelling involved is a big deal and that then sort of percolates down into issues of whether younger people want to spend all that time travelling around, travelling on out-of-town jobs. It is almost taking away a reality of life which is, you know, people have a house somewhere and live there and friends and all that stuff, and saying "oh, we are going to put you, you can work in Oslo five days a week." Come back at the weekends. That is a lot more of that than there used to be. And I suspect not just for us, but for everybody.
>
> (Managing Partner, USConsultancy1, London)

So what you are doing is that you are hiring not only people who are a mixture, a cultural mixture, but you also hiring people who are globally flexible. Who can work in New York today, and Singapore tomorrow, and Sydney next year. Okay? And that is what they want today. I would say the propensity now in your career is to have more changes and assignments in different locations. And the more time you get in your area of specialty, the longer you stay in that particular location doing a particular business. . . . you know, we are an organization of 17,000 people and anywhere in time we have got 800 to a thousand people in a foreign centre . . . and that number is growing.

> (Director of Human Resources [Board], USBank1, New York)

Furthermore, as the latter Director states, willingness to work abroad and engage in these programmes of global movement are increasingly linked to personal career success both within organizations and industries. These transnational service firms want employees who 'are the kind of people who are comfortable with time abroad' (Head of Training, UKBank2, London) and working abroad in this way was an expected and increasingly common working experience. In a sense, this is hardly surprising. Certainly in part because of the logistics of doing transnational business – people have to move to clients – but also because in these industries where transnational socialization is increasingly central to corporate success, those individuals who are valuable employees are precisely those people with an already existing transnational network of contacts and/or experience of the multiple contexts in which these firms operate:

> What we are aiming for is for our people to be gaining an understanding of how the business works in another national context, in another regulatory, language and cultural environment . . . those are the kind of people we need most.
>
> (Managing Partner, USConsultancy3, London)

However, the extent to which these strategies of engendering transnational socialization are successful must be assessed. The strategies employed by these transnational business-service firms are far from unproblematic and there are (perhaps intractable) difficulties with, in particular, global employee movements that will have to be addressed more adequately by these companies if they are to continue to extend transnational work practices.

The nub of the problem in seeking to engender transnational socialization is that employees remain strongly attached to national contexts.
Expatriate work has always been regarded as challenging and unattractive
for many (Wheelan & Hunger 1998) because of the many disadvantages of working abroad for long periods of time: people have to live in
new linguistic, cultural, social and physical environments often away
from their families and friends. Expatriate work may be unattractive for
parents who may not want to move their children from established
schooling or are constrained by a partner's employment (Beaverstock &
Smith 1996; Beaverstock & Bostock 2000). Whilst senior managers were
keen to relate the growing numbers of employee movements, they also
admitted to considerable organizational resistance to these strategies. As
the Managing partner in *USConsultancy1* I quoted previously explained,
the majority of the companies' consultants are clearly reluctant to
become 'truly global' in terms of their personal location:

> To be frank, it [policy of employee movement] is creating havoc
> because a lot of Europeans say well "I am a partner in the Italian
> practice, and first and foremost I feel Italian. Although I worked in
> financial services I have no more interest in this guy doing financial
> services in New York that the man in the moon. And if I can not find
> work in financial services I am quite happy to go and work in a utility
> company rather than be picked up and put on a financial services
> job in Oslo. That is the issue that you have."
>
> (Managing Partner, USConsultancy1, London)

Furthermore, many respondents acknowledged that successful transnational socialization is not the inevitable outcome of employee circulation or transnational training strategies. Global employee movements
do not necessarily produce either contact networks or contextual know-
ledge/understanding of the business of a different branch. In several
managers' views, this was in part related to different organizational
forms[10] of TNCs that had originated from different national economic
contexts:

> It's different, I'd say, in an American company as opposed to a Japanese
> or German one. Different countries have different attitudes to
> this...where the Japanese send their mid-managers out as a matter
> of course, and have done for years, it's a much newer thing for us
> here [UK]...[it] takes time to get a company to adapt to having all
> these people moving...like when we first sent out Equities people to

Singapore, there was nothing for them to do, and I admit a few don't settle in well. But, you know, we learn from that . . .

(Director, Human Resources, UKBank4, London)

Simply sending someone to the Tokyo, Singapore, Pittsburgh or Sidney obviously does not mean they will necessarily become socialized in that new context. This issue is clearly illustrated by the Japanese investment banks because of 'the wider cultural differences and barriers between the Japanese firm and what you might call the American-European model' (Partner, Japanese Clients, USConsultancy3, New York). As one respondent described, Japanese banks have for some time operated a more rigidly defined and pervasive employee circulation policy-practice as a standard feature of work practice than their Anglo-European counterparts:

I would say that the majority of the employees here are from Japan – Japanese. They come in for their three to five year stints. I guess you are familiar with the Japanese system of rotation management[11] and it is very alive and well in this company. This company is extremely – I would say it is one of the more traditional, conservative shoshas. *JapanBank5* or one of the others might be a little bit more progressive. So yes, all the managers are Japanese. In fact, we just have a rotation of the President of the Corporation so the last man has stepped down and he is going to be the new Chairman. He will be overseeing things. So even at that very highest level you have that rotation going on.

(Senior Analyst, JapanBank2, New York)

Other senior managers in Japanese investment banks who I spoke to suggested that this rotation management allowed them to be 'more global than some of [our] competitors . . . since [we] have for some years had many people spread around the globe' (General Manager, JapanBank3, New York):

We have been carrying out what you are saying is global working for some years . . . many Japanese firms moved out of Japan and set up a global network of offices in the early 80s. This was to follow new investment opportunities and because of that, managers in this company have then been rotated on a four-year cycle to gain knowledge and understanding of the company's global business.

(Senior Manager, JapanBank4, New York; paraphrased)[12]

However, this rotation management at the transnational scale was not seen by one consultant partner (who specialized in Japanese Financial Institutions) as being particularly effective in achieving transnational socialization. He argued that the rotation management strategies that he had experienced in Japanese companies did not permit the development of contact networks or client relations amongst the expatriate Japanese managers. Rather, as he describes, Japanese banks would rely on 'local' nationals to maintain contact networks:

> And one vein of thought says, "go get the names of the people with the client business and look at where they come from." They are all, you know, local people. The key guys. If you look at *JapanBank4* over in California, what do they do? They send this revolving set of Japanese guys over to look at it, so they are never going to trash it because there is never anybody there long enough. The top American guys are likely to feel "why should I come here? Because I am never going to be the top guy." It is going to be a Japanese guy who turned around and goes back to Tokyo after two or three years. Now that is not a global corporation ... it is a company that maybe operates globally, but it ain't a global company. Whereas some ... I mean, that may be a dimension of how you really understand whether your company is global or not. I think it has to have to do with their people policies.
>
> (Partner, US Finance, USConsultancy3, New York)

Interestingly, and I think tellingly, in this instance this partner's definition of a global corporation is centred around 'people policies'. This is significant because the implicit argument behind his comment is that employee policy and practice is crucial to the successful operation of transnational business-service activity. Japanese banks are ultimately often relying on American local employees for business success. Yet these people, who are central to the success or failure of the companies in the US market, can easily end up dissatisfied with their Japanese employer because senior managerial jobs are rarely open to Japanese expatriates 'who quite often don't have the contacts that are bringing in business' (Senior Business Analyst, JapanBank1, New York) (see also Wong 1999).

The ramifications of these potential problems faced by Japanese firms extend out, I think, to TNCs more generally. Although the Japanese firms may represent a more extreme example because of the considerable cultural differences experienced in an Anglo-American location, the last argument in this section is that, to a large extent, transnational social contact is something developed by individual employees in working practices – and this is despite the fact that the TNCs studied invested considerable time and effort in transnational socialization. Formal strategies of socialization play a relatively limited part in engendering social contact. In the end, management consultancies' and investment banks' success or failure depends again on the social abilities of their employees in this regard. The theoretical ramifications of this point are that to understand, for example, sectoral competitiveness in investment banking, the nature of multiple individual business relationships needs to be investigated. Individuals in these industries are the key. For this reason, I turn now to examine the nature of individual social relationships in depth. There are two stages to this: to look first at what elements of individual socialization are important in business practice and then second at how key individuals relate to these factors.

Transnational client relationships

I would say the investment banking world is extremely competitive and you have to have people available who understand the needs of clients on the ground, working with clients, forming a business relationship. That's the key – the relationship. And that is how you get business. You get business through direct face-to-face marketing. You get it through word-of-mouth. You get it also through advertising, of course, you get it through whatever. But in the business that we are in – more corporate rather than retail – it is primarily building relationships over time, having somebody face-to-face talking about what *USBank1* means, *USBank1* can-do. What we have done for other sort of similarly-situated companies and it is a gradual building of faith and understanding and trust. And trust is a big word. So you know you have got to have that face-to-face, you just cannot dial up on the phone and gain somebody's trust.

(Director of Human Resources [Board], USBank1, New York)

Much of the academic literature within the new economic sociology (Grahber 1993; Thrift & Olds 1996; Child & Heavens 1998) does make general claims for the significance of the social relations of business activity, as manifest in the transnational contact networks explored so far. However, this literature's concept of a 'contact' is too crude a term for what in reality are far more complex social relations of business than simple 'professional contact'. What do senior managers mean when they assert the importance of 'client relationships'? This analysis is expanded in two phases through this section. The first of these phases tackles the question of how 'social contact' in terms of employee–client dealings is relevant to successful business activity by considering in depth the ways in which the acquisition and retention of banking and consultancy business is intrinsically social.

To begin with there are the social practices of *acquiring new business*. Senior managers often suggested that a banker or consultant's 'client base is generally their most important asset in terms of how much business they bring in on a daily basis' (Managing Partner, USConsultancy5, London). When finding new business in investment banks, there was a heavy reliance on personal relations between bank employees and potential clients:

> Most of the primary equity business we do is either done through the personal connections that people have with clients, or the extent to which they work together with the general investment bankers . . . primary equity and investment banking will team up together to attack a certain client or they'll do it directly because they have the contact. And it's that – the focus on the client – which generates the business through both connection and product understanding. So we try to deliver to the client an understanding of what it is they're trying to achieve – which is obviously what the client needs. But also an understanding of what can be accomplished within the market. So you bring both product and client understanding together in trying to impress upon a client that he [sic] should come to us with business.
>
> (Managing Director, Equities and New Issues, UKBank3, London)

Neither management consultancy nor investment banking is an industry where business is attracted simply by tendering a low price in a marketplace. Reputation and the quality of employees is far more important – a fact most readily demonstrated by the dramatic demise of Arthur Andersen after its involvement in Enron's collapse in 2002. Once reputation and trust are lost, business-service TNCs' market is gone. Respondents in the study in this light regularly made comments along the lines that 'business does not come to you, you have to go and get it' (Associate Director, UK and European Bond Sales, USBank6, London), and the process of going after new business required direct and extensive social contact:

> It's essentially a question of going and calling on them [potential clients], and talking to them about strategy and tactics, talking to

them about their competitors, talking about their competitors' position in the market, talking to them about their needs for M and A, for finance, and from that into discussions of corporate structure. And so you delve in more and more, offer lots of ideas: have they thought about this? Have they thought about that? Would they like to change their balance sheet?

(Managing Director, UK Head of Corporate Finance, EuroBank3,
London)

And success in acquiring new business is not easy. Senior managers reflected the comments of one Managing Director, describing here how his firm goes about seeking new business:

Well, it depends very much on the product that you're talking about. No, it isn't easy to break in. Because as I say, they'll have twenty or thirty banks calling them, and they'll talk to three. So they have to make a choice. And they're much more comfortable...because most conversations are a step forward from a conversation you've had in the past; they're not about something new. So it's much easier to continue the next step, rather than break off, reset, go back ten steps and begin anew. So it's not easy, but it does happen. And with less strategic products you can make entry faster. And by making entry and showing them efficiency, skills and gaining their trust, you begin to open the doors. So you can attack in a different way. Attack from other areas which will gain credibility which will then open that strategic door.

(Managing Director, Equities and New Issues, UKBank2, London)

As this Director points out, 'most conversations are not new'. Cold-calling is 'a relatively rare phenomenon in the banking world' because there are quite 'tight business communities' (Executive Director, Global Fixed Income, EuroBank2, London) of relevant people in banking and major corporate clients who know each other. Partners in consultancy firms also made a similar point. However, this is not always a question of straightforward social relations between specific individuals. Senior managers regarded their relationship with clients as 'collective' within an organizational context – that is to say, their individual relationship was seen as something 'blended' with wider group relationships which they, as a team of colleagues, would (re)produce over time with a company:

We started with respect for the individual, the individuality. We pride ourselves on a level of individuality within the partnership. But this is a partnership. I don't know how we are expressing it today but it has to do with how we communicate, sharing goals and building a firm on the global basis. This is not one group of people fighting another group of people. There is a very strong notion about the individual in the wider group partnership – and evidently it is at the core of what we do. Our clients know that. We work very closely with them and team with them as a partner too. The key element is those long-term clients and the people. The long-term relationships. Those are fundamentally . . . those are our core. The core essence of what we are about and we talk about that globally. Recently we have begun to deal with that globally. We are effective in teams both internally and with our clients.

(Partner, USConsultancy3, New York)

Thus, in sectors with high employee mobility, groups of people perpetuate relationships with clients (firms' reputations) as well as a general circulation of specialist employees within firms in the industry (the individual). In either instance, reputation and recommendation figure highly in winning business:

The majority of our clients are in Asia, because that's where we're already very strong. But our clients are brought to us by winning deals which comes to us by word of mouth, or by winning deals because of a deal we've done for someone else and gone to them with the idea, or by doing it in competition with someone else because they want to do a deal and they have selected us because of our credentials from past deals.

(Director, Capital Markets, UKBank1, London)

Yet although it is not just a question of individuals, the ability of key employees to socialize (at the transnational scale) was highlighted by the majority of my respondents as being central to successful new business acquisition. Individuals form not only relationships of trust with potential clients, but because of the information-dense nature of business-service products, they are also crucial sources and suppliers of information with regard to product design:

And we watch very carefully what the clients show interest in. So we log the development of the market by seeing what the clients tend to do. We try to then discern trends: is one client doing something because he's [sic] a maverick, or is one client doing this because he's

[sic] the head of a product-based theme of what clients of that particular type want to be doing? What type of business is being sold? And in that respect we watch competitors very closely and we watch the deal-flow very carefully, so we are always studying what the population of clients in every country are actually doing, and using that information in trying to assess whether there is a new mood...

(Managing Director, Equities and New Issues, UKBank3, London)

Both consultancy and banking are centred around information-rich, tailored products – for example, a consultancy selling a package of IT research and restructuring to a firm, or an investment bank selling a portfolio of financial products to a transnational manufacturing company seeking to make a foreign investment. In that way, therefore, the function of client relations is often 'about identifying and understanding client needs' (Executive Director, Global Fixed Income, EuroBank2, London). These business-service firms can and do undertake this information-collection activity through a considerable array of secondary information sources (stock prices, corporate reports, news agencies), manifest in the ranks of 'industry analysts' in investment banks or 'research consultants' in management consultancy firms. However, the research suggests that when it comes to actively acquiring new business, specific information that determines whether a contract is signed or not emerges from individual business relationships within a potential client community:

So in every single geography, the people in that area have looked at the population of prospective clients, and we've sorted them into people we'd like to do business with, people we're prepared to do business with, people we're not prepared to do business with, people we're not in touch with ... so having got a definition of the population of clients, we use the people in the geographies in the investment banking line, to burrow into those clients, gain an understanding of what they're doing.

(Senior Manager, Investment Banking, USBank1, New York)

Academic discussion of the 'informational society' runs the risk, therefore, of emphasizing a world of limited social contact where information flows between huge and growing numbers of nodes in a network. However, a considerable amount of informational transfer – and perhaps the most significant pieces of information – is made between individuals in a face-to-face social relationship. It is not sufficient to pay lip-service to the idea that 'face-to-face' is still important: in short, very little transnational business in banking and consultancy is conducted without extended and protracted face-to-face contact which remains the most significant aspect of the business process.

This claim becomes more evident if I turn to consider not only the acquisition but also the retention of business activity. Senior managers in both industries were asked to describe what factors most important to their companies in retaining existing business activities. The answer received almost exclusively was that long-standing social relationships with clients are the key to future business:

> I think long-standing relationships are a big a source of the business. For example, our department has done deals before and has relationships with certain suppliers of equipment because we do vendor financing. We have a strong relationship with NEC, for example. So that is one-way because we have this network of offices all over the world, this global network: through all these offices we try to introduce business to each other via the branch network. So for example, there is somebody from Israel, from our Israeli office who is coming next week and he wants to talk to another Partner about opportunities in Israel. And we are interested in Israel, we have projects there now. So there is that kind of thing like where he might know some venture capital firm there and he will introduce... since he knows them in person, he will introduce them to us even though we do not know them. So that happens quite a bit.
>
> (Director, USBank6, New York)

In both industry sectors, managers suggested that a considerable bulk of their business is 'repeat business'. In other words, breaking into a new client-market is relatively hard. Business tends to be highly linked to previous contracts and existing firms tend to concentrate on the client firms that they have done a lot of work for before:

> I mean, a lot of our work is repeat business with large, significant clients. So what we try and do is focus – and this is the approach of the other consultancy firms – is focus now on the large significant clients and do large projects for them. As opposed to having a myriad of clients doing a myriad of different stuff for a lot of people – you know, it can be a lot of fun. It appeals to all of us to be able to do different work for different clients in different industries, but we

have focused-in on the larger clients doing large projects. And usually the larger projects – particularly in the world I operate which is Wall Street – those clients are always global.

(Partner, Financial Institutions, USConsultancy2, New York)

This is the same in investment banks as well as in the consultancy firms, despite some sectors of investment banking being well known for abstract market relations – the image of the stockbroker exploiting price differences with little or no regard or contact for the people behind the prices. As one banker explained, a lot of his company's most lucrative business is repeat business with long-term clients. Trading represents a relatively small proportion of the company's activities[13]:

The *USBank3* view, and I don't know whether I agree, is that you are better off cultivating a long-term stable relationship with whom you can do lots of business. Lots of repeat business. Rather than just chasing from trade to trade, because sometimes you don't necessarily want to do a trade with a client. You know, your trader would love you to do it but you have decided not to do it for the sake of a relationship . . . you see, the trader, he [sic] just wants to get the trade done. But trading is only one part of our business . . . so I, on the other hand, have the long-term relationship to consider.

(Senior Associate, Corporate Finance, USBank3, London)

It is in terms of these 'long-term relationships' that the crucial importance of 'transnational social contacts' becomes clear. In the consultancy industry, major contracts in, for example, consulting to 'Financial Institutions' are rare: there are only a few large, transnational financial institutions[14] that represent the market. Transnational consultancy firms who offer such a service have no choice but to compete at the global scale. Yet competing successfully against a competitor is largely dependent on the ability of these firms to hold onto their existing clients and become highly targeted, through extensive social relationships, to their needs:

So we tried to differentiate them in these markets because it was very difficult to distinguish between the players. A bit like consulting. What your clients are looking for are solutions and what you need to do is turn this business around so that we have an emphasis on client relationships. So you focus on a selected number of clients in a market, maybe 200, the people who generate enough business for you. And your people talking to these clients know what is going on and the issues, and behind their needs ... we will have a set of people who liase closely with the clients and they are the solution developers – they will say exactly what needs to be done. That means we are not trying to sell them something at a distance. We are looking at the state of the balance sheet and saying "what can we do?" What capital do they have, what is the most efficient way of financing that development? Discussing this with them. So we have a total relationship, not a product sales relationship. And behind those people are the people who deliver the solutions and then you have the back-office and operations people. And they will be supported by the typical makeup of IT, and so on. So it is actually taking the business that way whilst at the same time identifying their efficiencies which means that they will be able to give and take half of the staff. This emphasis needs investment. Because it is long-term.

(Managing Partner, Corporate Finance, USBank6,
London)

Having considered the social constitution of business acquisition and retention in a broad sense, however, the second phase of this section's analysis is to examine in depth the widely cited (Thrift 1994; Lee & Wills 1997; Leyshon 1998) but the little qualitatively scrutinized concept of 'trust'. I take the preceding discussion one step further by addressing the question of what it is that 'a long-term relationship' means, reinforcing the point that individual employees are the key to corporate success in business services.

The study suggests that trust as a key factor of business relations in these transnational service industries is again something manifest primarily through relationships between individuals. Much of the literature asserts the importance of trust (Lee & Wills 1997; Yeung 2000) in a way which is open to several possible interpretations. For example, a company may be trusted by its clients on the back of a reputation disseminated through various media. A given bank may gain business because of a common discursively constructed view in the investment community of that company being 'trustworthy'. However, within transnational management consultancy and investment banking at least, when senior managers speak of trust as being a crucial determining of social relations, what they are referring to is a factor constituted primarily in the relations between key individuals in their own and clients' firms. In short, trust largely originates between individuals in these business-service industries. As one manager explained, he sees a client's trust as developing on the back of direct experience of dealing with his company before:

> Corporate clients want to have their underwriters, their banks and they want to have points of reference all over the globe. And they don't want to deal with a hundred. They want to deal with one or two. So from a ... a user or banking-services point of view, why would you not want to deal just, say, with the two biggest? And that is also about trust: by that I mean experience of dealing with us, experience of our level of service, our reputation, of their key people respecting the opinion of our top people.
>
> (Partner, Financial Institutions, USConsultancy4, New York)

As this Partner notes, the crucial issue when it comes to a trusting business relationship is that 'their key people respect[ing] the opinion of our top people'. Trust is something that is engendered by individuals knowing and respecting other individuals. As I spoke with managers, I was, in fact, surprised by the extent to which business relations are not abstracted from individuals. For example, in investment banking where the literature certainly often presents the image of abstract global markets (Adam 1992; Kim 1999), one Senior Director undermined this idea quite dramatically as he pointed out that even in his Capital Markets division, the market was in fact often a synonym for individual relationships. If there were no trust relations between individuals, there was no market – 'it was difficult to sell anything':

> The advantage I would say is knowing your counterparts, feeling comfortable – dealing with other people is extremely important in this business. If you know who are dealing with ... not just having a name on a piece of paper but really knowing the person is really important. On the one side, I think the bank profits because it brings back business – it's a trust thing. It's also an advantage if you talk about the cross selling of products – if you don't know anyone in those locations, it is difficult to sell.
>
> (Managing Director, Head of Capital Markets,
> EuroBank3, London)

I do not want to extend this argument too far as there are clearly still many situations – in financial markets at least – where it is quite possible to trade in a market of faceless abstractions. However, as the following quotation demonstrates, even the most abstract of markets – the money markets – involve some degree of individual trust relationships:

> ...I, on the other hand, have the long-term relationship to consider. And that's why you have sales-people. If you let traders talk directly to clients, you see what I mean, you have no clients left...so that's why you have salesmen. That's certainly the view and it works. Have you heard of the 80:20 rule? Well, you can apply it to almost anything. The basic rule is...you get 80 percent done in 20 percent of the time. And it's amazing how it does work. I mean, generally this bank does 80 percent of its business with 20 percent of its clients. So clearly to maximize your profits you want to focus almost all your effort on those 20 percent of clients, and get even more business out of them. And do all the business. You want the relationship to be so close that you do all their business. Whether it is Foreign Exchange, Equities you name it, you do all their business. You are their first call. That's a bit of a term in banking, is 'first-call'. A 'first-call relationship'.
>
> (Senior Associate, Corporate Finance, USBank4, London)

Overall, therefore, it is not sufficient to suggest that transnational consultancy and banking are 'embedded' in sociality in some kind of facilitating fashion which acts as the context for pure 'economic' activities. The research discussed here has shown how sociality is at the centre of business activity in these TNCs. Whether or not business is 'done' is constituted and mediated through social relations within firms and, most especially, beyond firms in the form of client relationships. These client relations constitute transnational business activity – they are not a context within which it is 'embedded'. Although the social science literature does sometimes appear to use embeddedness in a similar way to this (Thrift 1997; McDowell 1997; Yeung 2000), too often the term simply serves to reinforce a theoretically limited distinction between the 'social' and 'economic' (Sayer 1994, 1997; Barnes 1996). In sum, therefore, the success or failure of transnational management consultancy and investment banking is predicated on the nature of social relations with clients. Furthermore, as the preceding discussion of how senior managers understand 'trust' within the context of these social relations indicates, the sociality of client relations in investment banking and consultancy often boils down to the relationships between groups of individuals. This is the final issue warranting closer examination in this chapter.

The key significance of individuals

> I just don't see how these niche players are going to survive in an increasingly globalized world. If they lose three key bankers in that environment, they have had it. If we lose three key bankers it is important, but we haven't had it. In Corporate Finance the focus has to be on the key people you have or don't have as the case may be. And the smaller you are, the more vulnerable you are to your best people packing up and leaving with their clients. That is just the way it is.
>
> (Director, UK Head of Corporate Finance, EuroBank3, London)

The words of the Director quoted above reinforce the culminating argument of this chapter: that individuals, and often key individuals, through the social relations they (re)produce, are crucially important in determining the success or failure of transnational business-service firms. This section examines more closely what it is about particular individuals in the transnational social context that makes them so important to these companies, arguing that the key significance of individuals rests on their ability to develop 'dense' face-to-face relationships with colleagues and potential clients. There are at least two different features of this relationship 'density' that are of particular significance.

The first feature of the dense social relations between individuals that respondents identified centres around the significance that informal information flows play in both the effective functioning of transnational service firms and in attracting/retaining clients. As one manager explained, 'there is a considerable volume of information in this business [that]...moves through less formal channels' (Manager, USConsultancy1, New York). However, that is not to suggest that 'off-the-record' flows of information are only important in consultancy and banking – much the same could probably be said of any workplace environment (Drew & Heritage 1992). However, informal information plays a more direct part in the practices of consultants and bankers than it does in other industries – something related directly to the informational rich nature of these firms' products and in the 'dense sociality' in their business activity. This proposition is illustrated through the words of one banker describing the nature of information dissemination in his workplace environment:

> Anything that is important and urgent is always communicated straight away. It's not some sort of formal thing or anything like

that. People tell you stuff all the time . . . I mean, you could be on the phone to your mum, frankly, and if you were just in your own little cubicle then the phone would ring and you would be on the phone and the tone would be engaged. Or you would get through to voicemail. And it could be some bloke wanting to trade 100 million . . . you know, instead, because that comes straight through to you, you're like, 'Mum, I got to go this guy wants . . .'. Okay, and that's kind of how it works. It's more stressful, but it means that everything important is known about quickly. And it even comes down to the point, the level, where if something is really import-ant, then someone will make a lot of noise about it. Like for example, if the Bank of England suddenly raises rates for whatever reason unexpectedly, then everyone on the floor will know about it whether they have seen the screen or not, because the traders, the foreign exchange traders, will be screaming. And if you are sitting twenty yards away, you'll be thinking "what the fuck [sic] is going on?" You look at the screens, and know within five seconds. If you were off down the hallway somewhere, you would have no idea. And you do.

(Senior Associate, USBank1, London)

This respondent is describing the trading floor of an investment bank, which is probably a more extreme environment than most consultants' and many bankers' workplaces. However, the way in which much important information is communicated, for example, simply by some-one swearing at you, is more widely applicable. Informal information flows play fundamental parts in shaping key decisions in the sense that in the social context of the transnational workplace, face-to-face contact between individuals can determine the form, terms and even the existence of business deals. A huge amount of information is being communicated between large numbers of people quickly and effectively through the intense social interaction of the working environment. In information industries these are often premium modes of communication where informal cultures are as, if not more, important than conventional meetings, telephone conversations and e-mail. The previous respondent expressed this point well as he continued:

You have people just shouting across the room and it is just really noisy, and that's very distracting so it's a skill to learn to be able to be on the phone and to talk sensibly. But I think the advantages in terms of advanced communication far outweigh the drawbacks, those relative disadvantages. Even if that communication isn't formal stuff. I mean, here there's no such thing as a meeting or appointment or anything. It's just, if you want to ask somebody something then you ask them. I can go up to the M.D. and just ... I interrupt him all the time if it is important. If it is not important, then he would be annoyed. But you just learn ...

(Senior Associate, USBank1, London)

As a further example of this, consider another banker responding to my question about how individual relations are important in his workplace. In this case the banker explains how face-to-face interaction is a much more effective and influential form of communication than telecommunications:

Another problem I would say is demonstrated by today's escapade that kept me upstairs, which is local interest. Now in this case – and this is funny – this deal today which we launched was too cheap and everybody wants it. And everybody and his brother [sic] wanted it. Now this deal was being run out of New York, okay? Now as part of the whole globalization process we are marketing – you know – US deals like that to European clients, and you know all the rest of it ... However, when it came to allocations on this deal, US clients generally got a much better deal than the European clients. Can you think why that might be? For a start the syndicate guys have got salesman face-to-face going "give me more bonds". And he's like, "sorry, got to go." Bang. End of argument. We don't get a look-in here in London. Whereas he's got some other salesman [sic] standing in front of his face in Wall Street going, "I'm not leaving here until you fucking [sic] give me ... more bonds".

(Sales Associate, UK & European Bonds, USBank4, London)

'Informal communication' also has a dimension within the organization beyond immediate face-to-face interaction in the form of rumours. Their impact on financial markets has been discussed in some sectors of the social science literature (Barker 1997), but as another of my respondents explained, the function of rumours extends throughout investment banking activity. Rumours circulate between and across companies and industries, and informal information flows to and from client organizations through social contact. And informal information is also significant in that sense because this kind of information transfer is generally faster than formal channels (that is memos, documents, contracts):

> I always say that one of the fastest ways at getting information is just rumours that go around. I mean, the fact that Korea was going to get an IMF package was around the market long before it was announced...a couple of weeks...so that was just because some bloke saw this...well, it was rumoured that it would be necessary...and this bloke saw this senior guy from the IMF turning up a Seoul airport, that was it. Next thing everybody knows about it...so that is the other way that they will get information. They will also get information from the sales force who are talking to clients, and they will get information from brokers.
>
> (Senior Research Analyst, USBank3, London)

Similarly, within consultancy there appears to be an acknowledgement amongst many respondents that informal information flow, mediated through relations between individuals, is important in the social practice of business:

> Yes, this business is all about information, and getting information across...so a lot is informal, over a coffee or in a bar when you're discussing the client after work. Like last week when we ended up virtually having a strategy meeting in the lobby because that's when someone raised a few key issues, literally as we were walking out of the door...and out of the proper meeting you can be, well, more frank than in there with the client.
>
> (Partner, USConsultancy2, New York)

This leads to my second point about the significance of individuals. Informal information flows in some ways relate to the wider issue of persuasion and negotiation with clients. Senior managers in both industries suggested that in the more contract-based areas of their business – corporate finance or M and A, for example – the team manager plays a key role in gaining business as a chief negotiator. Bankers and consultants alike suggested that the crucial function of senior staff was to 'carry the clients' (Partner, US Finance, USConsultancy3, New York):

> A lot of it might be contacts that you have, but it is also how good you are at what you do. Tom, the guy I was working for, when he first started four years ago, he came in a few months before me. You

know, nobody wanted to speak to us. Nobody really cared. He was really good at analysis, made some people some money and picked some good stocks and now everybody wants to hear what he has to say. And the clients now have realized this and they are like, "well, if this is a guy who is going to be able to sell my stock, he is the one I want to do my deal." So you get more business that way. I mean, there are some people who just kind of like the social strata or whatever. And can bring in business because of who they know – but more and more it is how good you are at what you do.

(Senior Analyst, EuroBank2, New York)

In that sense, being a successful bank or consultancy is about employing the right key figures – personalities, if you like, who not only are known amongst the community of (transnational clients) but also have the right kinds of social skills[15] that will persuade potential clients to do business with your firm:

The people who succeed in this company – I mean who move up the hierarchy – are those who have the ability to communicate well with and present the right image to clients . . . so you find the more senior guys are extremely good at listening to clients' needs, developing a sense of trust and partnership . . .

(Managing Partner, USConsultancy1, London)

Furthermore, the key senior banker or consultant is also important to the firm's ability to assess its client market. One senior manager told me that key individuals also provide a major source of information for companies about which clients are important and the direction that the firm should take in the marketplace. In that sense, key individuals are effectively these service TNCs' locus of market research and development:

Competitive banks come along with good ideas to a company week in, week out. And you can only do that if you have the feedback through the client relationships . . . it's also about us being able to assess potential clients as well. I mean, you know, it is no good hanging onto some clients. You are just not going to get anywhere. So the critical thing for service-orientated businesses is to hold on to the best people – the people with good judgement. If a good banker loses confidence in his firm, he will move. And then what? You know, those are the critical assets for the firm.

(Director, UK Head of Corporate Finance, EuroBank3, London)

In the light of the importance of certain key individuals, it is hardly surprising, therefore, that the loss of these key personality 'client carriers' was a major cause for concern. Losing such people is regarded as a serious blow to a division or company:

> I can promise you every time somebody is moved it creates a substantial problem and we have to manage it. It is easier with younger people because they are probably not carrying the client relationship. So they might be important members of a team but they are not the leader so maybe they are more dispensable. The older they get, the harder it gets.
>
> (Director, Human Resources, UKBank2, London)

Senior client-carrying individuals are crucial to banks and consultancies because they are the repository of 'a huge amount of information about the client' (Senior Manager, USConsultancy5, London) which is effectively 'locked' in the individual. The high salaries and the 'organizational scandal' created by the movement of key figures in these firms reflects the potentially severe problem that the loss of the social relations they 'carry' and the information they 'hold' presents for firms:

> If you are going to survive in this business [investment banking] in the long term ... I mean your senior people, the ones who know the clients, know what they want ... know how they work and the history ... they are the central issue. So we need to keep our top people like everyone else.
>
> (Executive Director, EuroBank1, London)

The importance placed on key individuals in both sectors is reflected in job descriptions situated in the transnational organizational structure. For firms to engender 'total, long-term relationships' at the transnational scale, individuals within business-service organizations are assigned through their position to act as overseers for important, lucrative client relationships at the functional level. Since major clients also tend to be major TNCs, in many of these firms key individuals have job titles such as 'global client relation manager':

> In terms of how we have a relationship with you know a *USBank6* or a big multinational, we will have ... we have a global leading client service Partner nowadays. A person who is responsible for that relationship overall. Now, in a lot of cases that would be somebody in

the states – for the American multinationals. But for, say, *EuroBank4* we would probably have as leading client service Partner someone in Germany... as we try to globalize those roles, that person is responsible for synchronizing our delivery of services to that client on a global basis. For example, take *USBank6*, a partner of mine Andy was always the lead client service Partner for *USBank6* from the consulting standpoint. So that meant that Andy just kept an eye on – not directly necessarily – but kept an eye on all the services we provided to *USBank6*. A few years ago we said "well, we are going to go global. We are global now after globalization and we need to have a global relationship, not just relationships in the UK, relationships in New York." So Andy is now the global lead client service Partner and his role is really just to co-ordinate everything. He keeps aware of what is going on in Hong Kong, Singapore, New York, London... all the places where we are doing work with *USBank6*. And he makes sure that from *USBank6*'s point of view, we are being the consistent, we are talking to each other.

(Partner, Financial Institutions, USConsultancy3, New York)

In fact we always have a global relationship manager. So if we are dealing with – I don't know – a steel company or whatever, there will be managers all around the world who will keep reporting in as we conduct business. Reporting in to the global relationship manager.

(Managing Director, UK Head of Corporate Finance, EuroBank2, London)

However, contrary to internal job descriptions and to the global-local discourses found in management and academic texts (Lessem 1987; Barnevik 1994), my suggestion is that the business acquiring and retaining activities of these firms in the transnational world economy are better not theorized through a scalar, local-global approach. The problem with this typology is that it obscures where the significant determining elements of 'doing business' are by reducing them to a scale. Senior managers are understood as being 'global' and they need staff who are conversely 'local' to be 'close to the business on the ground' (Partner, USConsultancy4, New York). However, this research suggests that senior managers and junior staff alike are simultaneously global, national, regional and local in their functions in the company. Both sets of actors are bound into the business process in a variety of ways that could be construed as global, local or neither of these scalar ideas. Informational flows may be 'global', but senior managers spend a considerable amount of time meeting and building relations with clients in 'local' locations. The point is that, 'yes, they are both of these scales and more', but that scale is not the key issue here. Consider, as an illustrative example, the self-contradictory view of one manager on transnational client relations:

> We are just saying to people that "you've got to be locally reactive to your people." And you have often got a person running that business who is not only running the country, but is also running the clients. You know, if you say to that guy "well, sorry from now on the client contact will be through London and some of your people will not report to you but will report to London." Then you are really changing the very nature of that person's job. And you are just going to make them a manager or an administrator or you are going to make them a client integrator. And that is certainly the shift which has been marked from very much globally, geographically controlled business to business at the product end.
>
> (Director, Human Resources, UKBank1, London)

This Director uses convenient, familiar scale-based concepts in a way which *misrepresents* the material social practices of transnational business. He wants 'locally reactive guys [sic]' who, through geography-product restructuring, are increasingly controlled through 'a global business product end'. By local, therefore, he is referring, in essence, to people who are able to meet and thereby collate information from clients because they are physically located in Kuala Lumpur or Los Angeles. Yet these senior global managers are also heavily involved in this social practice of transnational business. In a sense they are local too, or perhaps multiply-local in that they are involved in social relations in multiple national locations in the course of controlling and overseeing business activity. The point is that scale here is not especially useful. What is significant is the nature of social relations – this is the concept that has most use in exploring the question of whether, why and how transnational business activity occurs.

Conclusion: live it, breathe it!

> And it [employee turnover] is worse, of course, in this business. Because people are much more important. I am not saying that people are not important in manufacturing, but the same goes for

investment banking: people are the key. Their contacts, their know-ledge, their capabilities. I mean what is a consultancy firm? Aside from a few buildings, that's all we are: the people we have.

(Managing Partner, USConsultancy5, London)

'These guys live and breathe banking; it's all they do day in, day out!' (Managing Director, Equities and New Issues, UKBank1, London). These are the words of the Director of Equity and New Issues in one of the London investment banks; he is referring in this specific instance to his own employees within the division he runs, but in many ways his statement is applicable across both investment banking and management consultancy. Employees in both industries are heavily wrapped up in their work. Everyone knows that investment bankers work long hours (Budd & Whimster 1992; McDowell 1997), but the same is true in the management consultancy sector (Rassam & Oates 1991; Clark 1995). Business-service work in these sectors is highly social in the sense that social relations are at the centre of economic activity, and the outcome of this is the idea that employees 'live and breathe' their occupations. Investment bankers socialize together, discuss work informally, and spend substantial amounts of their waking hours either in the office or in the company of colleagues. As I discussed earlier, the companies themselves expend considerable time, effort and money seeking to engender social contact amongst their own employees. And they seek to employ those who have social contacts amongst a transnational community of clients.

In the academic literature these service TNCs, certainly in the case of investment banking, are too readily theorized as operating in an asocial economic context where social interaction takes second place to the logic of market and financial factors. In contrast, this study has shown how senior business practitioners in banks and consultancies alike regarded sociality, in the form of social relationships and contact, as a central feature of their businesses. There are a number of dimensions to this sociality. With regard to investment banks and management consultancies as TNCs, networks of social contact both within and beyond the boundaries of firms are crucial to the ability of a company to compete and succeed. Internal *transnational socialization* is regarded a functional necessity in order for transnational service companies, employing people in disparate locations around the globe, to operate successfully. Equally, if not more important, however, is the development and maintenance of external social contacts that are the primary media through which business is acquired and retained in banking and consultancy.

The key importance of both of these forms of contact network is further reinforced, of course, by the strategies employed by investment banks and management consultancies to engender 'transnational socialization'. In examining the various approaches described by respondents, I suggested that although these efforts do achieve success through training and circulation programmes – in terms of allowing contemporaries to meet and make external contacts in different locations – the success of transnational socialization is constrained by the difficulty of strategically producing the type of social relationships which firms regarded as probably most important: client contact. Deliberate strategies of external transnational socialization are limited because the key factor in whether or not firms gain business is often the relationship between specific individuals. It is these people, who maintain sets of client relations, who represent the most important assets that their firms possess.

Yet, whilst certain key individuals fulfill crucial specific roles, the study also showed that these individuals do not work in isolation. Key individuals are part of a wider set of social relations as some of the extracts quoted in this chapter have hinted at. This leads to another set of questions concerned with the nature of the collective social relations in business-service TNCs – an idea more usually captured in discussions of organizational and business culture. Questions of 'global corporate culture' will therefore be the subject of the next chapter and the last part of my integrated approach to theorizing and understanding transnational management consultancies and investment banks.

5
Global 'Glue'? Corporate Culture in a Transnational World

I've worked with a number of firms – I'm a consultant by background but I've worked in the past with consultants, banks, brokers, pharmaceuticals...and if you look at it, pose the question: can you create a global culture? I'm not sure you can. But if you ask can you create a culture that is aware and appreciates the diversity of the cultures that make up the firm, then, yes...yes, you can.

(Director, Head of Training, UKBank3, London)

There are different aspects of global culture, of corporate culture. There are operating principles, values, where people come from, how they work with each other and so on...so culture is pervasive. It is in everything we do...

(Senior Partner, USConsultancy2, New York)

Introduction

When I was wandering around the bookshops of downtown Manhattan and the City of London, awaiting my next appointment with some 'master of the universe',[1] I spent time scanning the titles in the business and management sections: a little literature research in what was otherwise dead time. And as I come to discuss the final part of this study, I cannot avoid remembering one particular instance that seems a salient anecdotal point of entry for my analysis in this chapter.

On the occasion I have in mind, I was half an hour early for an interview with a senior partner in USConsultancy3, whose offices were – at that time[2] – in the World Financial Center in New York. Since it was a hot, muggy New York July day outside, I decided to while away some time searching for any relevant business books in an air-conditioned book-store in the Center. I intended to (and did, in the event) speak at length to the partner concerned about the significance of the management literature and those books aimed at business practitioners. Once inside this particular bookstore I was not disappointed. The branch of whichever chain I was in appeared to be almost exclusively dedicated to business texts. I had little trouble finding a shelf full of (mostly) manual-style books instructing managers on how to go about 'changing stagnant corporate cultures' (Ward 1995; Pritchett 1996), creating a 'learning culture' in the workplace (Burgoyne & Reynolds 1997; Woods *et al* 1997), or creating effective and supportive 'managerial cultures' (Van der Erve 1993; Toft & Reynolds 1997).

Whilst I was browsing these shelves, two be-suited middle-aged busi-nessmen came over to the same section. I have no idea what sectors or companies they worked in, although they clearly worked nearby, or perhaps were going to a meeting somewhere. Within a couple of minutes one of the men had rifled the shelf I had been paying most attention to. To my slight surprise, he quickly proceeded to pay for four thick-volumed books before leaving with his companion. This business-man clearly thought that issues revolving around 'corporate culture' are worth spending a hundred and fifty dollars in a lunch hour. I have no idea why he so decisively wanted those books, but the experience served to focus my attention on the issue during the subsequent interview. The senior partner concerned, when asked about these corporate culture manuals, suggested that 'a lot of people certainly read widely on this kind of thing' (Senior Partner, Financial Institutions, USConsultancy3, New York). Corporate culture, in his opinion, was an issue 'on a lot of people's minds' and he told me that he thought it was 'if anything, even more important in transnational firms... [that] are so reliant on behaviours'. He didn't find it in the least surprising that business man-agers should value the type of business literature that I had noticed in the bookstore.

My starting point in this chapter, therefore, is that senior managers in some of the world's major business-service firms regard the concept of 'corporate culture' as crucial to the successful and effective functioning of their firms. Furthermore, this is a question of 'global', or as I prefer it, 'transnational corporate culture' – an idea I found firmly fixed in senior business managers' minds. As one Director noted, transnational corporate culture 'is what glues the firm together as a whole... [a] kind of global glue' (Senior Manager, USBank1, New York). 'Global corporate culture' is a term that many of the senior managers broached without prompting as soon as the idea of 'organizational culture' was raised, and it was seen as 'fundamental to the ability of a transnational firm to operate consistently around the globe' (Partner, US Finance, USConsultancy3, New York).

However, social scientific theorizations of 'global finance' and 'business globalization' have paid relatively little attention to corporate culture. Much of the existing literature on transnational firms tends to take for granted the organizational coherence of the TNCs it discusses (Pitelis & Sugden 1991; Schoenberger 1997; Dicken 1998). The issue of what binds these companies together across many national contexts has not really been addressed – or at least not beyond the more quantifiable issues of divisional structures (Daniels & Daniels 1994; Mourdoukoutas 1999), capital flows (Davidson & De la Torre 1989), and quite general discussions of the significance of information and communication (Guile & Brooks 1987; Graham *et al* 1990; Castells 1996; Pearce 1997). This wariness of dealing with cultural ideas in relation to transnational business is probably in part attributable to the fact that culture is another of those notoriously broad and ambiguous concepts. Most people understand the concept immediately in a general sense, but it becomes trickier to pin-down with forms of tight definition (Tomlinson 1999). Furthermore, what literature there is concerned with the 'social nature' of economic (business) activity is quite often unclear about issues of culture. Many social scientists fail to refer to culture – or at least avoid the issue – when discussing social embeddedness (Grahber 1993; Ingham 1996), or use the terms 'culture' or 'corporate culture', assuming an implicit shared understanding between the author and the reader (Schoenberger 1997; Kono & Clegg 1998).[3]

Corporate culture as a concept has been criticized as being 'woolly', 'ill-defined' and thus lacking much theoretical utility (Peet 1997). Even within the sizeable management literature which is clearly helpful in indicating what might be understood by corporate culture in general (for example, Hampden-Turner 1994; Ward 1995; Temporal & Alder 1999), there is very little writing that specifically engages with the object of my enquiry here: corporate culture at the transnational scale.[4] What work has been done has also often tended to try to reduce culture to quantifiable and generalized common variables relevant to all TNCs (for example, Brock *et al* 2000). Furthermore, most of the more popular corporate culture literature consists of manual-style books which tackle this issue to a limited extent, discussing, for example, the problems that American manufacturing firms have encountered when setting up operations in south-east Asia or China (Lessem 1990). Similarly, other business-oriented writers have addressed the cultural difficulties that Japanese firms face outside the national context of Japan (Kono & Clegg 1998; Yamashita 1998) or the cultural characteristics of different national management 'styles' (Bjerke 1999). Overall, the business studies/management literature is evasive and vague when it comes to discussing the culture of transnational firms. To a large extent, this may be accounted for by the fact that 'truly transnational firms', as respondents I have quoted elsewhere were quick to argue, 'are few and far between' (General Manager, USConsultancy1, London). So the issue of 'global or transnational corporate culture' is a new phenomenon that is relevant to a small, if growing, number of firms manifest in the listings of the Fortune Global 500. Whatever the reasons for its neglect or conceptual vagueness, this chapter tackles this theoretical gap.

Corporate culture, manifest at the transnational scale, is a central and significant determinant of the feasibility and success of transnational management consultancy and investment banking business. I do not want to engage here in a philosophical debate as to what, if anything, the concept 'culture' might mean in general, and so I am narrowing the idea to a discussion of what might otherwise be described as 'collective social practices'.[5] In other words, this chapter picks up from where I ended the last by broadening the focus on social relations as specific business practices into a wider examination of social relations in a collective and contextualized sense. Beyond the significance of sociality constituted through the micro-relations between individuals doing advanced service business in the transnational economy, attention now shifts to the production of collective social relations – or transnational corporate culture – that enables transnational investment banks and management consultancy firms to operate across the globe in an effective and competitive fashion. This means a focus on the way in which social relations in the workplace and with clients 'sit' in the wider context of society in terms of extra-workplace activities, attitudes and discourse-practices. Collective business practices in organizations are shaped by multiple influences: what some have described as national (Weinshall 1993; Hickson & Pugh 1995) or regional cultures (Saxenian 1994; Gertler 1997) and norms of social behaviour with regard to a whole variety of things including gender, custom, (in)formality and so on (Gherhardi 1995). In a transnational firm, the whole question becomes more complex as multiple geographical contexts are added to this melee. This is the 'messy reality' that in the following discussion is captured with the concept 'transnational corporate culture(s)'.

The first point to make is that the significance of transnational corporate culture(s) is not, however, easily reducible to the question of standardization. Having discussed the nature and significance of transnational corporate culture in a broad sense, the chapter examines how there exists a tension in transnational management consultancies and investment banks between cultural standardization and cultural diversity. This tension can be understood as the need for both *macro-cultural* and *micro-cultural tropes* for the success of transnational business activity. The concept of a cultural trope is used in the sense of a cultural manner or style that is shared and understood amongst social actors in a firm of organization. The word 'trope' implies the fluidity of cultural mores where there is no one specific form of behaviour/attitude but rather a range of behaviours shaped around a collective sense of understanding.[6] In that respect, macro-cultural tropes correspond to organization-wide forms of practice and behaviour that constitute the consistency of transnational organizational context, yet they must be complemented by numerous co-existing micro-cultural tropes that permit sensitivity to specific business contexts. With these concepts it is possible to develop an understanding of how corporate culture can be effectively theorized at the level of the global organization.

These arguments develop in a series of steps. The next section explores how senior business managers in investment banks and management consultancy firms understand the idea of transnational corporate culture(s). It suggests that the concept, when taken as a singular idea, corresponds to a degree of standardization in employee behaviour in the transnational context and that senior managers regard cultural issues as a key area through which these business-service TNCs compete. Furthermore, a shared transnational corporate culture is an important facet of organizational motivation for consultants and bankers and also represents a means of maintaining organizational control, coherence and communication. In this sense, transnational corporate culture is a central element of control in the transnational organization, particularly in what I term its role in *reflexive cultural regulation*. The section ends by considering how business-service TNCs seek to engender a sense of shared transnational corporate culture.

The third section then develops the proposition that the issue of transnational corporate culture is more complicated than simply the idea of cultural standardization within the TNC. It argues that the potential development of what might be understood as a coherent, singular *transnational corporate culture* is simultaneously limited and limiting. In terms of the limitation on achieving cultural standardization, the combination of continual organizational restructuring, high rates of employee turnover and the strength of localized subcultures within the transnational service firms in the study acts to inhibit the development of a strong sense of standardized transnational corporate culture. Instead, the research suggests that some degree of corporate cultural diversity is in fact crucial for successful transnational business activity. The activity of 'doing' transnational banking or consultancy requires heterogeneous individual and collective team behaviours that do not constrain the free-flow of information across the transnational context, and which do not exclude employees who differ from the dominant cultural mores.

The latter point is taken up in depth in the fourth and final part of the chapter which examines the tension between the need for cultural standardization and cultural diversity in these transnational service firms. I argue that, rather than being understood in opposition, the standardized and diverse elements of transnational corporate culture – as macro-cultural and micro-cultural tropes – are simultaneously crucial to business success in the transnational context. The realm of macro-cultural tropes is not separate or discreet from the variety of micro-cultural tropes to be found in any one business-service firm and thus the section explores how it is not a question of the need for standard 'global culture' versus the need for diverse 'local cultures'. In contrast, what is needed is the simultaneous and harmonious co-existence of multiple cultural tropes at a variety scales according to the cultural facets in question.

'Global Glue'? The need for 'transnational corporate culture'

I think it [*global corporate culture*] is just enormously important. For us, we work in a very decentralized way – which I think is a very appropriate, and essentially professional, type of environment. We do not have a lot of control systems. What I think we do have is a very consistent corporate culture around the globe, and it is that at the end of the day that results in a client – whether they are in London, or Bangkok, or Chicago – getting similar levels of service. It is that which allows one of our UK clients recently who I was working with around the globe – to say, "I don't know how you manage to provide such a seamless service". Now we could not do that if we didn't have such a strong, clear sense of global corporate culture.

(Managing Partner, USConsultancy4, London)

Q: But what are the advantages of a strong core culture?

A: I think it is . . . it ranges. It ranges from around secure service to the client, to differentiation from the competition, to motivation for the staff.

(Director, Capital Markets, UKBank3, London)

The Director and Managing Partner quoted above, like many of the respondents in my study, put considerable emphasis on 'a clear sense of global corporate culture' in their respective firms. Yet what exactly are they referring to when they talk about corporate culture being 'consistent' so that clients get 'a similar' and 'secure' level of service around the globe? I realized that many senior managers in both investment banking and management consulting referred to a series of common themes when they discussed why a strong common transnational corporate culture was important. In that sense, this section first addresses the question of *what* respondents consciously understand transnational corporate culture to be. At risk of reducing what is obviously a complex and contradictory field of opinion amongst the respondents in the study, I argue that in management consultancy and investment banking, three distinct aspects of transnational corporate culture are regarded by senior managerial staff as being important to a firm's success. These correspond to the standardization of behaviour, employee motivation in the transnational context and as a medium of transnational organ- izational coherence and control. In the latter part of the section, the way in which these business-service TNCs seek to engender transnational corporate culture in relation to these ideas is examined.

Defining transnational corporate culture

First, and cited by almost every senior manager I discussed this issue with, is the argument that having a strong transnational corporate culture means in effect that employee behaviour is to some extent standardized in the transnational context. In both investment banking and management consultancy, where social relations between individ- uals – as we have already seen – are crucial to corporate success, the idea of a transnational business culture in the singular corresponds to consistent shared forms of behaviour in the ways in which employees deal with each other and clients:

To be able to operate seamlessly in terms of services, so the culture of how you do business is the same no matter where the client is. So that means the same high standards of behaviour, of how you treat clients, of how you talk to them, how you provide the service. And that is the model. That is what the *USConsultancy7*'s of this world, the *USConsultancy2*'s work with.

(Partner, US Finance, USConsultancy2, New York)

Globalization is cultural. I mean, the logic for it from our point of view is that we serve multinational corporations...I mean we serve Exxon, General Motors or whatever and so on. They at GM or at Exxon operate seamlessly around the world as much as they can. So they expect their consultants to be seamless so that if they work with us in New York and Kuala Lumpur, they want to have the same standards, the same approaches, methodologies and so forth. So that...the business driver for globalization in the consulting world is to be able to serve our clients seamlessly and consistently.

(Managing Partner, USConsultancy5, London)

As the Managing Partner suggests, the advantage of a transnational business-service firm having a sense of unified transnational corporate culture arises through this 'seamless' operation around the globe. Clients receive the same standards of service, delivered in the same way, if the transnational service firm in question has a strong transnational culture. 'Consistency is definitely the key word' (Managing Director, Money Markets, EuroBank4, London). This applies equally to both the investment banking and management consultancy sectors. In both sectors, senior managers perceived there being 'clear drawbacks to having an inconsistent culture' (Director, USBank6, New York):

Many of our clients are global clients. What they don't want to say is, 'well, alright ringing them in Italy is good news, they're a good squad in Italy, but for Christ's sake [sic] don't ring them in Paris!' You can't afford that. You know, you've got to brand yourself and stand for something globally. So that wherever we ring *UKBank3*, we know we get this.

(Director, Head of Training, UKBank3, London)

Corporate culture is thus another arena of competition for these firms. Having a strong transnational corporate culture is perceived by senior managers as an advantage in attracting client firms. This competitive advantage derived from a strong sense of transnational corporate culture can, however, be loosely divided into two sets of arguments. On the one hand, it is about providing consistent service standards around the globe which potential clients know they can rely on and so they are attracted to the firm:

> And a client feels confident as they know they can find these stand-ards of behaviour ... [if they] know our people have been shaped by the same mould wherever. That certainly is an issue that I think gives *EuroBank2* some advantage in the global market ...
> (Executive Director, Global Fixed Income, EuroBank2, London)

On the other, it is about differentiating a firm's 'character' from that of the competition. Corporate culture, transmitted across the transnational context, is felt by senior managers to be a way in which they can distin-guish their own firm in a highly competitive transnational marketplace:

> I don't think the other global players differ very much in their statement of global culture: it's how they do it, how they practice it – that's where they differ. There are certain principles of business behaviour; there might be nuances in terms of the aggressiveness in terms of how one deals in the market ... You will see when you sit together with other companies who have a much stronger culture than we have ... I remember, for instance, when I was in New York in the late eighties you could actually see *USBank9* employees approaching you from a hundred metres: the way they dressed, the way they walked, the way they behaved – a very distinct culture. I would say also other big players are very interested in developing cultures.
> (Managing Director, Head of Human Resources [Europe], EuroBank2, London)

To take another example, a senior manager in one of the leading US transnational investment banks explained how he thought that his company was characterized by 'a polite culture':

> The second core value is respect. And that is the thing here which people say they feel it straight away – that is what I think they are referring to. It is how we interact with each other. And the Chairman and I put it how other senior managers put it, we try to model with each other the same behaviours we would display to our clients. Say we try to treat each other the same way we treat clients – with respect. And clients ... I have talked to clients and they will, they

attest to that. It is true. So it leads to a rather dignified, a rather ... I am trying to think of the word without being too pejorative ... somewhat understated, polite culture.

(Senior Manager, Operations, USBank1, New York)

This illustrates well what I mean by defining transnational corporate culture as the nature of collective social interaction in these firms. Corporate culture is generally understood as shared behavioural norms, accepted ways of communicating and practising business with clients. The same senior manager went on to explain how this 'polite culture' corresponded to a reputation for being probably more honest with clients than some of the more 'individualistic' American investment banking companies. Whilst such a view might be more rhetoric than reality of course, I encountered, interestingly enough, an anecdote from a more junior employee of the same bank in London that further illuminates this company's culture and vindicates the senior manager's view to some extent. The senior sales associate quoted below is responding to my question as to how he thinks USBank1's corporate culture is distinctive from that of competitors:

I think it is generally true that *USBank1*'s image is a lot softer than your *USBank4*'s, your *USBank5*'s who are known as commission houses ... I went to lunch today with one of the salesmen from *USBank4*, who literally every time there is a trade, he gets a percentage of it. And sometimes when their traders have got positions that they really want to get rid of, they'll get on top of a desk and wave a cheque around in the air – say, 'this is a cheque for a hundred thousand dollars and it goes to the first person who can sell this position'. Erm .. like you know they own 50 million whatevers, and they just want to get rid of it. They really want to get rid of it. You know, *USBank4* are right at the other end of the scale to us in terms of being very aggressive, just aggressive institutions, aggressive trading-type houses. Typically they will be very profitable some years – in good years for the markets – but a big proportion of their profits is either trading for their own book – you know, there is a lot less of that client business I was talking about. Or any client business they do do which goes along with that is, you know, going to be commission-driven and that's kind of the same thing. Because you can guarantee that that guy is not paying one hundred thousand dollars because that's a great bond to own. So he will try and jam someone with it.

You know, that's what it's called: 'jamming'. We don't do that, and it's about the culture.

(Senior Associate, UK and European Bond Sales, USBank1, London)

In essence, respondents thought their firms need a distinctive cultural 'character' so that potential client or business partner firms should, ideally, be aware of it as soon as they walk into the meeting room:

We have an extremely strong culture. Now ... there is no point asking anybody at *USBank1* because we have no objectivity, particularly those who have been a long time. But I am told it is very strong and I have spent a lot of time with entry-level trainees, and the career guys. It is particularly interesting to talk to people who come from the competition – who come from *USBank3* or *USBank5* – they will tell you that culture is very strong and very tangible. And if you ask them, 'When did you first experience it?', they will say, 'first contact'. And that is one of our strengths over and above a lot of the field, I think ... so that may give you some clues as to the nature of the culture.

(Senior Manager, Operations, USBank1, New York)

This leads to a second definitional element that senior managers in the case study firms referred to. The argument often made was that a strong sense of transnational corporate culture is an important facet of organizational motivation for staff. If employees feel part of a strong culture, with certain standards of service, 'and they are caught up in thinking they have to work to maintain [the firm's] good reputation' (Director, Head of Human Resources, UKBank4, London), then senior managers are of the opinion that they are likely to be more productive and generally 'better traders, financiers, sales guys or whatever' (Director, USBank6, New York):

I think having a strong corporate culture is helpful. I think it helps individuals align themselves with other individuals in the organizations so they all tend to pull in the same direction. But I don't think it matters that much at the moment to us because we are still so much in growth development ... so the desire pulls everyone together even if they've all come from different places, different perspectives, different histories and different ways of doing things ... er ... there is a common desire which, if you like, magnetize all the iron filings so they point in the same direction, but in a few years time, say 5 years time, it will be important.

(Managing Director, Equities and New Issues, EuroBank1, London)

A distinct transnational corporate culture is desired by those managing transnational business-service firms because it represents a medium for the communication and understanding of a common sense of purpose amongst, especially in the transnational context, a workforce that may be scattered in disparate locations:

> ... because it is just a much more pleasant experience to be in a place where everybody is rewarded and incentivized to function as a Partner, and many of us came out of the Wall Street cultures where it is much more, you know, you lock your desk when you go home at night. My client is my client; he [sic] is not the firm's client and that kind of thing. What you want are people in the firm working for the same collective goals, doing good business wherever they are. And that sense of purpose also means you can also do what is really important – to be able to mobilize and combine industrial expertise and transactional expertise as well as global understanding of the cultural, economic, sociological environment is the fundamental differentiation.
>
> (Partner, Financial Institutions, USConsultancy3, New York)

This is interrelated with a third definitional element of how senior managers understood transnational corporate culture: a common culture as a means of maintaining organizational control, coherence and communication. Consider, for example, how one senior manager explains how he regards corporate culture as being crucial to effective managerial control throughout the transnational organization:

> Culture, you know, is a nebulous, intangible sort of thing. But we make the point that it is probably more important than anything else we teach them because of the risk to an organization of messing up is so much bigger than the money that any of those individuals is going to make on the job. Which is a sort of rather sobering thought. I mean look at Nick Leeson in Barings ... he can bring down a 224-year-old bank. It doesn't take much. And I refer frequently to *USBank8*, *UKBank6* ... all these cases where people have come unstuck. Just pointing out that it is very easy to mess up. And the downside ... the *USBank8* case in 1991 when the trader was manipulating

the treasury market is a good case in point because, you know, they reckon he only made a few million messing around with the market and it cost the firm upwards of a billion dollars. And you know the final chapter of that book was written about a year ago when they were bought. And at the time in 1991 *USBank8* was the powerhouse on earth – it's brought the house down. So we talk about those stories and we study them, and we say, "you know, what can be done?" And one of the outcomes that we emphasize is that there is no protection against a rogue trader or somebody who wants to mess up. You can't ... no systems, no methodology will ever prevent it. The only hope you have is shared values which is what a corporate culture is. And a sense of responsibility ...

(Senior Manager, Operations, USBank1, New York)

So you really have to instil a sense of shared responsibility. We have six core values in the firm and I build the training around those six. And, you know, they are not different from anybody else's so it is a matter of emphasis. And the first one – probably the most important – is ethics. And that is what we were talking about when we say culture: business practices. What is acceptable and what is not.

(Head of Training, EuroBank1, London)

For the managerial upper echelons of transnational business-service firms, cultural factors become as much the focus of conscious attempts to restructure transnational corporations as the divisional and hierarchical reorganizations discussed in Chapter 3. As this manager explains, there is a limit to how much surveillance, feedback and information can be collected in large transnational firms operating in disparate locations. In that light, a shared sense of identity, responsibility and common purpose – manifest as a transnational corporate cultural facet – constitutes a major element of organizational control. This is not 'direct' control but peer regulation – what I term *reflexive cultural regulation*. One of the senior managers quoted above captured a description of what this constitutes later in the same interview:

I ask the trainees if you are working on a trading floor like this [indicates through office window] and you think that the trader is sticking tickets in the drawer, you know, is hiding trades because he has got a bad position and he is not reporting it. What would you do? And you know, the answer that you would expect and that you get is that, 'I would ask somebody about it. I would talk to my boss'. So of course the final question is: what if it is your boss? What are you going to do?' And you kind of press them on this...some of them say, 'I'd ask him or her'. Some people are vehement, "I'd kill him. He is risking the success of all the firm." That is what you want to hear...a sense of teamwork. And you want to leave them with the impression that there is a shared responsibility. If you are quiet...consider David X[7] over at *USBank5*, making pots of money for the firm like that. You are working in his group. You are aware that he is doing it, but let me tell you, he is making money. And we are all getting big bonuses. Now, are you going to think, 'Say Dave, I don't know how you are doing it? But good on you mate, stay with it!' That is kind of your attitude. I think that probably in every case, there were people around that individual who you knew what was going on or suspected but didn't want to do anything because, you know, who wants to mess with a good thing? So it's about generating a culture that prevents that kind of mind-set...

(Senior Manager, Operations, USBank1, New York)

In transnational banking and consultancy, therefore, transnational corporate culture is regarded as a key aspect of maintaining organizational coherence around the globe. Corporate culture is what ultimately holds these TNCs together, and the degree to which senior managers want to speak of a coherent form of global corporate culture represents for them an indication of the extent to which their firm is a consistent and competitive business at the transnational scale. Certainly in terms of how managers in both sectors define it, transnational corporate culture in a singular sense constitutes a degree of constancy, consistency and 'standardization in terms of collective behaviours, attitudes, beliefs, motivations, communication...and so on' (Managing Director, Head of Human Resources [Europe], EuroBank2, London). It is the 'global glue' that senior managers want to bind their transnational organizations together with:

With us, it [corporate culture] glues people together. It cements you into a culture of making money. I have always felt very strongly that everybody needs somebody to talk to or to report to, you know, if you are trading to bounce ideas off. And the more people work as a team, the more they talk to each other. And the more they talk to each other, the better the communication. And the better the communication, the more likely you are to avoid any sort of misunderstandings.

(Director, UK Head of Corporate Finance, EuroBank3, London)

In the light of this understanding, it is not surprising that respondents identified a range of strategies employed within transnational investment banks and management consultancies that are geared to engendering a standardized and shared set of cultural values amongst employees around the globe. This is the issue that I want to discuss next.

Generating a common global corporate culture

As with the social contact networks discussed in the preceding chapter, a number of organizational strategies designed to engender a standardized transnational corporate culture emerged from the study. These centre around processes of *aculturation*, where new and existing employees are instructed on how they are expected to behave in the business environment. Thus, again, there are two principal sets of organizational strategic practices aimed at engendering aculturation: recruitment and training.

The first set of strategic practices – and perhaps the most obvious in terms of transnational cultural standardization – concerns recruitment. Amongst human resources managers, there was a clear appreciation that in cultural terms, 'you are not going to completely change a person to fit whatever mould you've decided you want' (Head of Training, EuroBank2, London). Rather, it is a question of 'trying to recruit the type of people who fit your existing culture, who will blend in' (Director [Board], Corporate Head of Human Resources, USBank1, New York):

> Generally it is a case of perpetuating people like us... So the first step... and it does tend to happen at screening. We ask, 'Is he [sic] like one of us?' Would you fit in around here? And that is going on at the back of someone's mind even there at the front of their mind, they may be asking about your views on economics. In training, we pursue it very unashamedly... a heavy emphasis on cultural issues in the first few weeks and impressing upon them how we like to do things.
> (Senior Manager, Operations, USBank1, New York)

As this manager went on to explain, he regarded this 'cultural match' not simply as a definite, decided feature of an individual but also something that the company needed to work on nurturing. In short, having recruited the 'right type of person' who is regarded as culturally compatible, the bank needs to impress this new employee with a sense of their fitting in[8]:

> I believe from my work in recruiting and experiences in training, that getting them... the earliest point is the best point. The sooner the

better. On that basis, we make day one, the date they arrive, the first day of training, our goal the stated, articulated, printed idea was to exceed their expectations. We want them to go home at the end of the first day and pick up the phone and call Mom, spouse, sibling, mentor – whoever the key person is in their life – and say "you know, I was thinking all summer about whether I should have gone to *USBank3* instead of *USBank1*, let me tell you ... I just had the time of my life. This was the greatest day." And that is our goal. Because we believe that – it is kind of like imprinting – if you can make a good impact up front, everything else kind of falls into place.

(Senior Manager, Operations, USBank1, New York)

Thus, from the starting point of employee selection, there is an active attempt at replicating the sense of common, standard culture. Senior managers responsible for designing or implementing recruitment within these transnational organizations described how recruitment focused on identifying individuals who would be able to interpret the core business culture values; values that seemed common to many of these companies but which also would be interpreted and understood in a specific way that fitted the general realm of collective social practice in a given company. This point is best illustrated through an account given by a senior manager in one of the US investment banks:

We want those same core values just like everyone else: ethics, responsibility, honesty, accountability, integrity ... those are probably the main ones ... [and] you can find them in any textbook on recruiting for a healthy organization,[9] whether that's global or national ... But the issue then is really how your recruits understand and take-on those ideas. I'm sure *USBank6* look for honesty and integrity, but the fact is that – certainly from what's happened there historically – their culture of integrity is not as water-tight as ours. They're more into risk-taking, it's more aggressive, more competitive ... so that's what fitting in is about: people who'll best share your understanding of what it means to deal with clients with integrity.

(Senior Manager, Capital markets, USBank3, New York)

In that context, many of the human resources managers suggested that 'getting people young' (Director of Human Resources, UKBank2, London) is regarded as important. Engendering a common culture is certainly easier with people who have not been working in a different organizational culture, and may be less willing to adapt to a new set of collective behavioural norms:

> We put an enormous effort into moulding our own people...only when this really functions on the graduate side do you grow and develop people through the organization, allowing a strong culture. If you are in an expansion mode as we have been in this market-place, and bring in all these new high-flyers with their own opinions, then its very difficult to change people who have a strong experience from another company and convert them into *EuroBank4* people...they will always have elements of a small sub-culture. Only over time can you change this.
>
> (Executive Director, Global Fixed Income, EuroBank4, London)

> Q: So people are stamped with the firm they come from?
>
> A: Well, I think people can be predisposed to say, 'if he comes from X, he'll be like so-and-so'. And some of those are exaggerated, and out of date. But I mean certainly you could look at certain firms in the marketplace, and people perceive that they will be of a type. And to a considerable extent there is truth in it – I mean, after half an hour in a room with some guy I don't know in this industry, I could have a pretty good stab at guessing who he works for just from what type of person he is.
>
> (Head of Training, EuroBank3, London)

This last quotation reinforces the argument for taking the idea of distinctive corporate cultures seriously. Although not the focus of my analysis here, there is a social scientific literature, mainly within organizational sociology, that has explored the extent to which it is possible to differentiate the organizational cultures of different firms (Frost 1985; Gherardi 1995; Schein 1997). Different organizations exhibit different cultural mores, although not perhaps coherently enough to correspond to a uniform idea of culture (Frost 1991). In the case of transnational business services, although the criteria that senior managers identified when asked about their culture often appear to be fairly common across firms and both industries, the cultural context of interpretation and practice in specific organizations appears to vary considerably.[10] Recruiting people with experiences of working in other companies in these industries is to some extent seen by senior managers as a 'drag' on their ability to blend into an existing corporate culture in the new firm. Furthermore, employees lower down the internal hierarchy of these firms are also aware of these cultural differences. For example, cultural differences are manifest in the extent to which one employee's self-assessment of their own 'match' to a given firm's culture figured in decisions about which company to apply to work for:

> So in terms of our culture, yes it does work globally, coming back to your question. It's a real mystery how – I'd love to know exactly how it does work. But it does. It's partly because people like me are very impressionable and come in when they arrive and they don't forget it. And also of course they are going to select people who fit in – you know, there is a definite thing there. I don't think I would have got hired by *USBank7*, because I'm too... I'm not brash, I'm not outwardly aggressive enough. And I think that is very important. The kind of people you recruit, and the kind of indoctrination you give them. Now, as you start to get into this hire and fire culture and bring outsiders in from *USBank6* and *USBank8*, you are obviously going to dilute that. And that's the worry. *USBank1* typically has not been a hire and fire type of place. They bring people up the various departments...
>
> (Senior Manager, Corporate Finance, USBank1, London)

The second set of strategic practices, however, and as the last quotation illustrates, concerns training programmes and activities. There are at least three major issues that are significant to the way in which training is geared to engendering shared cultural values and behaviours. First, the quotation above refers to training practices as processes of 'indoctrination' – a clear allusion to induction and training programmes within the transnational firm that are geared directly to engendering *shared values* and a *sense of common identity and belonging* amongst new recruits. When I took up this point with the man who designed the training programme in question in USBank1, his answer revealed a surprisingly explicit cultural objective to training activities:

> Yes, I guess it is a kind of indoctrination. For that reason our training is centralized in New York. Anybody who is hired as a professional – that is a university graduate – goes to New York to train. And this training program I am talking about is what you call the induction, we call it the core training. And we spread these, we tell the stories and talk about these issues and try to get them early with impressing upon them our values, in the hopes it will keep us out of trouble at

the end of the day. We want them to leave that programme with a clear idea of what it means to work for *USBank1*.

(Senior Manager, Operations, USBank1, New York)

This senior manager had designed all of USBank1's 'global training programme'.[11] He speaks of the need to 'impress' values on new recruits early through this training medium. From talking to other employees in the same investment bank who had experienced this training programme, it became apparent that 'impressing values' corresponds to quite an intensive and memorable process:

I agree that it ['global' corporate culture] is very strong. Part of the reason is that it is an old firm, and it's been around since the end of the 19th century. And not only is it an old firm, but they make you aware that it is an old firm, that it has all these old traditions. Like on the training program we had a course of lectures about the *USBank1* culture going right back to the founder and a history and the roots ... and there are all sorts of quotes [sic] all over the place like "a first class business in a first-class way". And there is this other one which I always remember which is "do not do any deed which you would not want known to your fellow man". And they really drum that into you. Really heavily.

(Associate, UK European Bond Sales, USBank1, London)

I think one of the most important reasons why they do that ... is to get you really sort or brainwashed with corporate culture. And also really attached ... if you spend five months of your life with a firm in somewhere that is not your home and therefore you are entirely dependent on the firm, you are emotionally going to get attached to the company as well in terms of just your pay packet. You are going to make friends with people plus its five months, it's a really good time ... and I know that's definitely part of the logic behind it. There are all sorts of additional ties. It's not really globalization, but it is certainly ... well, globalization is part of it but there is the other thing ... because of course you have got people from all over the world there, it certainly increases your confidence that you can just phone up any of the offices, and know someone there. And know how to talk to them, find out how to address whatever problem. So it builds the kind of situation that you could basically phone up anyone anywhere and they are going to be friendly and pretty helpful. That's the culture they want.

(Associate, UK Corporate Finance, USBank1, London)

Second, training programmes are often centralized at the global scale which considerably facilitates the creation of shared cultural values. For example, in USConsultancy1 – one of the largest USconsultancy firms – all new recruits are sent to a dedicated 'training centre' which the firm owns near Chicago. Once there, new recruits spend three to four weeks attending lectures, seminars and business training lessons that are, in part, also to do with inculcating a common set of attitudes, values and behaviours:

> Every cohort goes out to Chicago to *USConsultancy1*'s business school where we put them through our global induction course...like going back to college really: lectures and seminars every day, role-playing exercises, as well as some basic technical and numerical skills...it's also about instilling values though...[about] exposing people to the kind of mindset and ways of doing things we want in our consultants...
> (Senior Partner, USConsultancy1, London)

This is a common strategy that I found in other consultancy firms, and also in investment banks:

> But more and more because of...say you have transactions in New York or...say in South Africa, you fly in people from London, New York, Zurich, possibly some other place who all sit in one room and deal with each other. You've got to deal with each other and communicate, and this makes it very complicated. And for this you must have some form of standards, practices and behaviours. So that's the point of all this induction and training: to get people quickly up to speed so they're all comfortable in a meeting, able to talk the same language metaphorically, if you like...
> (Managing Director, Head of Human Resources [Europe],
> EuroBank3, London)

These 'intensive few weeks' (Senior Partner, USConsultancy1, London) of induction training serve not just to engender social contact in a general sense – as discussed in the last chapter – but equally importantly, they generate an understanding of 'how things are done in this firm' (Senior Partner, USConsultancy3, New York).

Thus, and the third point I want to make, is that training is about instilling values and attitudes that senior managers wish to be a feature of the company's business practices. As another training director explained:

> We have a global intake of a 100 young people – 112 this year – and what we're trying to say at the end of it: do we have them all, irrespective of whether we'll do business, to a common shared understanding of what are the standards here that we deliver by, what's your knowledge-base standard, what's your client-delivery standard? So you start to work on that. You follow that up by – obviously the head office here is London. So we do a lot of support work with technical education but then we take that to other parts of the world. So in terms of globalization, I'll take a squad of people with me on December 3rd, and we'll be in Singapore for a week, and we'll deliver something like 45 programmes that week. Now what does that mean? It means about common knowledge, common standards, understanding the products, client-delivery service is of a nature, that wherever we are in the world we can look at a client and say 'we deliver to this standard; our people are to this standard.' Right? So behind all of that, we're trying to do that on a global scale.
>
> (Head of Training, EuroBank2, London)

The training experience is thus about engendering new employees with a 'deep' cultural understanding of business practice in that particular firm. Most of the senior managers in these service TNC firms described their desire, not surprisingly, to engender 'trust', 'responsibility', 'team skills' and so forth. But these terms could be lifted directly from the pages of any managerial handbook. Training, as a material practice in contrast, is about getting people to understand specifically 'how we do things around here':

> We are proud of our culture, it is very strong, it is something that we work hard to perpetuate. But we also recognize that it is not the only way. You know, I think it is fairly clear that you only have to look at our competition who are very good, world-class competitors to know. And they have very different cultures and yet they are just as effective. So there is no one solution. But we do believe that there is a solution which works for you ... it doesn't really matter what the culture is as long as it is broadly appropriate to the industry in which you find yourself.
>
> (Managing Director, Capital Markets, UKBank3, London)

For example, if you were to mess up, *USBank1* people might say, "Gosh Andrew, that is not the best idea." That's how it would probably be articulated at *USBank1*. But at *USBank6* or somewhere, they would probably say, "that sucks!" Same message, different culture. So if you start missing the signals, you find yourself on the outside looking in. You suddenly find that you are not getting it. And that is harmful to your career and to the company.

> (Senior Manager, Operations, USBank1, New York)

The latter extract is taken from my discussion with the man who designs USBank1's recruitment and training strategy worldwide. The relative specificity of a given (transnational) corporate culture is reiterated in his point about seeking to aculturate employees so that they are able to operate in the interpretative and behavioural community of the firm – the idea that they must not 'miss signals'. As a partner in a consultancy firm similarly expressed, it is a question 'of people operating on the same wavelength' (Senior Partner, USConsultancy5, London) with regard to attitudes and behaviours.

This leads to a fourth way in which training is concerned to engender standardized corporate cultural norms: aculturating employees into standardized group and team behaviour. Many human resources managers regarded, in the words of one managing director, engendering 'an effective culture team behaviours' (Managing Director, Capital Markets, UKBank3, London) as a crucial training objective (Williams *et al* 1993). Little wonder then that both the recruitment criteria and assessment procedures in banks and consultancies – along with post-recruitment training – are heavily focused on the concept of teamwork and how team behaviour can be developed:

> Teamwork is the next one. Having a team culture. You know, there is not a firm or a company in this kind of industry that doesn't have teamwork. So the challenge we put to them is what is so great about teamwork? Why do we go on about teamwork? And the answer in our industry I think hinges on two things which are related. One is the complexity of what we do is just too difficult to do it all by yourself. So the days of the star ... you know, 'I came to Wall Street to make my millions and screw everybody else'. You just can't do it. You just cannot crunch the numbers or deal with the complexity by yourself. And secondly – a related point – is the need for speed. You can't do it fast enough either because everybody is racing to be the first with a proposal to the customer or a new structure or derivative

product whatever. So speed and complexity dictate that you must work in a team.

(Director, Head of Human Resources, EuroBank3, New York)

Yet in the transnational business-service firm, the effective functioning of teams is heavily caught up in the culture of the workplace. In these service TNCs where social relations is the backbone of business success, it is no simple task to engender a uniform team culture. New employees often come from diverse national cultural contexts; developing effective 'transnational team behaviour' is therefore an objective of training practices in these firms. The density of cultural understanding/ knowledge required to achieve this is a key factor leading to transnational employee movements in training and working experiences. 'There is simply no substitute for exposing someone to another culture...whether in the office or in the country you're trying to deal with' (Managing Director, Global Head of Money Markets, UKBank5, London):

To do business in Japan, having Japanese consultants to help us understand how to do that effectively and to understand and appreciate the culture...it is invaluable. You cannot read enough books to get it right. And that's true generally....You learn much more about the culture of how we do business here in the first ten minutes after you join, I'd say, than you ever can from anything in a book or a memo.

(Senior Partner, USConsultancy4, New York)

Transferring people between offices world-wide. I called them training programs, but often they are more aculturalization...if you understand what I mean, because that is not a word. I think that is very important. Teams that work across offices I think help spread it out.

(Managing Partner, USConsultancy5, London)

Thus, to summarize the argument so far, in transnational investment banks and management consultancies, senior managers regard the idea of global or transnational corporate culture as crucially important. Although there is no clear shared definition of the concept, in a broad sense senior managers consider transnational corporate culture as being important to issues of organizational coherence, functionality and control in the transnational context. Culture 'glues' otherwise physically disparate individuals together in terms of shared values, objectives and, perhaps most importantly, in the nature of business behaviours. In that light, within these service industries, TNCs actively seek to engender a degree of cultural standardization in their employees. The strategic organizational practices concerned with this aculturalization process are focused largely on recruitment and training activities. However, I want to take the argument a step further by problematizing this idea of transnational corporate culture in a singular sense as I turn to examine the constraints that affect it.

Stuck in the glue-pot: the limits of cultural homogeneity

Whilst senior bankers and management consultants readily described the advantages of transnational corporate cultural standardization, the interviews reveal considerable variations in the extent to which standardization was feasible, or indeed desirable. The central argument of this section is that despite the wishes of those designing 'global recruitment and training strategies' – and to some extent contrary to the management and business literature discussing (transnational) corporate culture (Frost 1985; Schein 1997; Cameron & Quinn 1999) – the potential development of a coherent singular transnational corporate culture is simultaneously limited and limiting. This argument is elaborated first through the discussion of three factors that inhibit the development of a strong sense of standardized transnational corporate culture: continual organizational restructuring, high rates of employee turnover and the strength of localized subcultures within transnational firms. I then examine why too great a degree of cultural homogeneity is undesirable and has potentially negative influence on the success of transnational service business. Overall, therefore, the section explores how the nature of transnational cultural context is more complicated than simply cultural standardization.

To begin with, consider the limits to the development of a uniform, standardized transnational corporate culture. First, senior managers in both the investment banking and management consultancy sectors recognized that there are considerable limiting 'organizational realities' on generating a common transnational corporate culture. In particular, 'the sheer pace of globalization' (Partner, Financial Institutions, USConsultancy3, New York), manifest in terms of the drive towards mergers in these business-service sectors, means that many companies 'find themselves in a near continual state of upheaval' involving 'dramatic changes of staff, policy and strategy' (Managing Director,

Head of Human Resources [Europe], EuroBank4, London). In such a business environment, it was seen to be difficult to develop and promote organizational cultural consistency:

> Well, we have just merged with *EuroBank5* in Europe which means there's a lot of upheaval at the moment: people leaving, managers coming in from London. They have ideas about how to do things differently obviously...so it's pretty hard to see how we can have a strong sense of corporate culture. My guess is that *EuroBank5* will try and integrate us some way, but all the printed stuff...you know, mission statements and 'the *EuroBank5* way'...no-one is really paying that much attention to it.
>
> (Senior Analyst, EuroBank3, New York)

In industrial sectors where dramatic restructuring occurs in direct response to competitive necessity, many companies are undergoing radical changes. Continuing business transnationalization – in the form of the new office openings and the extension of business activity into more centres around the globe discussed in Chapter 3 – is seen by many senior managers as undermining attempts to engender a common, standardized corporate culture. Likewise the industry-wide trend in both sectors towards mergers amongst firms also strongly inhibits efforts at generating cultural consistency. As one of the senior managers at USBank2 described, contemporary transnational expansion is eroding older mechanisms within former 'multinational' structured firms for (re)producing a coherent corporate culture:

> Q: Why is so much emphasis placed by these books [management texts] on the idea of corporate culture – especially in a global sense?
>
> A: I have often wondered why that was and the most plausible explanation that I have heard is around the subject of culture and controls. It was certainly easier to manage a culture and maintain control if you have a small number of branches...The unfortunate reality nowadays though is that with more and more branch offices, that becomes harder and harder to achieve. And the clients won't wear it...
>
> (Director, Human Resources, USBank2, New York)

In short, despite the ambitions and rhetoric of many of the senior managers, the development of transnational business activity within business-service TNCs is itself a powerful force that hinders the development of coherent corporate cultures.

Secondly, inherently high rates of employee turnover in both the investment banking and management consultancy sectors also hinder development of a single transnational corporate culture. In these well-paid and highly skilled sectors, employees enjoy a relatively strong bargaining position in a (increasingly transnational) labour market (Brint 1991; Beaverstock 1996; Beaverstock & Boardwell 2000). Many of the companies where I interviewed were at the time experiencing annual turnover rates of up to thirty per cent. A number of senior managers identified this as a key element in limiting the development of any strong sense of corporate culture in their organizations:

> I think it [employee turnover] is a problem that you have to tackle but I think it is a mixed effect. Because you know you could have a situation where there is minimal turnover and the problem is the retention level. That people are not moving on when they need to move on. And I think there has been that here.... We are at 11 or 12 percent here so that is relatively healthy – you'd be doing well to get it much lower in this industry. But of course the problem is it means you don't have undying loyalty and therefore people will be more demanding in that way and they will be more demanding of their managers and leaders.
>
> (Head of Training, EuroBank1, London)

However, in addition to the high rates of turnover, a number of managers concerned with recruitment and training also pointed out that their employees came from an increasingly diverse social background. A number of case studies have documented the increasingly 'meritocratic' composition of advanced service employees in global cities such as London (Thrift *et al* 1987; Budd & Whimster 1992; McDowell & Court 1994) and New York (Brint 1991; Fainstein *et al* 1992; Beaverstock & Smith 1996). Such shifts in the last twenty years or so are a consequence of changing class formations and life experiences in national societies as a whole (Savage *et al* 1992), in conjunction with the changing requirements of business services as these industries have expanded. (McDowell 1997; Leyshon 1998). However, as one Managing Director pointed out, both transnational mergers and organic growth were leading to an increasingly diverse nationality/background of employees. 'With an increasingly global workforce drawn from many countries around the world' (Executive Director, Global Fixed Income, EuroBank4, London) it becomes difficult to *aculturate* people into a strong sense of corporate culture. EuroBank1 provided a good example:

Q: Does *EuroBank1* have what you'd describe as a distinctive corporate culture? And is there an active way in which this is encouraged or produced?

A: Erm...I don't think there is really. *EuroBank1* is I would guess...er...easily half of the people come from the outside. The average life of the four thousand people within the business is probably less than three years. The company as a whole is eleven years old, so it is a polyglot of histories. I think the one thing that draws them together is the desire to succeed.[12] It's an up-and-comer, rather than one of the elite, so it aims to get people who have a desire to become one of the elite, and know what it takes to get there. That, if anything, is the one thing which draws them together, but there's no conscious perspective of what our culture is or should be.
(Managing Director, Equities and New Issues, EuroBank1, London)

Third, however, both these limitations on a uniform transnational corporate culture – organizational and employee constituted constraints – relate to a third and less tangible limitation: the strength of local cultures within transnational firms. By local cultures I mean the differential cultural practices across a given transnational firm's operations – as one Director put it, 'any kind of global corporate culture is restricted by the extent of different subcultures within your organization' (Managing Director, Capital Markets, UKBank3, London). Given that many of the transnational business-service firms in the study have grown historically through a continuing process of (foreign) mergers,[13] a number of senior managers described distinct 'sub-cultures' within their firms. For example, one Director explained it was difficult 'to get a newly acquired American firm to adopt the cultural norms of the British buyer' (Managing Director, UK Head of Corporate Finance, EuroBank3, London). Another Partner in a consultancy firm involved in a number of investment banking mergers described the same kind of problem as a US firm expanded the scope of its transnational operation through the acquisition of a foreign firm:

The American viewpoint is very much we have got to be seamless on a global basis and there is a natural tendency for people in American-based companies to say "we drive it out of America" and then we are back to this cookie cutter[14] thing. And I see that a lot when US companies buy foreign ones... I think, speaking on behalf of the rest of the world where I used to spend most of my life, I think there is resentment towards that. That has always been a certain amount of resentment towards America because A, it is powerful and B, it is successful. Those are natural human characteristics. There is also a lot of pride in local culture and the way we do things and they just see it as the Americans trying to force everybody to do it their way. So I think we have at least two different mindsets...

(Partner, Financial Institutions, USConsultancy1, New York)

This quotation leads into the second phase of my argument here: that there was a recognition (although perhaps not consensus) amongst senior managers that a common transnational corporate culture is not a wholly desirable goal. That is, a standardized transnational corporate culture in these service TNCs, should they manage to develop or impose such a characteristic too strongly, presents a number of limitations on the ability of firms to do successful business. Again, there are a number of related threads to this argument.

First, if a transnational firm exerts itself in attempting to recruit people who will fit 'our culture' (Director, USBank7, New York), then it runs the risk of restricting the quality and range of skills inherent in a company's workforce. As a number of human resources senior managers voiced, 'too tight a concentration on hiring the right kind of people [is] a bad thing' because 'it makes for narrow employees' (Head of Training, EuroBank1, London):

So back to that – you know, people like us interviewing – you really want to try not to get just the middle of the bell-curve. You really want to be diverse in every way. Diversity not only of gender or race or nationality but also of particular degrees. What we call undergraduate majors. So we've got music majors and French majors and history majors. When you think, 'well why don't you just hire business majors?' Well the answer is because they are all the same. You are not getting new ideas. We find that Latin scholars are rather good at proprietary trading, for example. They just sort of see things in the totality rather than getting too focused.

(Managing Director, USBank5, London)

When it comes to management consultancy and investment banking business activity, there is a fine line to be walked between ingraining certain cultural norms and retaining a degree of 'team heterogeneity'. Many senior managers, having already argued for the value of common cultural norm, would then suggest that corporate cultural diversity is simultaneously both necessary and desirable. The reason for this, as one human resource Director described, is that it is 'vital to good business practice':

> So we look for heterogeneous teams. Of course, inherent in that as you would imagine is that they are inherently less stable. And if you are not careful, and particularly after a certain size, they start breaking down into homogenous teams. People start clumping together. You know, we all went to Cambridge right so we all start hanging out together. We are all Brits. We are all white. We are all guys, you know, whatever. So you have ... it puts ... managing heterogeneous teams is a skill. And so we focus in on training managers to help them to keep teams together. To keep them vibrant and vital and creative without falling apart ... without becoming unstable.
>
> (Director [Board], Global Head of Human Resources, USBank1, New York)

> But then we and everyone else knows – and I think you can safely make this point for banking or consultants – that in fact, okay, you have got teams, but back to the point I made earlier, you don't want them to be homogenous teams because this will lead to lack of creativity. It is not as creative as a heterogeneous team.
>
> (Director, Human Resources, USBank4, New York)

When I inquired further as to what the advantages of some elements of cultural heterogeneity might be, the consensus amongst those I asked is best described as a mixture of local sensitivity, creativity and innovative capacity. In short, the last two issues at least can be summed up in the argument that too strong a notion of a uniform culture stifles the ability of banks and consultancies to generate new – and potentially competitively advantageous – ideas. In industries dealing in knowledge-rich (Clark, 1997) service products, the implications are clear:

> In this kind of business ... you have to have the ability to be creative, to think up new ideas, new products, new ways of doing business ... that's what happened in the 80s of course, but it's still true ... banking these days, I often say, is about lateral thinking.

> Coming up with something new that the client needs... and that requires local knowledge, flexibility...
>
> (Executive Director, Global Fixed Income and Currencies, EuroBank2, London)

However, with regard to the issue of local sensitivity, senior managers recognized that in operating a transnational service business, having employees with an awareness of different national and regional cultures is also distinctly advantageous. Transnational corporate cultural diversity is therefore an inevitable and desirable outcome of these companies (increasingly) employing professional staff from multiple national contexts.

Second, too standardized a corporate culture adversely affects the individual social relations and the personal interactive elements of gaining and doing successful business that I discussed in the last chapter. Having too strong a transnational corporate culture and recruiting people who 'fit' these cultural norms too closely potentially inhibits the process of gaining and doing business. In the socially interactive business of investment banking and management consultancy, products are most competitive when 'tailored' to the needs of the client. And in a world of diverse cultures, to compete transnationally these firms need a diverse mix of employees able to adapt to cultural diversity, thus enabling the organization to have that tailoring ability in multiple different market contexts.

This issue is perhaps most visible in several of the Japanese firms where there exists the most obvious cultural differences from the Anglo-European form. Japanese firms, even those with substantial transnational operations, are generally typified by a distinctive Japanese corporate culture (Kono & Clegg 1998; Sakai 2000) that can create competitiveness-related problems across a range of industrial sectors (and see also Viney 1997; Yamashita 1998) for their non-Japanese operations. There has been much debate around this issue in the on-going Japanese economic downturn from the mid-1990s (Fumitoshi 1999; Yoshikawa 2000). In the Japanese investment banks that I studied, a number of employees identified the apparent 'strength of the Japanese corporate idea' (Partner, Japanese Clients, USConsultancy3, New York) as a factor inhibiting the competitiveness of the US or UK office:

> I find that the clients, if they are western, do most of the talking. The Japanese are more passive – not maybe in the thinking up ideas but just the way they are presenting themselves. They tend to ask more

questions rather than answering them and I think they are pretty minimalist in their communication. They say what they need to say, they don't do a lot of the schmoozing kind of verbose sort of speak that a lot of businessmen engage in ... For example, we had a presentation the other day at this company that are seeking equity investment from us. So they came and gave us the spiel [sic] – they were from Boston you know, younger guys, and I sort of have a personal connection with one of them and so set it up. And afterwards I asked what their impression was of the presentation and they said, "I don't know what they were thinking" – because usually with Japanese they will just sit there and they will not say anything. There is no expression on their faces. So there is definitely that feeling more than maybe in other meetings – with other western people it might be a little bit more up-front and communicative, even if a lot of it is just fluff. A lot more interaction. And I'm sure that that puts some people off a Japanese firm like this and maybe loses the company some business ...

(Senior Business Analyst, JapanBank4, New York)

As this Anglo-American analyst[15] went on to explain, she found herself acting as a kind of 'cultural interpreter' in certain business meetings because of her knowledge and understanding of Japanese corporate culture:

I felt even myself a bit frustrated because there is also a language barrier. Most Japanese managers ... even if they have studied English and they know they have a great working vocabulary in what they do, it is still pretty hard to find someone that is fluent, who is truly fluent in a natural way with their English. The guys in my group have great English. One of them is lagging a bit and so he is taking in-house English classes which is also commonplace, but I was in a meeting with him in Atlanta and I am sort of looking on ... I don't say as much. I don't want to step on his toes. But there were a couple of times when I could see that all these lawyers and sales and marketing people gaining eye contact – almost to try to get it more from me because they could not get it from him. And they knew that I understood him. So it was kind of interesting in that way in terms of cultural differences.

(Senior Business Analyst, JapanBank4, New York)

My proposition, therefore, is that too strong a cultural standardization – in this case based on a national cultural background – is problematic for transnational firms attempting to compete in multiple national contexts. Furthermore, it is clear in this context that the circulation of employees at the transnational scale also serves multiple purposes. Whilst it engenders common culture and transmits standardized practices in some arenas of business activity, it is simultaneously a key tool for engendering cultural diversity within the firm: 'so US people go out to Tokyo and take our culture with them' while they also 'learn about the local needs of the Japanese office, how the markets work, how doing dealing there is different...' (Partner, Japanese Clients, USConsultancy3, New York).

This relates to a third limitation of cultural standardization: constraining the transmission of information through the transnational corporate context. Transnational business-service firms – as information-rich business organizations operating in many different national economies, regulatory frameworks and cultural contexts – are liable to be constrained by poor information-transmission (and hence weak products) if they attempt to over-standardize business cultural attitudes and practices. To do business successfully in Tokyo requires different behaviours, information sensitivity and attitudes than in New York:

> We learn a lot from those people who have gone out there sometimes not knowing a whole lot about that local marketplace and culture. They will then feed that back and, yeah, it could result in a change in a way that we operate there. Absolutely. And again with our clients I have seen that as well. I have seen situations where a client was making a decision out of New York for a Tokyo subsidiary, and then all of a sudden they send out a new branch manager or someone out there who spends time out there. And based on actually living, working and actually being out there, they will feed information back to New York and change things. That information coming back will change the way they decide to operate that branch from there forward. It is complicated but if you keep people in their silos and reward them for silo-like behaviour, then you will not end up with anything successful. If on the other hand you want some kind of global operation, you have got to figure out a way to support people jointly and you have got to rotate them about. And that is a general principle. It is very high level but that is, I think, it.
>
> (Partner, Japanese Clients, USConsultancy2, New York)

This is not just a question of the relatively obvious and problematic cultural differences between Anglo-American and Japanese business.

Too strong a corporate culture represents a potential limitation on the internal functionality, and hence indirectly on the competitiveness, of consultancies and banks even within the Anglo-American context. One Partner in a major USconsultancy firm recounted his experience of how cultural differences had become a severe problem within one of his client investment banks as they 'tried to co-ordinate a big deal across the Atlantic' (Partner, Financial Institutions, USConsultancy4, New York):

> We were doing some work for a large broker-dealer... they were trying to decide on which of a number of existing systems to use to support their back-office. So it was kind of a big decision. And a lot of the requirements were global... What was kind of interesting was we arranged a video conference-call between the folks in New York and the folks in London.... I have never done a video conference-call before where, I swear to God, there were daggers coming across the Atlantic through the cable: hostile was not the word. It was just awful. And nothing got achieved in that meeting and it was just very frustrating... because the people in England just did not want to be part of the conversation. And of course the Americans at the end, I said to them, "Gee, you know, it looks as though you don't have great communications with your counterparts." And they said, "yes, well, you know we are going to tell them what to do anyway." And I thought, 'well, there you go'. I understand it now. So I think the cultural issues are real, they are deeply significant.
>
> (Partner, Financial Institutions, USConsultancy4, New York)

This quotation illustrates how, as transnational service firms have expanded – especially through merger-led growth – organizational cultural conflicts have emerged at the transnational scale. Firms operating in different national business contexts clearly have different, contextually specific subcultures that are not fully compatible with transnational corporate cultural homogenization. To quote a manager in another Anglo-American investment bank that had experienced a transatlantic merger, American bankers neither want, nor think it appropriate to try 'to become too European in (our) corporate culture' (Senior Manager, EuroBank2, New York).

In summary, therefore, the second phase of the argument in this chapter is that the issue of transnational corporate culture in investment banking and management consultancy is more complex than simply corresponding to the standardization of behaviours in the transnational organizational context. There are a number of factors constraining the degree to which cultural homogenization within the transnational firm is achievable in practice. Organizational restructuring, employee turnover and the existence of 'local', contextually-specific subcultures in transnational corporate organizations mean that the strategic practices aimed at engendering cultural standardization described in the previous section can only be, and are, limited in their effect. However, and furthermore, the standardization of transnational corporate culture in a singular sense also potentially limits the competitiveness of service TNCs. Too great a degree of common culture constrains the ability of firms to recruit diverse, flexible and creative employees who can adapt and conduct successful business in a world of diverse cultural forms. In short, while perceived as important by senior managers, too strong a transnational corporate culture is also problematic. The last part of the chapter takes up this apparent contradiction by developing a theoretical framework for understanding the relationship between the need for some degree of cultural standardization on the one hand and on the other, the simultaneous need for cultural diversity in the transnational firm.

Culture or cultures? Macro- and micro-cultural tropes in the transnational firm

> We at *USConsultancy3* – it is the same kind of thing with investment banks – we are actually, well, it is about rotations. And by that I mean not just sending people out to conquer the world but also sending Partners out to Australia, to the Czech Republic ... wherever. We also bring some of their guys there over to here, and I see the same practices going on in some of the investment banks, doing the same kind of thing. They are trying to make sure that they do get rotations so that they can absorb the culture in both environments. Appreciating the differences – as opposed to a few years ago when I think it was a lot more unsubtle ... a lot more, especially with the US companies. You know, we would go there and just tell them what to do: which meant fitting in with our culture.
>
> (Partner, Financial Institutions, USConsultancy3, New York)

Many senior managers operationalized 'global corporate culture' as an umbrella term for both the standardization and homogenization of behaviours and attitudes, and also the pluralized idea of multiple heterogeneous corporate cultures to theorize the necessity of 'adapting business behaviours to local markets and contexts' (Director [Board], Global Head of Human Resources, USBank2, New York). There are clearly many tensions here. Rather than being understood as oppositional features, my argument is that the standardized and diverse elements of transnational corporate culture need to be theorized as simultaneously crucial to business success. Furthermore, the theoretical binary opposition of 'standardized, global' culture in the singular against 'diverse, local' cultures in the plural insufficiently captures the complexity of transnational cultural context. Rather, it is more productive to understand the culture within transnational firms as sets of competing 'cultural tropes' that are meaningful at different scales and in different contexts.

This approach entails, therefore, the view that a binary global/local and one/many divide cannot easily be made relevant to the issue of culture at all. If corporate culture is taken to be collective social attitudes, practices and behaviours, then any degree of consistency and commonality is only ever partial in form. No two business deals are conducted in precisely the same way, different employees reflect attitudes and forms of business practice differently. For example, in similar circumstances the behaviour of a banker from a certain firm in New York may have many similarities to that of a colleague in London, but it is not exactly the same.

The point is that corporate culture, like culture in general, is not something that academics, bankers, consultants or any one else understands as a highly consistent well-demarcated concept. Cultural tropes do not require a high degree of match to another case before they have meaning: several investment bankers being perceived as being 'honest' with a client in completely different deals constitutes enough of a trope for a firm such as UKBank2 to regard itself/be regarded as having 'a polite culture' (Director, Head of Human Resources, UKBank2, London). In that sense, therefore, culture itself is a concept that only really gains any full meaning in a given context: as numerous writers have discovered, it is very hard to theorize 'culture' of any form in general (Tomlinson 1999). Consequently, this apparent contradiction between cultural standardization and diversity is better theorized as the necessary co-existence of both macro-cultural and micro-cultural tropes. In exploring this proposition, I consider first the notion of macro-cultural tropes as part of the transnational corporate cultural context, before turning to discuss their relationship with micro-cultural tropes.

First, therefore, by macro-cultural trope, I refer to what thus far has been identified as the need for cultural standardization within transnational firms. As the first section explored, in both transnational banks and consultancies organization-wide attitudes and forms of behaviour are crucial to business success. Such cultural tropes need to be transmitted to every employee, no matter where they are on the planet. Hence, the macro-cultural tropes of corporate culture are ideal standards of behaviour identified by managers, including integrity, honesty, reliability and politeness.

> I think it's a question of having identification with your employer, with the company you represent. It helps because it also makes my opinion...should make in its behaviours somewhat predictable because you have certain patterns of behaviour.
>
> (Managing Director, Head of Human Resources [Europe], EuroBank4, London)

Thus, in engendering a 'common corporate culture', what is in fact being encouraged is predictable consistency amongst employees on certain specific sets of cultural characteristics that are deemed important to business success by senior management. However, these tropes are not a unified corporate culture *per se*. Macro-cultural tropes are generalized cultural facets that may or may not be applicable in a given business context, as opposed to a set of many standardized cultural behaviours. As one training Director explained, the cultural tropes that correspond, as he termed them, to 'core competencies' in a good investment banker only become fully realized in the actual process of doing business – social practices that are potentially infinitely diverse in terms of behavioural nuances in any given context:

> A: For example, we have a programme improving managerial competency...we have just started with something like this...so that's how we are trying. These core competencies, they are flowing out around the globe so we have – within Investment Banking[16] – we have some standard competencies for good investment bankers around the globe.
>
> Q: Could you give any examples?
>
> A: Well, customer focus, definitions...it's the definitions around what kind of behaviours people express if they are good investment bankers so it's various...er...six to eight different competencies. And we do this through resource feedback which is also something which helps us to understand globalization because human resource

feedback can be done not only within the division but also it can be done with global customers, and it appears from different locations...

(Managing Director, Human Resources, EuroBank2, London)

Thus, global training is not so much about developing a singular corporate culture, but instilling a series of transferable cultural tropes that can be applied to any business situation. However, where senior managers described the limitations of 'too strong a culture', this reflects not so much the inherent problems of having one corporate culture but more the over-extension of macro-cultural tropes to the degree where they excessively penetrate the numerous and highly diverse sets of social practices that constitute transnational business activity. For example, as another managing director in a European investment bank pointed out, the problem of having too standardized a common culture really arises when common understanding impeaches into the realm of 'implementation':

I think people are trying to get some shared common understanding of some principles or some values. I think the mistake is to look for total homogenous implementation solutions. I mean, you've got to really come up with your umbrella, if you like, of broad principles and trust the local delivery. And the local delivery may actually look a little bit different depending where you are.

(Managing Director, Head of Training, EuroBank1, London)

This brings me to the second issue: what this Director identifies as the value of 'local delivery', I prefer to define as micro-cultural tropes. Such a distinction is based on the argument that when it comes to effectively theorizing local corporate cultures, territorial scale is only one of several defining features. The idea of a micro-cultural trope is useful because it not only encapsulates the territorial limitation of, for example, an office in a given national market context but also the temporal/organizational/social limitations of cultural diversity in the transnational organization. Where senior managers argued for cultural heterogeneity in their firms, this should be understood not as a contradiction, fighting against the need for a common global corporate culture, but another spectrum of multiple-cultural tropes required to successfully do business at the transnational scale. These micro-cultural tropes, corresponding to what managers tend to refer to as 'local cultural sensitivity' (Director (Board), Corporate Head of Human Resources, USBank1, New York), enable transnational consultancies and banks to adapt to multiple contexts for the collection and interpretation of crucial business knowledge and information. For example, business-service firms need a corporate culture in their Korean office that is sensitive and aligned with a whole set of different micro-cultural tropes than in their Peruvian one:

> One of the distinct advantages is if you...it is not just enough to understand the language, you have to understand culture. Okay? And if you really do business in India or if you want to do business in Korea or you want to do business in Peru or wherever – Turkey – you have got to have people who not only can speak the language but understand the culture...you know, have a good sense of local rules, regulations, customs but also have a feel for what is good business and what is not good business. And unless...if you are not a national of that country, you have got to spend some time there to really understand. So you know we send people to Berlitz all the time but we want individuals who can not just represent this organization but also to understand the culture, the mores, the values, the rules and regulations...we want people who can actually represent this firm with the highest integrity and understanding. And so people who have grown up in that culture and know what it takes to do business the way we want to do business in that culture.
>
> (Senior Partner, USConsultancy1, New York)

> I think one of the most difficult issues is the cultural issue. People think they understand each other, but they don't: from the arrogant West, if you like, we don't understand the mores...people crossing their legs in front you to us doesn't mean much, but it can mean in certain countries one of the most terrible offences. I know that that exists, I don't know in which countries that is a problem, and so unwittingly I could be offending somebody terribly, perfectly unintentionally. But nevertheless that's a big issue. And I think for an international business, we try to decentralize as much to the local environment. At the same time you want to have continuity of standards and of approach. That does mean you're going to have to shuffle the cultures around. And not understanding enough about them makes that quite difficult. As a young organization, we don't have...for example, any one from Taiwan in London. So here it's a bit too localized.
>
> (Managing Director, Equities and New Issues, EuroBank5, London)

Yet as this manager points out, these numerous micro-cultural tropes present in any business-service TNC must co-exist in mutual interdependence with the wider macro-cultural tropes that constitute the consistency of the transnational organizational context. It is not a question of the need for standard global culture *versus* the need for multiple local cultures but the simultaneous and harmonious co-existence of multiple-cultural tropes operating at a variety of scales according to the cultural facet in question:

> There is a certain amount of trepidation about globalization. Because it is seen as you know . . . standardization is a good thing up to a point but you don't want to just standardize everything and become just a global culture, in a global market-place any more than you likewise don't want a set of local cultures tacked together uncomfortably. And every company does that differently – I mean I think they all need to do it, but there's no one way. So what works here does not necessarily work everywhere else. And we are still finding our way through it.
>
> (Partner, Financial Institutions, USConsultancy6, New York)

Thus, the implication of the need for the organizational absorption of a (vast) array of micro-cultural tropes is reflected in the growing multi-nationalism to be found among the employees of these firms. Locals are already aculturated into the urban, regional or national culture where a given office is located and their knowledge capital is used to translate the specific context of that office to the wider functioning of the transnational firm:

> The kind of general theme is you need local presence, local people who understand the culture and you also need standard methodologies and stuff and training made available . . . I mean, for example, if you want to do business with the Japanese, you really need Japanese people in your firm to do that. I think it would put you at a disadvantage if you did not have that.
>
> (Partner, Japanese Clients, USConsultancy3, New York)

> The other important thing for us is that we believe in having locals in overseas offices. We don't believe it makes sense to have Brits running an office in Frankfurt. It is terribly important that we really are a global organization. The more non-Brits we have in the organization, the more multicultural we will be anyway. The Americans

used to insist on Americans running all their overseas offices. They have now cottoned-on to the fact that you need locals. And there is a lot of talent in Europe. The markets are less developed than they are here so the Anglo-Saxon countries are ahead in terms of investment banking, but there are a number of good people in those markets who you can employ sensibly to work for you. And it goes down well with the clients. It really is becoming a global industry now. Ten years ago there were very few French investment bankers. They were bankers but not investment bankers. Or German investment bankers. But now the industry is a real global industry as opposed to a Anglo-Saxon industry.

(Director, Head of Human Resources, UKBank2, London)

In that sense, the standard training and induction programmes run by many of the investment banks and consultancy firms studied are not so much about generating a homogenous transnational corporate culture. Rather they are better understood as attempts at familiarizing and training new recruits in interpreting and implementing the macro-cultural *behaviours*, *attitudes* and *practices*[17] that the transnational firm desires them to combine with their micro-cultural capital in specific business contexts:

Oh yes. Not true anymore. You're seeing a real marked difference of an intake of British, European, South-east Asian, Australian and American influx coming in. And they as a young body of people as you bring them together – and they stay with us say for three months – what you've got at the end of it, is virtually an international network and a set of international cultures . . . and it's about teaching them our values while also keeping their understandings of different countries in the company.

(Managing Director, Head of Training, EuroBank1, London)

However, this is not just a situation where business-service TNCs require people with an understanding of different micro-cultural tropes in just one specific context: the value of, for example, a German consultant who understands the cultural mores of Frankfurt as a financial centre is not restricted to any one given context. That German consultant can bring his or her cultural understanding to bear on the wider needs of other transnational clients who have part of their business in Germany. And such a client can make simultaneous use of the diversity of cultural understanding and interpretative ability within the transnational consultancy by buying the experience of Japanese-, British- and

American-aculturated employees as well. Furthermore, many consultants and bankers, such as the senior managers I interviewed, can be understood as being multi-aculturated in many different local markets. Although partially, therefore, it is not *wholly* a question of local culture brought to bear on local client business. Both micro- and macro-cultural tropes are not discreetly scalar in this way:

> I think it is how you serve global clients. We are a US firm but we serve a German company with mostly Germans, but when the Germans try to do that here [the US], they just pull a couple of Americans on board. Do they serve the company globally? Not really. And that is to say, you know, we talked about a bank this morning with operations in Tokyo and in London and in the U.S. and we have a team and we go to that bank and we serve it with a global team with a representative global dispersion. And we can talk the cultures separately, country by country. We have a Japanese partner, we have a UK-based partner. They get together along with others who take an international perspective and we can serve them in a seamless way. Then you are a global company. But if you show up and say "we are Japanese-based and we have a Japanese team and we will find an American here or there..."
>
> (Senior Partner, USConsultancy4, New York)

Thus, the realm of macro-cultural tropes is not separate or discreet from the variety of diverse micro-cultural tropes to be found in any transnational business-service firm. The two are interrelated in a way that undermines attempts to pigeon-hole them into scalar conceptualizations – the use of the words 'global' and 'local' by many senior managers notwithstanding. Macro-cultural tropes, as the following quotation demonstrates, are shaped and influenced by the array of micro-cultural tropes implicated in a transnational firm's business practices, as well as vice versa:

> What I am saying is you can't... you have to accept that your offices overseas are going to have an overlap with the way you do business. Obviously they have got to have the same ethical culture, the same sort of integrity. But you have accept there are different ways of doing business. And you actually have to encourage people to come up with new ideas and different ways of doing business. And I think if you have a single omnipotent culture: (a) I think you are kidding yourself, and (b), I think it stifles innovation. And I think you'll find

that in all the firms I know including *USBank1*, there is not one culture, or at least not one complete culture. Yes, you should have your rule books, yes, you have a culture, but I think each of them in their heart of hearts, would accept that in Germany and Milan there are slight . . . there are local cultures which are overlaid onto the corporate culture. And I think that is a natural way of doing business and I think that will continue.

(Senior Partner, USConsultancy4, London)

The final point to emphasize in all of this, therefore, is that it is not possible to differentiate the need of these firms for standardized cultural norms from the simultaneous need for cultural diversity within the transnational organization. Furthermore, the nature of the transnational cultural context in the service firms studied is not, at the level of industry-wide generalization, a concept that can be developed any further without engaging directly in the specifics of a given firm's context. In order to expand such a theorization of corporate culture in any transnational business-service firm, research needs to be carried out into the specific operations of individual companies. This was not the task I set out to achieve here.

Conclusions

There are different aspects of global culture, of corporate culture . ∵. and it's in everything we do.

(Senior Partner, USConsultancy2, New York)

The central argument of this chapter has been that cultural issues are crucially important to transnational investment banks and management consultancy firms. As the Senior Partner quoted above states neatly, culture pervades everything, even in the transnational context. My goal, therefore, has been to tackle the gap I identified in the existing literature concerned with corporate culture by addressing the question of what global or transnational corporate culture is through the development of my concept of transnational corporate culture(s).

In analyzing the way in which transnational corporate culture is understood by senior managers, the research showed that considerable importance is placed on transnational firms having a strong common, shared corporate culture. In investment banking and management consultancy, this need for a standardized transnational corporate culture is perceived to revolve around the desirability of shared forms of behaviour.

Consistency and coherence in the way in which employees treat and deal with clients is important to the success of these service businesses, and shared cultural values thus correspond to the medium through which these behaviours are transmitted through the transnational organization. A shared transnational corporate culture is also important in terms of differentiating firms from their competitors and in ensuring that in a spatially dispersed transnational organization, there is sufficient coherence in terms of information flows, practices and strategies. In this way, the idea of a singular transnational corporate culture is understood as the 'glue' that is needed to bind together large and complex transnational organizations; it is the less tangible socially constituted set of factors that determine whether or not the divisional structures described in earlier chapters actually cohere.

As a consequence, therefore, transnational investment banks and management consultancies expend considerable time and money in seeking to engender a common sense of corporate culture in the transnational context. This is an important issue in recruitment, as firms seek to take on people who will 'fit in' and help reproduce the existing corporate culture. Furthermore, training programmes are geared to processes of aculturation that aim to expose employees to certain cultural norms deemed desirable within the firm and to help engender a sense of shared identity and culture.

Yet as the chapter moved on to argue, although a standardized transnational corporate culture in a singular sense is needed for all of the above reasons, there is also a simultaneous need for cultural diversity in the transnational organization. In examining how cultural standardization in practice has certain limits, and also potentially limits firms' competitiveness, the discussion showed how transnational cultural context needs to be theorized as being more complicated than simply a question of the development of a singular transnational corporate culture. In these transnational business-service firms, a standardized transnational corporate culture is hard to achieve as a consequence of continual processes of organizational restructuring, high rates of employee turnover and the continued prevalence of subcultures within the firms. Furthermore, too much cultural standardization constrains the ability of firms to recruit diverse, flexible and creative employees who can adapt and conduct successful business in a world of diverse cultural forms.

Transnational management consultancies and investment banks thus need both cultural homogeneity and diversity in order to compete successfully in the contemporary global economy. Culture, within the transnational corporate context, is better understood as corresponding to a series of cultural tropes that co-exist and are transmitted across varying scales through the transnational firm. The need for a singular 'global' corporate culture identified by managers is better theorized as the need for macro-cultural tropes that are necessary for the firm's success and competitiveness wherever it seeks to undertake business activity. These 'tropes' are decontextualized ideas rather than 'complete cultures' because they only really become fully meaningful in a given business context – for example, 'honest' business behaviour is something desirable in any deal but the specific form that that will take depends on the context of the given deal. Yet, in addition to macro-cultural tropes, transnational service businesses also need a whole array of micro-cultural tropes in circulation at fewer but less extensive scales within the organization. These are the 'local knowledges' that many senior managers also recognized the need for, embodied in the recruitment of local nationals who have appropriate 'knowledge capital' for a given marketplace.

However, the end-point of this argument again feeds back into the wider concern throughout this book with how transnational business might be better theorized. The argument that transnational corporate culture needs to be understood as corresponding to a broad set of cultural tropes operating at a variety of scales relates to my overarching point that globalization is a poor generalized concept for capturing and understanding the processes of transnational business. To reiterate, *it is not a question of global culture versus local cultures*. The binary division of global–local only serves to cloud the complexity and interrelatedness of different cultural tropes within the transnational corporate context that become fully comprehensible only when applied in a given specific organization in a given business context. That is why the kind of theory I have tried to advocate throughout this chapter and earlier ones is inherently flexible and sensitive to being applied in different corporate contexts.

Thus, the theoretical framework for understanding transnational corporate culture in terms of the concepts that are transferable beyond the case of investment banking and management consultancy is not intended to be a final vocabulary. Like the concepts proposed in the preceding chapters, this is not an overarching theory that can be simply applied to other cases. In that sense perhaps the most important objective in developing this kind of theoretical approach is to outline a new theoretical approach to TNCs that can allow issues of organizational culture to be taken seriously rather than be regarded as ambiguously intangible and, therefore, not a worthy object of study. This requires a different conceptual and methodological emphasis than is currently favoured within the academic literature. For as the senior manager quoted above reiterates, for the last time in this study, corporate culture in the transnational firm he works for is a crucial element in determining business success. Which makes either ignoring or over-simplifying it far more problematic than just representing a blind-spot in the field of academic enquiry.

6
Conclusion – Capturing the Complexity of Transnational Business

> The literature advocating globalization is far too simplistic. While there are some economic drivers of globalization there are extremely strong cultural and political barriers preventing the development of a single world market . . . For most manufacturing sectors, and all service sectors, regionalization is more relevant than globalization.
>
> (Rugman 2001: 18)

In his recent book *The End of Globalization* (2001), Alan Rugman argues from a business-school oriented perspective that the academic debate on globalization has been largely simplistic and misguided. He criticized academic theorists of globalization for misunderstanding the nature of TNCs' activities in the contemporary global economy and equating them with the emergence of integrated global markets and business practices. Rugman argues that there is no evidence for true (economic) globalization: the global economy, along with the world's largest TNCs, is becoming more oriented towards the three main regional trading blocs – North America (NAFTA), Europe (EU) and Asia-Pacific (ASEAN). Very few truly global corporations exist, corresponding only to a small number of the very largest manufacturing TNCs who sell homogenous products across the globe. Rugman regards the social scientific discussion of globalization as having ignored the complexity of business activity in today's global economy, in favour of a general theoretical story about globalization as a far-reaching and pervasive phenomenon.

It is these important questions identified by Rugman that were taken up by the research presented in this book. In examining investment banks and management consultancies as examples of contemporary business-service TNCs, the research has shown in a variety of ways that a generalized approach to theorizing globalized business is extremely limited in helping us to understand the complex nature of contemporary business activity. As Rugman recognizes, and as I explored in Chapter 2, the academic debate on globalization appears to be simplistic in the kinds of arguments it makes. The world is not populated by numerous truly 'global corporations', and the activities of TNCs are not directly comparable nor necessarily even similar between firms and across sectors. In that sense, there is far more complexity to economic globalization than the story of TNCs 'taking over the world' with the help of the neoliberal international trading system. Yet, overall, the research I have presented also casts doubt on the validity of Rugman's argument that it is 'regionalization' rather than 'globalization' which better explains the nature of contemporary world economy. The complexity of contemporary global business runs much deeper than globalization versus regionalization.

In that sense, I have in this book sought to move beyond the self-evident truisms and generalized descriptions found in the globalization literature, and examine in depth the complex nature of transnational business activities within some of the world economy's most important informational and financial-service firms. Without repeating too much of the analysis from earlier chapters, by way of conclusion I want to revisit what I regard as the most significant insights from each of the four conceptual 'cuts' made at understanding the complex nature of transnational business activity in these firms. From that basis, I make a series of recommendations for business practitioners and other policy-makers before ending with a comment on the future direction of research into transnational firms and business activity.

Business-service industries in an era of globalization

In examining the first of the conceptual cuts at understanding transnational business activity – *organizational form* – the research suggested that there are significant dangers in relying upon the more easily quantifiable indicators of organizational globalization. Using numbers or even geographical dispersal of corporate branch offices across the planet provides only a very crude indication of the degree to which a TNC operates across the global economy. Knowing a company's presence in various countries reveals little about the nature of their business operations in that nation-state and allows the theorist no understanding of the relationship between those branch offices and the firms' top management and strategists. Indeed the research showed that using such data can be misleading, as amongst the firms studied there was a clear 'marketing preference' to convey an image of globality even where this was poorly developed in functional or market-share terms. Such a finding has important implications for the globalization debate, given that much of the literature relies heavily on this kind of numerical data.

In contrast, the detailed qualitative research in this study revealed that in management consultancies and investment banks, the distribution, function and relationships between branch offices are complex and varied between firms and industries. Different TNCs in these business-service sectors, depending on their specific specializations and strengths are present and active to a greater or lesser degree in different centres around the globe. However, what does emerge from the research in this book is a general trend amongst firms in both industries towards ongoing internal divisional restructuring to enable their corporate organizations to deliver business-service products at the global scale. This entails most often a shift, in organizational form, away from the more conventional 'multinational' or 'geographical' model where divisions are set-up around states or regions towards a functional or product-driven form – a finding to some extent reflecting a long-standing view of the evolution of TNCs as informed by research into manufacturing companies (Franko 1976; Bartlett & Ghoshal 1993). In this shift, divisions are increasingly based around products that are managed at the global scale. Such a general shift in the organizational form of consultancies and banks certainly appears to be informed by a shared understanding amongst senior managers of what globalization 'is' and the pressure it places on firms to compete more effectively in the global economy. In particular, in these business-service sectors, these restructuring processes are being driven by a combination of (as in manufacturing sectors) economies of scale and scope but also by the need to better serve client firms who are themselves increasingly transnationalized. However, such shifts in organizational form are far from unproblematic. Both consultancies and banks face difficulties in achieving greater organizational globality with respect to employee's general resistance towards global working-practices, and in terms of retaining effective managerial control at the global scale.

This issue of *managerial structure* represented the second key concept in my theorization of transnational business activity in these service industries. The study suggested that this shift in organizational form at the divisional level within both consultancies and banks does not correspond to a simplistic form of centralization at the global scale. In examining how power and control is constituted and (re)produced in these TNCs, attention is turned to the formation, operation and functioning of management hierarchies. In exploring qualitatively the relationships through the management hierarchy of firms in both industries, I suggested transnational control is better understood as a much more *diffuse* concept than the influential image of centralized control in the head office. The power relations that transnational management hierarchies allow to be actualized permit the transmission and dissemination of centralized power throughout the organization without necessitating too heavy an involvement in individual business decisions by the centre. Furthermore, the divisional shift towards a product rather than a geographical-oriented form is in part the result of these firms' struggle to find internal power formations that generate adequate and effective forms of control for senior management in the transnational context.

In both information-centred industries, an important factor in these shifts in organizational form and managerial structure is the mediating role of information technology. However, the research suggested that IT should be understood as playing an important part in facilitating (but not driving) business transnationalization. Most importantly, the role of IT cannot be separated from the social practices of transnational business. Such a finding offers a clear indication of the weakness of parts of the globalization literature's tendency to place technology at the centre of understandings of business transnationalization. In contrast, in these business-service sectors, IT is less important than the social interactive aspects of transnational business activity because it is the nature of sociality that fundamentally has most influence on the profitability and success of management consultancies and investment banks.

This argument was taken up in shifting the analysis to a third key concept – *interpersonal relations*. In a contrasting approach to the firm-level analysis of much management theory, this study examined in depth how social actors – employees – actually 'do' transnational business in management consultancies and investment banks. In that sense, a number of abstract factors such as business networks, often quite crudely quantified 'numerically' in management studies research, were examined from an in-depth qualitative perspective. A number of key conclusions were drawn in respect of the role of these business networks. First, it is clear that both internal and external social networks are crucial to successful transnational investment banking and management consultancy. Internal networks facilitate the acquisition of business by enhancing a transnational firm's capacity for rapid and effective internal communication. They are also one of the key issues that affect the quality of service that clients receive. Yet equally important are external contact networks that are central to a firm's ability to acquire and retain business. External contacts and individual relationships in the form of long-term relationships with client firms, particularly manifest in the crucial significance of 'repeat business', are central to the activity of 'doing' transnational banking or consultancy. It should be therefore emphasized once again that anyone – academic, business manager or policy-maker – who wishes to develop a better understanding of the *competitiveness* of individual firms or these service sectors as a whole must therefore focus their attention on these interpersonal networks. No matter how competitiveness, profitability or general business success are measured or assessed, in these people-centred service industries, it is ultimately social relations that are a core defining factor.

As a consequence of this central importance of interpersonal relations, the research also revealed how considerable money, time and effort are spent by transnational business-service firms in attempting to 'engender' effective forms of social contact and networks. *Transnational training* involves sending new and existing employees on induction and training courses together as TNCs seek to promote the formation of internal contact networks at the global scale. Such an objective is also reflected in strategies of *global movement* where existing employees move between locations throughout their careers in circulation programmes that are to a large extent about socializing them through the transnational context of the firm. These movements of employees play a crucial part in creating coherence in the TNC, especially in these business-service industries where the quality of 'products' is reliant on the ability of employees to work together as effective teams at the transnational scale.

Third, in considering the relative significance of different kinds of interpersonal relations, it was argued that client relationships are the most important factor in determining the competitiveness and thus the success of transnational investment banks and management consultancies. Relationships between key senior employees and their counterparts in client firms, often cultivated over some time, are central to the acquisition and retention of much consultancy and banking business even when competing in global markets. I argued, therefore, that 'trust' as a key factor in business relations, at least in these business-service firms, is manifest primarily through relationships between *specific individuals*.

The research suggested that individual personal relationships between key 'client-carrying' senior personnel is central to many (although not all) management consultancies and investment banking businesses. In that sense, client relations *constitute* transnational business activity – they are not a context within which it is 'embedded' as is often implied by writing within economic sociology. Although perhaps a symptom of the terminology of embeddedness, the implication that economic relations exist independently of social relations between business practitioners is misplaced. They are not 'embedded' in social relations because they can never be 'extracted' or 'disembedded' from those relationships. In that sense, the implication for theorists of business is that the debate around 'embeddedness' needs to shift direction insofar as placing social relations at the centre of economic theory rather than around its margins.

This was further reinforced by my fourth argument concerning inter-personal relations – that it is also this key significance of certain indi-viduals that is very often also the crucial factor affecting *business success* in global markets. In both of these business-service industries, this signi-ficance rests on an (often senior) individual employee's ability to develop 'dense' face-to-face relationships with colleagues and potential clients. This density of relationships is manifest particularly through flows of informal information and in social skills concerned with persuasion and negotiation. Thus, being a successful investment bank or manage-ment consultancy is about employing the right key personalities who are known amongst the community of (global) clients and who possess the necessary kinds of social skills. Clearly, care must be taken not to forget the importance of the organizational and institutional contexts in which key business people operate. However, my point is that far too little attention has been paid to these crucial social relations in any depth. Those who wish to understand transnational business more effectively need to move beyond the rather generalized descrip-tive and undeveloped measurement of 'important social factors' built around questionnaire surveys that have tended to be favoured by management studies.

Finally, in the last stage of the research analysis, this concern with the sociality of transnational management consultancy and banking merged into the discussion around the final key concept: *transnational corporate culture*. The research suggested that the idea of a standardized transnational corporate culture in the singular, although widely used by senior managers in these business-service firms, is an inadequate conception of the nature and significance of culture in business transnationalization. Rather, I have argued that there is a tension between the need for cultural standardization and cultural diversity in transnational consultancies and investment banks. It is true that to an extent there is a clear need for cultural standardization, understood as collective social practices, in terms of 'gluing' a physically disparate organization together. Senior managers, therefore, see such standardization as important for a firm's competitiveness, ensuring a degree of constancy and consistency in employee behaviour. Consequently, as with social contact networks, transnational investment banks and management consultancies spend considerable time and money seeking to engender a common sense of corporate culture through recruitment and, in particular, training strategies and practices. These activities are often designed to *aculturate* new and existing employees into certain forms of behaviour and attitude.

However, the research also showed how too great a degree of cultural homogenization can be problematic for business-service TNCs. It argued that standardization is both limited in the degree to which it is realistically achievable and limiting in the constraints it can impose on the TNC as a global organization. The research produced a number of overall points in this regard. First, a homogenous transnational corporate culture is, in fact, an unachievable goal because of the practical realities of transnational organizational form. Corporate expansion, mergers, rapid employee turnover and the continued existence of different sub-cultures, all work to prevent and inhibit the development of a strong singular sense of corporate culture in transnational investment banks and management consultancies. Second, and furthermore, too standardized a corporate culture is also an undesirable goal because of the restrictive impact it has on the skill base of employees, the limitations it imposes on the crucial social contact networks identified in Chapter 4 and the negative impact it has on the transmission of information through firms whose business is highly information-rich.

Thus, to highlight the central argument of the fifth chapter, the idea of global corporate culture needs to be theorized as the simultaneous need for both micro-cultural and macro-cultural tropes within the organization. Macro-cultural tropes correspond to the organization-wide cultural facets that senior managers perceive as global corporate culture: integrity, reliability, team-work and so on. Yet also crucial to the success of transnational banking and consultancy are micro-cultural tropes that correspond to what senior managers described as 'local sensitivity' which enables firms to adapt to multiple contexts for the collection and interpretation of business knowledge and information. However, as often suggested by social scientists and business commentators, it is not a question of a simplistic global versus local scale to corporate culture. In the same way that theorizing organizational form through simplistic divisions between global, regional and local structures clouds the complexity of organizational form, or the idea of social-embeddedness at different scales conceals the complexity of social relations involved in 'doing' transnational business, the binary division of global–local obscures and misrepresents the complexity and interrelatedness of different cultural tropes within TNCs in these industries.

Implications for business practitioners and policy-makers

The theoretical conclusions reached through each aspect of this study have a series of implications not only for business practitioners within management consultancy and investment banking but also in other transnational firms beyond the business-service sector. Likewise, these issues must also be of interest to anyone seeking to develop a policy perspective on these business-service sector industries and are likely to be helpful more widely in facilitating understanding of the activities of TNCs in regional and national economies more generally.

First is the question of the general concept globalization. Setting aside wider questions about how (if at all) this concept should be theorized and deployed, the discussion in the first chapter of how senior consultants and bankers understand the term offers some clear warnings for business managers and others. In identifying the multiple (and often contradictory) understandings of globalization amongst business managers, it is clear that a great deal more caution needs to be taken in using this concept. There are good arguments for avoiding using the term as an unproblematized description of the world at all because it conceals a complex web of power relations and implicit assumptions. For business managers, despite its advantage in supporting (neoliberal) business ideals, it also acts as a hindrance. Not all the phenomena subsumed in the term are beneficial or unproblematic for transnational firms. Likewise, for policy-makers the term needs to be critically engaged with, and broken-down into a less generalized form, if policies are to be developed that can adequately cope with the complexity of practices and phenomena surrounding business transnationalization. Globalization, in short, needs to be regarded with extreme and critical caution by those who seek to tackle its complex 'reality'.

Second, my analysis of transnational organizational form in Chapter 3 is most significant for business managers with regard to the issue of organizational control in the transnational context. Whilst the discussion illustrated the development and necessity of some degree of 'diffuse' managerial control, business managers need to critically address the extent, at least in business-service industries, to which it is desirable to centralize control. Investment banking and management consultancy are highly social forms of business activity where the centrality of social relations and dense information flows suggests that the model of the 'truly global firm' discussed by some managers is likely to be severely constrained by business necessities. There was no clear consensus on the best kind of transnational organizational form amongst senior managers, and problems were already becoming apparent with the 'global product-led' model. This suggests that senior managers would be well advised to be cautious in shifting organizational form too rapidly to structures that may be highly detrimental to the competitiveness and success of the company. Furthermore, the evidence from this discussion of organizational forms offers some supporting evidence for the potentially disastrous consequence that under-resourced or too quickly implemented central control structures can have for firms such as investment banks. Certainly, the cases of Barings Bank in 1996 and Allied Irish Bank in 2001 represent examples where inadequate global control structures were a central feature in allowing 'rogue' trading activities to take place. The globalization of organizational form requires a balance between centralization and diffuse control structures that permit the complexities of these kinds of service businesses to be appreciated by senior management. Organizational globalization in this light has to be about more than the concentration of managerial power in key offices.

Third, and relatedly, my arguments about the role of information and communication technologies in organizational globalization suggest that TNCs should pay more attention to the nature of the human–technology interface in the transnational context. Technology strategies need to be more effectively co-ordinated with the social practices of 'doing' transnational business, rather than continuing to regard technology as discreet and separate from the sociality of business. Such a shift in approach might enable transnational banks and consultancies to develop more effective and cost-efficient strategies for using existing technologies and could facilitate the development of new technology–practice nexi that enhance the firm's competitiveness. Without an appreciation of how the people doing global business make use of technology in relation to an individual TNC's business, costly and wasteful expenditures on information technology can easily be made on the basis of a vague appreciation of their centrality to investment banking and management consultancy business. IT strategists within companies therefore should be close in knowledge terms to the practitioners who generate revenue, rather than being partitioned off as a separate 'support' division. The more IT strategists and providers understand the needs of business practitioners in their working context, the better able they will be to maximize benefit through this mediating tool.

Fourth, and arising from the analysis in Chapter 4, the key significance of social relations in transnational management consultancy and investment banking means that, although they are already prioritized to some degree, the development of transnational social relationships could be better facilitated by these TNCs. Senior managers need to place more importance on training and socialization strategies that integrate more of their employees into transnational contact networks. In industries where annual rates of turnover are high, it is also important for these firms, as they transnationalize their business, to hold on to more of their key employees. In a world of transnational business, engendering transnational social contact is increasingly more difficult, time-consuming and expensive than it was previously when firms conducted business mostly in just one or two urban environments. As transnational organizations grow larger, therefore, they need to be accommodating to the more demanding working conditions of 'global work' if they are to retain increasingly valuable key employees.

Fifth, and finally, the discussion in Chapter 5 suggests that the ambiguous and woolly idea of corporate culture needs to be taken more seriously by business practitioners in management consultancies and investment banks. Business-service firms, as actors in a knowledge-dense and especially social form of business, are crucially dependent on cultural issues for success – much more so than in a manufacturing firm where the final product not heavily influenced by employee behaviour. Business managers need to be more cautious in too quickly adopting managerial 'fads' (Shapiro 1998) concerning the benefits of a strong corporate culture and more discerning in thinking about which and what kinds of cultural facets can be effectively promoted. This involves spending time considering what 'macro-cultural tropes' are important, and what strategies for engendering strong macro-cultural transmission least interfere with the co-existent need for diversity in the transnational business-service firm. Similarly, there is a need to develop more coherent and sophisticated strategies for the successful nurturing of multiple micro-cultural tropes in the TNC. In the firms I studied there is no clear appreciation of or strategy to develop different forms of cultural trope and much discussion of corporate culture showed little appreciation of the specific cultural needs of individual firms. In investment banking and management consultancy, competitiveness is heavily bound into the development of transnational-cultural tropes and as such cultural issues cannot afford to be regarded as marginal or unimportant on that basis that culture is an intangible idea.

Future research into transnational business

Finally, I want to end with some thoughts about the implications of this study for future research trajectories in the social sciences into transnational business. The overarching conclusion that can be drawn from all the different aspects of my analysis of transnational consultancy and banking is that global business activity in these sectors is far more complex and difficult to theorize than much of the current academic literature acknowledges. In both carrying out the research, talking to business managers and writing this book I have become increasingly aware of the limitations of different academic disciplinary perspectives in understanding transnational firms and business activity. A dominant element in this critical position is my unease with those who seek to rely excessively on 'generalized' theories of globalization or quantitative surveys in their arguments about the nature of transnational economic activity. Certainly, I think that much of the research and analysis presented through this book bears witness to the problems with adopting one methodological or theoretical stance when trying to grapple with the complexity of contemporary global business activity.

In that respect, each of my conceptual 'cuts' – *organizational form, management structures, social relations and transnational corporate culture* – represented an attempt to offer a more detailed, qualitatively grounded analysis of what has been occurring in two of the most important industries in today's increasingly global economy. These concepts certainly draw heavily at times on the arguments made within the existing academic literature but in allowing these ideas to emerge from the research process itself, the value of a strongly interdisciplinary perspective has I hope become apparent. This is not to suggest that one discipline or another has not provided important understandings of transnational business from within existing disciplinary frameworks, nor that a given research methodology is inappropriate. Rather it is more an argument that academic theory needs to break out of its methodological and disciplinary constraints if it is to more effectively produce theory of relevance to anyone seeking to understand the evolving nature of TNCs and the global economy. Whilst clearly not without its own methodological and conceptual limitations, the approach developed through this book represents an attempt to take a substantial step in this direction.

Notes

1 'Globalization Theory' and the Complexity of Global Business

1 For example, Wallerstein's work (1974, 1979, 1984) on world systems theory (see also Taylor 1993) represents an attempt at developing a historical-materialist framework for the evolution of human societies that, in its argument concerning the 'global scope' of the capitalist world system, corresponds to a proto-globalization theory.

2 This perspective is informed by both a social science critique pointing to the limitations of a methodology overly focused on quantitative techniques and also the view that modelling is an inappropriate and impoverished approach to understanding social relations (Holmwood & Stewart 1991; Hammersley 1992; Croon & Vijver 1994). This methodological debate is particularly applicable to the study of social relations amongst 'elites' such as those who form the focus of this study (Dexter 1970; Hughes & Cormode 1998; Herod 1999).

3 Ranked by captalization.

4 Ranked according to numbers of professional employees. These numbers are likely to have declined with rationalization in these sectors in the 00s (although accurate data was not available at the time of going to press). The relative rankings are unlikely to have been much affected by this process.

5 For a critical assessment of the strengths of the 'depth interview' in this respect, see Devine & Heath (1999); Mason (2002).

6 Chief Financial Officer.

7 Chief Executive Officer.

8 A construction that bears a striking resemblance to Rostowian ideas of progressive development (Rostow 1978, 1990).

9 For example, the websites of Accenture (www.accenture.com) and Deloitte (www.dc.com).

2 Rethinking the Transnational Firm

1 Although already by the 1960s, some commentators had started to (prematurely) describe MNCs as 'global corporations' (Doremus *et al* 1998).

2 For example, *Strategic Management Review, International Business Review, Transnational Corporation* and *Academy of Management Review*.

3 Global Investment Banking and Management Consultancy

1 And also the nature of 'globalized' cities and their significance to transnational business activity (Jones 2002).

2 The description is ambiguous, but includes firms that also describe themselves as strategic as well as management consultancies. I did not include firms whose primary business was IT or other forms of consultancy.

3 Although, of course, there are a considerable number of transnational service firms amongst the Fortune Global 500 largest. For example, in 2001, Deutsche Bank was the largest business-service company in the world, positioned twenty-ninth by revenues (Source: Fortune Global 500, available at www.pathfinder.com/fortune/global500/index.html).

4 The products of investment banking are obviously both 'financial' and 'informational' in nature, whereas consultancy firms provide only 'informational' products. In that sense, senior managers told me that size was more of a limiting factor on transnationalization in the investment banking industry. Small banks are financially constrained by the amount of capital they have available to fund products – a problem not faced by consultancy firms.

5 This point has been made by a number of other quantitative-focused studies (Beaverstock *et al* 2001) based on supposition from numerical indicators.

6 For a discussion of existing and new 'products' in contemporary investment banking, see Liaw (1999).

7 Meaning large, lucrative contracts.

8 There is considerable evidence of the same process occurring in other service sectors, for example, accountancy (Beaverstock 1996) and advertising (Karanteng 1996).

9 A large capital base allows banks to serve large transnational clients. Smaller banks do not have access to the capital to make (or even organize the syndication of) the kinds of loans increasingly demanded by the largest TNCs.

10 This appears to be a development of the market for syndicated loans that emerged in the 1980s, where large loans were spread between a syndicate of banks with one acting as the key broker.

11 Foreign Exchange.

12 Within management studies, with regard to manufacturing TNCs, there has been a longstanding debate about organizational change and the nature of these kinds of geographic versus functional managerial matrices (for example, Franko 1976; Robock & Simmons 1989; Dunning 1993a).

13 USBank8, a smaller US bank, was acquired by EuroBank3 in 1997. USBank7, a US brokers, merged with USBank3 in 1998.

14 By 'financial structure' I mean the way in which internal financing is institutionally formalized in transnational organizations.

15 A figure cited in 'One Global Firm' (USConsultancy1 1996).

16 Senior managers in USConsultancy3 in fact contradicted this view in reporting a shift towards 'global remuneration'.

17 This senior manager is referring to skill-based groups within the company when he refers to 'schools'.

18 For example, see Kogut *et al* (2001), Sutcliffe & McNara (2001) and Willman *et al* (2002).

19 The deregulation of financial business in global cities since the late 1970s has led to the emergence of many 'new' forms of financial product (Valdez 1997).

20 Merchant banking developed in western Europe during the sixteenth and seventeenth centuries as Europeans colonized the new world and invested in business ventures. Merchant banking thus refers until the twentieth century to

banking investment in trade and what limited foreign direct investment occurred. However, in the latter part of the twentieth century the operations of 'investment banks' have greatly diversified in terms of the nature of investments made. Merchant 'trade' represents only one aspect of contemporary non-retail banking.

4   'Doing' Global Business

1   Enron's collapse was not based so much on lack of managerial control as a flawed model and bad management (Blackburn 2002).
2   See Valdez (1997) for a wide-ranging introduction to these products.
3   And not all bankers, as various scandals have revealed!
4   One closer to the assumptions of neo-classical economic analysis – that is, perfect competition and lack of market failures.
5   Six of the firms I interviewed in, were amongst the top fifty largest firms in the Fortune Global 500 (2000).
6   The emergent transnational communities literature tends not to be concerned with this issue. See, for example, Whitley (1999) and Beaverstock and Boardwell (2000).
7   Although, of course, the literature concerned with these cases suggests this argument by implication (Yeung 2000).
8   A 'shosha' is a distinctively Japanese form of business organization. It is the name given to one of the largest investment-financing corporations which, in contrast to Anglo-American investment banks, takes considerable 'hands-on' involvement in investments with regard to management of projects. The shosha is therefore more than a financial organization.
9   Professional employees at graduate entry and above, as opposed to clerical and administrative staff.
10 The organizational forms of TNCs vary between industries and it is clearly related to the historically specific circumstances of corporate development in different national economies (Dunning 1993a; Dicken 1994).
11 For a detailed discussion of rotation management in Japanese firms see Harukiyo & Hook (1998).
12 This respondent refused to be recorded and so the quotation is a paraphrased version taken from shorthand notes.
13 In USBank1, taken from the Annual Report 2001, proprietary trading and investing corresponded to 40 per cent of pre-tax income in 2001 (USBank1 2002). In other words, 60 per cent of income arose from client-based activities.
14 This does not just include investment banks, but also, for example, government institutions, insurance companies and pension funds.
15 For detailed studies of the social relations of the work-place, also see Pringle (1988), Leidner (1993), Schoenberger (1997) and McDowell (1997).

5   Global 'Glue'? Corporate Culture in a Transnational World

1   In Tom Wolfe's *The Bonfire of the Vanities (1987)*, investment bankers are described as 'masters of the universe' to convey the unprecedented power they increasingly possess as a consequence of financial globalization.

2 Subsequently, of course, these offices were badly damaged as a consequence of the 2001 terrorist attacks.

3 Which is not to say that Schoenberger (1997) or Kono & Clegg (1998) do not make important arguments, just that their understanding of corporate culture is too vague sometimes to be useful.

4 Although see, for example, Garsten (1994) and Casson *et al* (1996).

5 Whether or not this is what culture 'means' is not the issue, because this is a reasonable definition of the meaning of what the respondents in my study were more-or-less talking about when they used the term 'corporate culture'.

6 'Trope' comes from Latin (tropus) and Greek (tropos) and is used in this sense to mean a manner or style of culturally mediated behaviour.

7 The name of the individual concerned has been changed.

8 See Jones (1998) on the gendered nature of these criteria and the recruitment process.

9 See, for example, Wanous (1980) and Herriot (1989).

10 This is just within an Anglo-American sample primarily – the differences from the Japanese firms are even more acute.

11 This interviewee is a very senior human resources and operations manager in USBank1. He provided me with hard copies of all the company's major training programmes, many of which he had written personally in close-contact with the Director on the company's Board responsible for Human Resources.

12 This suggestion is probably a good example of what a senior manager wants to present as an external image of the company.

13 Again, for example, the merger of Dillon Reed with SBC Warburg in 1997, Morgan Stanley and Dean Witter in 1998 or SBC Warburg and UBS in 2000.

14 A metaphor for standardization – that is one cookie-cutter produces the same product anywhere.

15 This analyst in fact came from a mixed Japanese–American background. One parent was Japanese and she had lived in Japan for part of her life, also speaking fluent Japanese. She therefore felt well positioned to comment on the interaction of Japanese/American culture from a personal perspective.

16 The title of an internal divisional structure.

17 By using the prefix 'macro-' I want to convey the transferability of these cultural tropes across multiple different contexts, rather than the less-transmittable, more specific tropes of a given business deal in a specific location.

References

Abrahamson, E. (1996) Management fashion. *Academy of Management Review*, 21, 1: 254–285.

Adam, N. (1992) Regulating global financial markets (London: Economist Intelligence Unit).

Agenor, P. (ed.) (1999) The Asian financial crisis: causes, contagion and consequences (Cambridge: Cambridge University Press).

Ahoroni, Y., Nachum, L. & Daniels, P. (2000) Globalization of services: some implications for theory and practice (London: Routledge).

Altenbas, Y. & Molyneux, P. (1993) Scale and scope economies in European banking (Bangor: Institute of European Finance, University College of North Wales).

Alvesson, M. (1995) Management of knowledge-intensive companies (Berlin: Walter de Gruyter).

Andersen, O. (1993) On the interrationalization process of firms: a critical analysis. *Journal of International Business Studies*, 2: 209–231.

Archibugi, & Michie, J. (1995) Technology, globalization and economic performance (Cambridge: CUP).

Arup, C. & Soloway, A. (2002) The new World Trade Organization agreements: globalizing law through services and intellectual property (Cambridge: CUP).

Ashkensas, R., Ulrich, D., Jick, T. & Kerr, S. (1995) The boundaryless organization: breaking the chains of organizational structure (San Francisco: Jossy Bass).

Augar, P. (2001) The fall of gentlemanly capitalism (London: Penguin).

Axford, B. (1995) The global system (Cambridge: Polity).

Barker, R. (1997) Information flows between finance directors, analysts and fund managers: a study of accounting information, corporate governance and stock market efficiency (Cambridge: Judge Institute of Management Studies).

Barnes, T. (1996) Logics of dislocation (London: Harvester Wheatsheaf).

Barnet, R. & Cavanagh, J. (1995) Global dreams: imperial corporations and the new world order (New York: Simon and Schuster).

Barnevik, P. (ed.) (1994) Global strategies: insights from the world's leading thinkers (Boston, Mass.: Harvard Business School Press).

Barrett, M. (1997) Globalization and the employment relationship: towards an explanatory framework (London: South Bank University, Centre for International Business Studies).

Bartlett, C. & Ghosal, S. (1989) Managing across borders: the transnational solution (London: Century Business).

Bartlett, C. & Ghoshal, S. (1993) Beyond the M Form: toward a managerial theory of the firm. *Strategic Management Journal*, Winter Special Issue 14: 23–46.

Bauman, Z. (1998) Globalization: the human consequences (Cambridge: Polity).

Beauregard, R. (ed.) (1989) Atop the urban hierarchy (New Jersey: Rowman and Littlefield).

Beaverstock, J. (1991) Skilled international migration: an analysis of the geography of international secondments within large accountancy firms. *Environment and Planning A*, 23: 1133–1146.

Beaverstock, J. (1994) Re-thinking skilled international labour migration: world cities and banking organisations. *Geoforum*, 25: 325–338.

Beaverstock, J. (1996) Subcontracting the accountant! Professional labour markets, migration, organizational networks in the global accountancy industry. *Environment and Planning A*, 28, 2: 303–325.

Beaverstock, J. & Boardwell, J. (2000) Negotiating globalization, transnational corporations and global city financial centres in transient migration studies. *Applied Geography*, 20, 3: 277–304.

Beaverstock, J. & Bostock, A. (2000) Migration, embedment and networks: highly-skilled international labour migration within Singapore's financial district. Presented at the 96th Annual Meeting of the AAG, Pittsburgh, 4–8 April.

Beaverstock, J. & Smith, R. (1996) Lending jobs to global cities: skilled international labour market migration, investment banking and the city of London. *Urban Studies*, 33, 8: 1377–1394.

Beaverstock, J., Smith, R. & Taylor, P. (2001) Geographies of globalization: US law firms in world cities. *Urban Geography*, 21, 2, 95–120.

Beck, U. (1999) What is globalization? (Cambridge: Polity).

Bell, J. (1995) The internationalization of small computer software firms – a further challenge to 'stage' theories. *European Journal of Marketing*, 29, 8: 60–75.

Bell, J., McNaughton, R. & Young, S. (2001) Born-again global firms: an extension to the 'born-global' phenomenon. *Journal of International Management*, 7: 173–189.

Bharat, V. (1997) Theory of the Global Firm (Oxford: OUP).

Bjerke, B. (1999) Business leadership and culture: national management styles in the global economy (Cheltenham: Edward Elgar).

Blackburn, R. (2002) The Enron Debacle. *New Left Review*, 14, 2: 26–53.

Bloomfield, B. (ed.) (1997) Information technology and organizations: strategies, networks, and integration (Oxford: Oxford University Press).

Bloomfield, B. & Daniela, A. (1995) The role of management consultants in the development of information technology: the indissoluable nature of socio-political and technical skills. *Journal of Management Studies*, 33, 1: 27–46.

Bradley, S., Hausman, J. & Nolan, R. (eds) (1993) Globalization, technology and competition: the fusion of computers and telecommunications in the 1990s (Boston, Mass.: Harvard Business School Press).

Brannen, J. (ed.) (1992) Mixing methods: qualitative and quantitative research (Aldershot: Avebury).

Braudo, R. & Macintosh, J. (1999) Competitive industrial development in the age of information: the role of co-operation in the technology sector (London: Routledge).

Bresnen, M. (1990) Organising construction: project organisation and matrix management (London: Routledge).

Brint, S. (1991) Upper professionals: a high command of commerce, culture and civic regulation. In Mollenkopf, J. and Castells, M. (eds) *Dual City: Restructuring New York* (New York: Russell Sage Foundation).

Brock, D., Barry, D. & Thomas, D. (2000) 'Your forward is our reverse, your right, our wrong': rethinking multinational planning processes in light of national culture. *International Business Review*, 9: 687–701.

Brotchie, J., Batty, M., Blakely, E., Hall, P. & Newton, P. (eds) (1995) Cities in competition (Melbourne: Longman).

Bryson, J. & Daniels, P. (eds) (1998) Service industries in the global economy (Cheltenham: Edward Elgar).

Budd, L. & Whimster, S. (1992) Global finance and urban living (London: Routledge).

Buiter, W., Corsetti, G. & Pesenti, P. (1998) Interpreting the ERM crisis: country-specific and systemic issues (Princeton, N.J.: International Finance Section, Dept. of Economics, Princeton University).

Burgoyne, J. & Reynolds, M. (eds) (1997) Management learning: integrating perspectives in theory and practice (London: Sage).

Cameron, K. & Quinn, R. (1999) Diagnosing and changing organizational culture: based on the competing values framework (Harlow: Addison-Wesley).

Cantwell, J. (1995) The globalization of technology: what remains of the product cycle model? *Cambridge Journal of Economics*, 19: 155–174.

Carrell, M., Elbert N. & Hatfield, R. (2000) Human resource management: strategies for managing a diverse and global workforce (London: Dryden).

Carrington, M., Langguth, P. & Steiner, T. (1997) The banking revolution: salvation or slaughter?: how technology is creating winners and losers (London: Pitman).

Casson, M. (1991) Enterprise and competitiveness: a systems view of international business (Oxford: Clarendon Press).

Casson, M. (1995) The organization of international business (Aldershot: E. Elgar).

Casson, M., Loveridge, R. & Singh, S. (1996) The ties that bond?: some observations on corporate culture in the multi-national corporation (Birmingham: Aston Business School Research Institute).

Castells, M. (1989) The informational city (Oxford: Blackwell).

Castells, M. (1996) The rise of the network society (Oxford: Blackwell).

Castells, M. (2000) The global economy. In Held, D. & McGrew, A. *The Global Transformations Reader*, pp. 251–259 (Cambridge: Polity).

Cerny, P. (1994) The dynamics of financial globalization: technology, market structure, and policy response. *Policy Sciences*, 27: 319–342.

Cerny, P. (1997) The search for a paperless world: technology, financial globalization and policy response. In Talalay, M., Farrands, C. & Tooze, R. (eds) *Technology, Culture and Competitiveness*, pp. 153–166 (London: Routledge).

Cerny, P. (1998) Globalisation, governance and complexity (Leeds: Centre for Industrial Policy and Performance, University of Leeds).

Chaffey, D. (ed.) (1999) Business information systems: technology, development and management (Essex: Pearson Educational).

Chen, J. (1998) Economic effects of globalization (Aldershot: Ashgate).

Cheng, L. & Kierzkowski, H. (2001) Global production and trade in East Asia (London: Kluwer Academic Publishing).

Child, S. & Heavens, S. (1998) The social constitution of organizations and its implications for organizational learning (Cambridge: Judge Institute of Management Studies).

Clark, G. & O'Connor, K. (1995) The informational content of financial products and the spatial structure of global finance. Available from the author, School of Geography, University of Oxford.

Clark, I. (1997) Globalization and fragmentation: international relations in the twentieth century (Oxford: OUP).

Clark, I. (1999) Globalization and international relations theory (Oxford: OUP).

Clark, T. (1995) Managing consultants: consultancy as the management of impressions (Buckingham: Open University Press).

Clarke, T. & Clegg, S. (1998) Changing paradigms: the transformation of management knowledge for the 21st century (London: HarperCollins Business).

Cohen, R., Felton, N., Nkosi, M. & van Liere, J. (eds) (1979) The multinational corporation: a radical approach: papers by Stephen Herbert Hymer (Cambridge: CUP).

Coleman, W. (1996) Financial services, globalization and domestic policy change (Basingstoke: Macmillan).

Colombo, M. (ed.) (1998) The changing boundaries of the firm: explaining evolving inter-firm relations (London: Routledge).

Corley, T. (1989) The nature of multi-nationals. In Teichova, A. (ed) *Historical Studies in International Corporate Business*, pp. 43–56 (Cambridge: CUP).

Crabtree, B. & Miller W. (1999) Doing qualitative research (London: Sage).

Croon, M. & Vijver, F. (eds) (1994) Viability of mathematical models in the social and behavioural sciences (Lisse: Swets and Zeitlinger).

Currie, W. (1995) Management strategy for IT: an international perspective (London: Pitman).

Czerniawska, F. (2001) Management consultancy (Basingstoke: Palgrave Macmillan).

Daniels, J. & Daniels, C. (1994) Global vision: building new models for the corporation of the future (New York: McGraw-Hill).

Daniels, P. (1993) Service industries in the world economy (Oxford: Blackwell).

Daniels, P. & Moulaert, F. (1991) The changing geography of advanced producer services: theoretical and empirical perspectives (London: Belhaven).

Dassbach, C. (1989) Global enterprises and the world economy: Ford, General Motors and IBM – the emergence of the transnational enterprise (New York: Garland).

Davidson, W. & De la Torre, J. (1989) Managing the global corporation: case studies in strategy and management (New York; London: McGraw-Hill).

Deloitte & Touche (1998) The global millennium: a world without borders (New York: Deloitte Touche).

Deloitte & Touche (2000) Fast course, smart moves. Corporate Annual Report.

Deloitte & Touche (2002) Necessary journeys. Corporate Annual Report.

Denzin, N. & Lincoln, Y. (eds) (1998) Strategies of qualitative inquiry (London: Sage).

Deutsche (1997) Global investment banking. Internal Brochure (London: Deutsche Bank).

Devine, F. & Heath, S. (1999) Sociological research methods in context (London: Macmillan).

Devinney, T., Midgley, D. & Venaik, D. (2000) The optimal performance of the global firm: formalizing and extending the integration–responsiveness framework. *Organization science*, 11, 6: 674–695.

Dexter, L. (1970) Elite and specialized interviewing (Evanston: North Western University).

Dicken, P. (1994) Global-local tensions: firms and states in the global space-economy. *Economic Geography*, 70: 101–128.

Dicken, P. (1998) Global shift (3rd Edition) (London: Chapman).

Doremus, P. (ed.) (1998) The myth of the global corporation (Chichester: Princeton University Press).

Doz, Y. & Prahalad, C. (1991) Managing MNCs: a search for a new paradigm. *Strategic Management Journal*, 12: 145–164.

Drew, P. & Heritage J. (1992) Talk at work: interaction in institutional settings (Cambridge: Cambridge University Press).

Dunning, J. (1988) Multinationals, technology and competitiveness (London: Allen & Unwin).

Dunning, J. (1993a) The globalization of business (London: Routledge).

Dunning, J. (1993b) Multinational enterprise and the global economy (Wokingham: Addison-Wesley).

Dunning, J. (1997) Alliance capitalism and global business (London: Routledge).

Dyer, J. (1996) Specialized supplier networks as a source of competitive advantage: evidence from the auto industry. *Strategic Management Journal*, 17, 4: 271–291.

Dyer, J. (2000) Collaborative advantage: winning through extended enterprise supplier networks (Oxford: OUP).

Eade, J. (ed.) (1997) Living the global city: globalization as local process (London: Routledge).

Eden, L. & Potter, E. (eds) (1993) Multinationals in the global political economy (New York: St Martin's Press).

Fainstein, S., Gordon, G. & Harloe, M. (eds) (1992) Divided cities: New York & London in the contemporary world (Oxford: Blackwell).

Ferguson, M. (2002) The rise of management consultancy in Britain (London: Ashgate).

Financial Times (1998) The Revolution in Risk Management. In '*Mastering Finance*', Report with London Business School.

Financial Times (1999) Europe set to remain overbanked. *Article 28/7/99*.

Fincham, R. (1999) The consultant–client relationship: critical perspectives on the management of organizational change. *Journal of Management Studies*, 36, 3: 335–351.

Flood, P., Gannon, M. & Paauwe, J. (1995) Managing without traditional methods: international (Wokingham: Addison-Wesley).

Franko, L. (1976) The European multinationals: a renewed challenge to American and British big business (London: Harper and Row).

Friedland, L. (1992) Covering the world: international television news services (New York: Twentieth Century Fund Press).

Frost, P. (1985) Organizational culture (London: Sage).

Frost, P. (1991) Reframing organizational culture (London: Sage).

Fry, M. (1997) Globalization, financial market opening, and foreign capital inflows (Birmingham: International Finance Group, Birmingham Business School, University of Birmingham).

Fukuyama, F. (1993) The end of history and the last man (London: Penguin).

Fumitoshi, T. (1999) Manipulations behind the consumption tax increase: the Ministry of Finance prolongs Japan's recession. *Journal of Japanese Studies*, 25, 1: 91–106.

Gang, Y. (1992) Chinese transnational corporations. *Transnational Corporations*, 1: 125–133.

Garsten, C. (1994) Apple world: core and periphery in a transnational organizational culture (Stockholm: Department of Social Anthropology, Stockholm University).

Geneen, H. & Bowers, B. (1999) Synergy and other lies: downsizing, bureaucracy, and corporate culture debunked (London: St Martin's Press).

Gertler, M. (1997) The invention of regional culture. In Lee, R. & Wills, J. (eds) *Geographies of Economies*, pp. 47–58 (London: Arnold).

Gherardi, S. (1995) Gender, symbolism and organizational cultures (London: Sage).

Ghoshal, S. & Westney, E. (1993) Organization theory and the multinational corporation (Basingstoke: Palgrave Macmillan).

Giddens, A. (1984) The constitution of society (Cambridge: Polity Press).

Giddens, A. (1990) The consequences of modernity (Cambridge: Polity and Blackwell).

Giddens, A. (1999) Runaway world: how globalization is reshaping our lives (Cambridge: Polity).

Gill, S. (ed.) (1997) Globalization, democratization and multilateralism (Basingstoke: Macmillan).

Goldstein, M. (1998) The Asian financial crisis: causes, cures, and systemic implications (Washington, D.C.: Institute for International Economics).

Gordon, M. (1994) Finance, investment, and macroeconomics: the neo-classical and a post Keynesian solution (Aldershot: Elgar).

Graham, J., Matthews, A. & Graham, D. (1990) Macmillan directory of technology in global financial markets (London: Macmillan).

Grahber, G. (ed.) (1993) The embedded firm: the socio-economics of industrial networks (London: Routledge).

Grandori, A. (ed.) (1999) Interfirm networks: organization and industrial competitiveness (London: Routledge).

Granovetter, M. & Swedberg, N. (1994) The handbook of economic sociology (Princeton: Princeton University Press).

Grant, R. (1991) The resource-based theory of competitive advantage: implication for strategy formulation. *California Management Review*, 33: 114–135.

Gray, J. (1998) False dawn: the delusions of global capitalism (Cambridge: Granta).

Green, C. & Ruhleder, K. (1995) Globalization, borderless worlds, and the tower of babel: metaphors gone awry. *Journal of Organizational Change Management*, 8: 55–68.

Greider, W. (1997) One world ready or not: the manic logic of global capitalism (New York: Simon Schuster).

Griffin, K. (1996) Studies in globalization and economic transitions (Basingstoke: Macmillan).

Grunwald, J. & Flamm, K. (1985) The global factory: foreign assembly in international trade (Washington, D.C.: Brookings Institution).

Guile, B. & Brooks, H. (eds) (1987) Technology and global industry: companies and nations in the world economy (Washington, D.C.: National Academy Press).

Hall, P. (1984) The world cities (London: Weidenfeld and Nicolson).

Hammersley, M. (1992) Social research: philosophy, politics and practice (London: Sage).

Hampden-Turner, C. (1994) Corporate culture: how to generate organisational strength and lasting commercial advantage (London: Piatkus).

Harrington, J. (1991) Organizational structure and information technology (New York: Prentice-Hall).

Harrison, M. (1994) Diagnosing organizations: methods, models, and processes (London: Sage).

Hart, O. & Moore, J. (1997) Default and renegotiation: a dynamic model of debt (London: Suntory-Toyota International Centres for Economics and Related Disciplines, London School of Economics and Political Science).

Harukiyo, H. & Hook, D. (eds) (1998) Japanese business management: restructuring for low growth and globalization (London: Routledge).

Harvey, D. (1989) The condition of postmodernity (Oxford: Blackwell).

Harvey, D. (1996) Justice, nature and the geography of difference (Oxford: Blackwell).

Harvey, D. (2000a) Spaces of hope (Edinburgh: EUP).

Harvey, D. (2000b) The limits to capital (2nd Edition) (Oxford: Blackwell).

Harvey, M., Speier, C. & Novicevic, M. (1999) The impact of emerging markets on staffing the global organization: a knowledge-based view. *Journal of International Management*, 5: 157–186.

Hassard, J. & Holliday, R. (eds) (1998) Organization – representation: work and organization in popular culture (London: Sage Publications).

Healey, M. & Rawlinson, M. (1993) Interviewing business owners and managers: a review of methods and techniques. *Geoforum*, 339–355.

Hedlund, G. (1994) A model of knowledge management and the N-form corporation. *Strategic Management Journal*, 15: 73–90.

Heenan, D. & Keegan, W. (1979) The rise of third world multinationals. *Harvard Business Review*, 1: 101–119.

Heetje, A. (ed.) (1988) Innovation, technology, and finance (Oxford: Blackwell).

Held, D., McGrew, A., Goldblatt, D. & Perraton, J. (1999) Global transformations (Cambridge: Polity).

Helleiner, E. (1994) States and the re-emergence of global finance: from bretton woods to the 1990s (London: Cornell University Press).

Hendershott, P. (1977) Understanding capital markets (Lexington: Lexington Books).

Henwood, D. (1997) Wall Street (London: Verso).

Hepworth, A. (1992) Geography of the information economy (London: Belhaven).

Herod, A. (1999) Reflections on interviewing foreign elites: praxis, positionality, validity, and the cult of the insider. *Geoforum*, 30: 313–327.

Herring, R. & Litan, R. (1995) Financial regulation in the global economy (Washington D.C.: The Brookings Institute).

Herriot, P. (ed.) (1989) Assessment and selection in organizations: methods and practice for recruitment and appraisal (Chichester: Wiley).

Hert, R. & Imber, J. (1995) Studying elites: using qualitative methods (Thousand Oaks, CA: Sage).

Hertner, P. & Jones, G. (1986) Multinationals: theory and history (Aldershot: Brookfield VT).

Hickson, D. & Pugh, D. (1995) Management world-wide: the impact of societal culture on organizations around the globe (London: Penguin).

Hirst, P. & Thompson, G. (1999) Globalization in question (2nd Edition) (London: Sage).

Holmström, B. & Roberts, J. (1998) The boundaries of the firm revisited. *Journal of Economic Perspectives*, 12, 4: 73–94.

Holmwood, J. & Stewart, A. (1991) Explanation in social theory (Basingstoke: Macmillan).

Holton, R. (1998) Globalization and the nation-state (London: Macmillan).

Hopkins, A. (ed.) (2000) Globalization in world history (London: Pimlico).

Howells, J. & Michie, J. (eds) (1997) Technology, innovation and competitiveness (Cheltenham: Edward Elgar).

Howells, J. & Wood, M. (1993) The globalization of production and technology (London: Belhaven Press).

Hu, W. (1992) Global Corporations are national firms with international operations. *California Management Review*, 34.

Hughes, A. & Cormode, L. (1998) Guest editorial: researching elites and elite spaces. *Environment and Planning A*, 30: 2098–3000.

Hutton, W. (1995) The state we're in (London: Jonathan Cape).

Hymer, S. (1976b) The international operations of national firms: a study of foreign direct investment (Cambridge: MIT Press).

IMF (2000) International capital markets: developments, prospects and policy issues (Washington, D.C.: IMF).

IMF (2001) International capital markets: developments, prospects and policy issues (Washington, D.C.: IMF).

Ingham, G. (1996) Review essay: the new economic sociology. *Work, Employment and Society*, 10, 3: 549–566.

Jackson, D. (1998) Profitability, mechanisation and economies of scale (Aldershot: Ashgate).

Jenkens, L. (1996) Office location in a post-industrial urban environment (Aldershot: Avebury).

Jervis, R. (1997) System effects: complexity in political and social life (Princeton: Princeton University Press).

Johanson, J. & Vahlne, J. (1977) The internationalization process of firms: a model of knowledge development and increasing foreign commitments. *Journal of International Business Studies*, 8, 1: 23–32.

Johanson, J. & Vahlne, J. (1990) The mechanism of internationalization. *International Marketing Review*, 7, 4: 11–24.

Jones, A. (1998) (Re)producing gender cultures: theorising gender in investment banking recruitment. *Geoforum*, 29, 4: 451–474.

Jones, A. (2002) The global city misconceived: the myth of 'global management' in transnational service firms. *Geoforum*, 33, 3: 335–350.

Jones, G. (1992) Transnational corporations: a historical perspective (London: Routledge).

Jones, G. (1996) The growth of international business (London: Routledge).

Jones, G. & Schroter, H. (eds) (1993) The rise of multinationals in Continental Europe (Aldershot: Edward Elgar).

Kamel, R. (1991) The global factory – analysis and action for a new economic era (Philadelphia, PA).

Kane, F. (2002) Another barings? We should be so lucky. Article in *The Observer*, 17 March.

Karanteng, J. (1996) The advertising industry in Europe: changes and development towards the 21st century (London: FT Telecoms and Media Publishing).

Keltner, B. (1995) Relationship banking and competitive advantage: evidence from the US and Germany. *California Management Review*, 34: 107–126.

Khan, K. (ed.) (1986) Multinationals of the South (London: Francis Pinter).

Kim, H. (1999) Globalization of international financial markets: causes and consequences (Aldershot: Ashgate).

King, A. (1990) Global cities: post-imperialism and internationalization of London (London: Routledge).

King, R. (2000) Risk management (London: Scitech).

Knight, G. (1999) International services marketing: review of research 1980–1998. *Journal of Service Marketing*, 13, 5: 347–360.

Knight, G. & Cavusgil, S. (1996) The born global firm: a challenge to traditional internationalization theory. In *Advances in International Marketing*, pp. 11–26 (New York: Jai Press).

Knight, K. (ed.) (1977) Matrix management (Aldershot: Gower).

Knight, R. & Gappert, G. (eds) (1989) Cities in a global society (London: Sage).

Kofman, E. & Youngs, G. (eds) (1996) Globalization: theory and practice (London: Pinter).

Kogut, B., Kunreuther, H. & Bowman, E. (2001) Introduction to focused issue: risk, managers, and options in organizations. *Organization science*, 12, 5: 579–581.

Kogut, B. & Zander, U. (1993) Knowledge of the firm and the evolutionary theory of the multinational corporation. *Journal of International Business Studies*, 24: 625–645.

Kono, T. & Clegg, S. (1998) Transformations of corporate culture: experiences of Japanese enterprises (Berlin: Walter de Gruyter).

Kozul-Wright, R. & Rowthorn, R. (1998) Transnational corporations and the global economy (Basingstoke: Macmillan).

Lall, S. (1983) The new multinationals (Chichester: John Wiley).

Langhorne, R. (2001) The coming of globalization (Basingstoke: Palgrave).

Langworth, R. (1987) Complete history of the Ford Motor Company (New York:)

Lechner, F. & Boli, J. (eds) (2000) The globalization reader (Oxford: Blackwell).

Lee, R. & Wills, J. (eds) (1997) Geographies of economies (London: Arnold).

Leeson, N. (1997) Rogue trader (London: Warner Books).

Legge, K., Clegg, C. & Kemp, N. (eds) (1991) Cases in information technology, people and organisations (Oxford: Blackwell).

Leidner, R. (1993) Fast food, fast talk: service work and the routinization of everyday life (London: University of California Press).

Lessem, R. (1987) The global business (London: Prentice Hall).

Lessem, R. (1990) Managing corporate culture (Aldershot: Gower).

Lewis, M. (ed.) (1999) The globalization of financial services (Cheltenham: Elgar).

Leyshon, A. (1995) Annihilating Space?: the speed-up of communications. In Allen, J. & Hamnett, C. (eds) *A Shrinking World?* (Oxford: Oxford University Press).

Leyshon, A. (1997) True stories? Global dreams, global nightmares and the writing of globalization. In Lee, R. & Wills, J. (eds) *Geographies of Economies* (London: Arnold).

Leyshon, A. (1998) Geographies of money and finance III. *Progress in Human Geography*, 22, 3: 433–446.

Leyshon, A. & Pollard, J. (1997) Globalization, conventions of restructuring and the regional reorganisation of banking. Paper given at RGS/IBG Conference, Exeter, January 1997.

Liaw, T. (1999) The business of investment banking (Chichester: John Wiley).

Lim, M. & Teoh, K. (1986) Singapore corporations go transnational. *Journal of South East Asian Studies*, 17, 2: 336–365.

Lipson, C. (1985) Standing guard: protecting foreign capital in the nineteenth and twentieth centuries (Berkeley, CA: University of California Press).

Llewelyn-Davies (1997) Four world cities: a comparative study of London, Paris, New York and Tokyo: summary report. Llewelyn-Davies Planning (London: Llewelyn-Davies).

Lo, F. & Yeung, Y. (1998) Globalization and the world of large cities (New York: United Nations University Press).

Lowenstein, R. (2001) When genius failed (London: Fourth Estate).

Madsen, T. & Servais, P. (1997) The internationalization of born globals: an evolutionary process? *International Business Review*, 6, 6: 561–583.

Majury, N. (2002) Framing the restructuring of financial services: markets and globalisation. *Progress in Human Geography* (Forthcoming).

Martin, R. (1994) Stateless monies, global financial integration and national economic autonomy: the end of geography? In Corbridge, S., Martin, R. & Thrift, N. (eds) *Money, Power and Space* (Oxford: Blackwell).

Martin, R. (ed.) (1998) Money and the space economy (Chichester: Wiley).

Maskin, Q. & Xu, C. (1997) Incentives, scale economies and organizational form (London: Centre for Economic Performance).

Mason, J. (2002) Qualitative researching: asking, listening and interpreting. In May, T. (ed.) *Qualitative Research in Action*, pp. 225–241 (London: Sage).

McCluhan, M. (1962) The Gutenberg galaxy: the making of topographic man (Toronto: Toronto University Press).

McDowell, L. (1997) Capital culture (Oxford: Blackwell).

McDowell, L. & Court, G. (1994) Gender divisions of labour in the post-Fordist economy: the maintenance of occupational sex segregation in the financial services sector. *Environment and Planning A*, 26: 1397–1418.

McKinsey (1993) Manufacturing productivity (Washington, D.C.: McKinsey Global Institute).

Mittelman, J. (ed.) (1997) Globalization: critical reflections (London: Lynne Reinner).

Mittelman, J. (2000) The globalization syndrome (Princeton: Princeton University Press).

Modelski, G. (2000) Globalization. In Held, D. & McGrew, A. (eds) *The Global Transformations Reader*, pp. 47–54 (Cambridge: Polity).

Morgan Chase, J.P. (2001) Annual Report (New York).

Morgan Chase, J.P. (2002) Annual Report (New York).

Morrison, A., Ricks, D. & Roth, K. (1991) Globalization versus regionalization: which way for the multinational? *Organizational Dynamics*, 19: 17–19.

Mourdoukoutas, P. (1999) The global corporation: the decolonization of international business (London: Quorum).

Murtha, T., Lenway, S. & Bagozzi, R. (1998) Global mind-sets and the cognitive shift in a complex multinational corporation. *Stategic Management Journal*, 19: 97–114.

Neuman, L. (2000) Social research methods: qualitative and quantitative approaches (London: Allyn and Bacon).

Newman, I. & Benz, C. (1998) Qualitative–quantitative research methodology: exploring the interactive continuum (Carbondale, IL: Southern Illinois University Press).

Nohria, N. & Ghoshal, S. (1997) The differentiated network: organizing multinational corporations for value creation (San Francisco: Jossey-Bass).

North, D. (1985) Transaction costs in history. *Journal of Economic History*, 42: 566–576.

O'Brien, R. (1991) Global financial integration: the end of geography (New York: Council on Foreign Relations Press).

O'Donnell, S. (2000) Managing foreign subsidiaries: agents of headquarters, or an interdependent network? *Strategic Management Journal*, 21: 525–548.

OECD (1996) Globalisation of industry: overview and sector reports (Paris: OECD).

Ohmae, K. (1995) The end of the nation state (London: Harper Collins).

Papadakis, V., Liokas, S. & Chambers, D. (1998) Strategic decision-making processes: the role of management and context. *Strategic Management Journal*, 19, 2: 115–148.

Pauly, L. & Reich, S. (1997) National structures and multinational corporate behaviour: enduring differences in the age of globalization. *International Organization*, 51: 1–30.

Pearce, R. (1990) The internationalization of research and development by multinational enterprises (London: Macmillan).

Pearce, R. (1997) Global competition and technology: essays in the creation and application of knowledge by multinationals (Basingstoke: Macmillan).

Peet, R. (1997) The cultural production of economic forms. In Lee, R. & Wills, J. (eds) *Geographies of Economies*, pp. 37–46 (London: Arnold).

Pitelis, C. (1993) The transnational corporation, international state apparatuses and deindustrialization (Cambridge: Judge Institute of Management Studies).

Pitelis, C. & Sugden, R. (eds) (1991) The nature of the transnational firm (London: Routledge).

Porter, M. (1990) The competitive advantage of nations (London: Macmillan).

Price Waterhouse Coopers (2001) Annual Report (London: PWC).

Pringle, R. (1988) Secretaries talk: sexuality, power and work (London: Allen and Unwin).

Pritchett, P. (1996) Culture shift: the employee handbook for changing corporate culture (Washington, Tyne and Wear: Pritchett and Associates Inc.).

Pryke, M. & Lee, R. (1995) Place your bets: towards an understanding of globalization, socio-financial engineering and competition within a financial centre. *Urban Studies*, 32: 329–344.

Raines, P. & Brown, R. (2001) From 'international' to 'global': the Scottish enterprise global companies strategy and new approaches to overseas expansion. *Regional studies*, 35, 7: 657–662.

Ramanujam, P. & Vines, D. (1989) Commodity prices, financial markets and world income: a structural rational expectations model (London: Centre for Economic Policy Research).

Rassam, C. & Oates, D. (1991) Management consultancy: the inside story (London: Mercury).

Richards, M. (2000) Control exercised by US multinationals over their overseas affiliates: does location make a difference? *Journal of International Management*, 6: 105–120.

Roberts, S. (1994) Fictitious capital, fictitious spaces: the geography of offshore financial flows. In Corbridge, S., Martin, R. & Thrift, N. (eds) *Money, Power and Space*, pp. 91–115 (Oxford: Blackwell).

Robock, S. & Simons, K. (1989) International business and multinational enterprises (4th Edition) (Boston: Irwin).

Rosenberg, J. (2001) The follies of globalisation theory (London: Verso).

Rostow, W. (1978) The world economy: history and prospect (London: Macmillan).

Rostow, W. (1990) Theorists of economic growth from David Hume to the present: with a perspective on the next century (Oxford: Oxford University Press).

Rowe, C. (1992) The management matrix: the psychology of interaction (Henley-on-Thames: Waller).

Rugman, A. (2001) The end of globalization (London: Random House).

Ruigrok, W. & Tulder, R. (1995) The logic of international restructuring (London: Routledge).

Sakai, J. (2000) Japanese bankers in the city of London: language, culture and identity in the Japanese diaspora (London: Routledge).

Sanchez, R. (ed.) (1999) Beyond the boundaries of the firm: integrating theories of the firm and theories of markets (Oxford: Permagon).

Santangelo, G. (2001) The impact of the information and communications technology revolution on the internationalization of corporate technology. *International Business Review*, 10: 701–726.

Sassen, S. (1994) Cities in a world economy (London: Pine Forge Press).

Sassen, S. (2001) The Global City (2nd Edition) (Princeton: Princeton University Press).

Savage, M., Barlow, J., Dickens, P. & Fielding, A. (1992) Property, bureaucracy and culture (London: Routledge).

Saxenian, A. (1994) Regional advantage: culture and competition in Silicon Valley and Route 128 (London: Harvard University Press).

Sayer, A. (1994) Cultural studies and 'the economy', stupid. *Environment and Planning D: Society and Space*, 7: 253–276.

Sayer, A. (1997) The dialectic of culture and economy. In Lee, R. & Wills, J. (eds) *Geographies of Economies*, pp. 16–26 (London: Arnold).

Scarbrough, H. & Corbett, M. (1992) Technology and organization: power, meaning and design (London: Routledge).

Schaberg, M. (1999) Globalization and the erosion of national financial systems: is declining autonomy inevitable? (Cheltenham: Edward Elgar).

Schein, J. (1997) Organizational culture and leadership (San Francisco: Jossey-Bass).

Schoenberger, E. (1997) The cultural crisis of the firm (Oxford: Blackwell).

Scholte, J. (2000) Globalization: a critical introduction (Basingstoke: Palgrave).

Scott, A.L. (1997) The limits of globalization (London: Routledge).

Sethi, S. & Thompson, G. (2000) Optimal control theory (New York: Kluwer).

Shapiro, E. (1998) Fad surfing in the boardroom: reclaiming the courage to manage in the age of instant answers (Oxford: Capstone).

Shipman, A. (2002) The globalisation myth (London: Icon).

Short, J. & Kim, H. (1999) Globalization and the city (Harlow: Longman).

Silverman, D. (2000) Doing qualitative research: a practical handbook (London: Sage).

Sklair, L. (1992) Sociology of the global system (London: Prentice Hall).

Sklair, L. (1998) Globalization and the corporations: the case of the California. *Fortune Global 500*, IJURR 22, 2: 195–215.

Smelser, N. & Swedberg, R. (1993) The handbook of economic sociology (Princeton: Princeton University Press).

Smith, R. & Walter, I. (1997) Global banking (Oxford: Oxford University Press).

Spybey, T. (1996) Globalization and world society (Cambridge: Polity Press).

Stopford, J. & Wells, L. (1972) Managing the multinational enterprise (New York: Basic Books).

Strange, S. (1996) Casino capitalism (Orig. publ. 1986) (Manchester: Manchester University Press).

Strange, S. (1998a) Mad money (Manchester: Manchester University Press).

Strange, S. (1998b) Globaloney? *Review of International Political Economy*, 5, 4: 704–711.

Streitz, N., Siegel, J., Hartkopf, V. & Konomi, S. (eds) (1999) Cooperative buildings: integrating information, organization, and architecture (Berlin: Springer-Verlag).

Sturdy, A. (1997) The consultancy process – an insecure business? *Journal of Management Studies*, 34, 3: 389–413.

Sutcliffe, K. & McNara, G. (2001) Controlling decision-making practice in organizations. *Organization Science*, 12, 4: 484–501.

Talalay, M., Farrands, C. & Tooze, R. (eds) (1997) Technology, culture and competitiveness (London: Routledge).

Taplin, I. & Winterton, J. (eds) (1997) Rethinking global production: a comparative analysis of restructuring in the clothing industry (Aldershot: Ashgate).

Taylor, P. (ed.) (1993) Political geography of the twentieth century: a global analysis (London: Belhaven).

Temporal, H. & Alder, P. (1999) Corporate charisma: how to achieve world-class recognition by maximising your company's image, brands and culture (London: Piatkus).

The Guardian (2000) Dresdner counts human cost of merger, Article on March 11.

The Guardian (2001) DrKW cry freedom in face of alliance, Article on March 30.

Thomas, R. (1995) Interviewing important people in big companies. In Hert, R. & Imber, J. (eds) *Studying Elites Using Qualitative Methods*, pp. 3–17 (Thousand Oaks, CA: Sage).

Thrift, N. (1994) On the social and cultural determinants of international financial centres: the case of the city of london. In Corbridge, S., Martin, R. & Thrift, N. (eds) *Money, Power and Space* (Oxford: Blackwell).

Thrift, N. (1997) The rise of soft capitalism. In Herod, A., O Tuathail, G. & Roberts, S. (eds) *An Unruly World: Globalization, Governance and Geography*, pp. 25–71 (London: Routledge).

Thrift , N. (2000) Performing cultures in the new economy. *Annals of the Association of American Geographers*, 90, 4: 674–692.

Thrift, N. & Leyshon, A. (1997) Money space (Oxford: Blackwell).

Thrift, N. & Olds, K. (1996) Refiguring the economic in economic geography. *Progress in Human Geography*, 20, 3: 311–337.

Thrift, N., Leyshon, A. & Daniels, P. (1987) "Sexy greedy": the new international financial system, the city of London and the South East of England. Working papers on producer services, University of Bristol and Service Industries Research Centre, Portsmouth Polytechnic.

Tickell, A. (1996) Making a melodrama out of a crisis: reinterpreting the collapse of Barings Bank. *Environment and Planning D: Society and Space*, 14: 5–33.

Toft, B. & Reynolds, S. (eds) (1997) Learning from disasters: a management approach (Leicester: Perpetuity Press).

Tomlinson, J. (1999) Globalization and culture (Cambridge: Polity).

Travi, V. (2001) Advanced technologies: building in the computer age (Boston: Birkhauser).

Trompenaars, F. (1993) Riding the waves of culture (London: Random House).

UNCTAD (2001) World Investment Report 2001: Investment, Trade and International Policy Arrangements (New York: United Nations).

USBank1 (2002) Annual Report 1996 (New York: *USBank*).

USConsultancy1 (1996) One Global Firm. Internal Report (Chicago).

USConsultancy2 (1998) Internal Strategy Report (London).

Valdez, S. (1997) An introduction to global financial markets (London: Macmillan Business).

Van der Erve, M. (1993) The power of tomorrow's management: using the vision-culture balance in organizations (Oxford: Butterworth-Heinemann).

Vatter, H. & Walker, J. (1996) History of the U.S. economy since World War II (London: M.E. Sharpe).

Viney, J. (1997) The culture wars: how American and Japanese businesses have outperformed Europe's and why the future will be different (Oxford: Capstone).

Walford, G. (ed.) (1994) Researching the powerful (London: UCL Press).

Wallerstein, I. (1974) The modern world-system: capitalist agriculture and the origins of the European world-economy in the sixteenth century (New York: Academic Press).

Wallerstein, I. (1979) The modern world-system II: Mercantilism and the consolidation of the European world economy 1600–1750 (New York: Academic Press).

Wallerstein, I. (1984) The politics of the world economy (Cambridge: CUP).

Wanous, J. (1980) Organizational entry: recruitment, selection, and socialization of newcomers (Reading, Mass.: Addison-Wesley Pub. Co).

Ward, M. (1995) Why your corporate culture change isn't working – and what to do about it (Aldershot: Gower).

Washington Post (1998) German bank seeks US link, *Article 12/7/98*.

Waters, M. (1995) Globalization (London: Routledge).

Weinshall, T. (1993) Societal culture and management (New York: W. de Gruyter).

Wheelan, T. & Hunger, D. (1998) Strategic management and business policy: entering 21st century global society (Harlow: Addison-Wesley).

Whitley, R. (1999) Divergent capitalisms: the social structuring and change of business systems (Oxford: OUP).

Wilkins, M. (1974) The maturing of the multinational enterprise: American business abroad from 1914 to 1970 (Cambridge, Mass.: Harvard University Press).

Wilkins, M. (1991) The growth of multinationals (Aldershot: Edward Elgar).

Wilkins, M. (1994) Comparative hosts. *Business History*, 36.

Williams, A., Dobson, P. & Walters, M. (1993) Changing culture: new organizational approaches (London: Institute of Personnel Management).

Williams, M. (2002) Generalization in interpretive research. In May, T. (ed.) *Qualitative Research in Action*, pp. 125–143 (London: Sage).

Willman, P., O'Creevy, F., Nicholson, N. & Soane, E. (2002) Traders, managers and loss aversion in investment banking: a field study. *Accounting, organizations and society*, 27, 1–2: 85–98.

Winfield, I. (1991) Organisations and information technology: systems, power and job design (Oxford: Blackwell).

Wolfe, T. (1987) The bonfire of the vanities (New York: Verso).

Wong, H. (1999) Japanese bosses, Chinese workers (Hawaii: University of Hawaii Press).

Woods, M., Fedorkow, M. & Smith, M. (1997) Modelling and learning organisation (Bradford: University of Bradford, Management Centre).

Yamashita, H. (1998) Competitiveness and corporate culture (Aldershot: Ashgate).

Yeoh, B. (1999) Global/globalizing cities. *Progress in Human Geography*, 23, 4: 607–616.

Yeung, H. (1997) Business networks and transnational corporations: a study of Hong Kong firms in the ASEAN region. *Economic Geography*, 73, 1: 1–25.

Yeung, H. (2000) Embedding foreign affiliates in transnational business networks: the case of Hong Kong firms in Southeast Asia. *Environment and Planning A*, 32, 2: 191–200.

Yeung, H. (2002) Entrepreneurship and the internationalization of Asian firms (Cheltenham: Edward Elgar).

Yeung, H. & Olds, K. (eds) (2000) The globalization of Chinese business firms (London: Macmillan).

Young, P. & Tippins, S. (2000) Managing business risk: an organization-wide approach to risk management (New York: Amacom).

Yoshikawa, H. (2000) The long stagnation of the Japanese economy during the 1990s and macroeconomic. *Économie internationale*, 84, 4: 13–34.

Zukin, S. & DiMaggio, P. (eds) (1990) Structures of capital: the social organisation of the economy (Cambridge: Cambridge University Press).

Index

Beck, U. 3
business meetings
  effect on travel 82–3
  importance of personal/social
    contact 81, 83–4
  IT-based *vs* face-to-face 81–2
  regularity of 82
business-service industries
  and branch offices 179–80
  in era of globalization 179–85
  future research into 188–9
  implications of research on 185–8
  interpersonal relations 181–3
  managerial structure 180–1
  organizational form 179–80
  and transnational corporate
    culture 183–5

Castells, M. 74, 85
client relationships
  and acquisition/retention of new
    business 114–15, 119–20
  collective aspect 115–16
  and face-to-face communication
    118, 183
  and importance of individuals
    116–18, 122, 182
  and information transfer 117–18
  long-term 119–20
  meaning of 113–14
  and repeat business 118–19
  social science literature on 113, 122
  and transnational socialization
    113–22
  and trust/reputation 114, 120–2, 182
communication 86, 186
  face-to-face 118, 123
  informal 123–6
  and international business
    meetings 81–4
  role of (IT) 75–80
contact networks, *see* social
  relationships

control, *see* power/control
corporate culture 20, 38
  see also global corporate culture;
    transnational corporate culture

Doremus, P. 33–4

employee–client contact
  centrality of 103–4
  crucial to acquiring/retaining
    business 98, 101
  and importance of individuals
    100–1
  and knowledge of needs,
    trust, negotiation,
    communication 98
  and local/global knowledge 102–3
  quality of 101–2
  social aspects 99–100
employee–employee contact 93, 131
  and acquisition of new business 94
  benefits/advantages of 95
  centrality of 103–4
  and communities of practice
    94–5, 96
  diasporic network 94
  lack of 97
  promotion of 96, 98
  relevance of 94
  external networks, *see*
    employee–client contact

financial globalization
  as abstract phenomenon 89
  academic literature/debates on
    89–90
  corporate/government response
    to 90
  critics of 90
  and fictitious capital 89, 90
  as good example of pure market 90
  new economic sociology view of 90
  popular image of 88–9